Reflective Practice
in Social Work

Sara Miller McCune founded SAGE Publishing in 1965 to support the dissemination of usable knowledge and educate a global community. SAGE publishes more than 1000 journals and over 800 new books each year, spanning a wide range of subject areas. Our growing selection of library products includes archives, data, case studies and video. SAGE remains majority owned by our founder and after her lifetime will become owned by a charitable trust that secures the company's continued independence.

Los Angeles | London | New Delhi | Singapore | Washington DC | Melbourne

6th Edition

Reflective Practice in Social Work

Andy Mantell
Terry Scragg

Learning Matters,
A SAGE Publishing Company
1 Oliver's Yard
55 City Road
London EC1Y 1SP

SAGE Publications Inc.
2455 Teller Road
Thousand Oaks, California 91320

SAGE Publications India Pvt Ltd
B 1/I 1 Mohan Cooperative Industrial Area
Mathura Road
New Delhi 110 044

SAGE Publications Asia-Pacific Pte Ltd
3 Church Street
#10-04 Samsung Hub
Singapore 049483

First published in 2007 by Learning Matters Ltd. Second edition published in 2010 by SAGE/Learning Matters. Third edition published in 2013. Fourth edition published in 2016. Fifth edition published in 2019. Sixth edition published in 2023.

Library of Congress Control Number: 2023930692

British Library Cataloguing in Publication Data

A catalogue record for this book is available from the British Library

Editor: Kate Keers
Development editor: Sarah Turpie
Senior project editor: Chris Marke
Marketing manager: Camille Richmond
Project management: TNQ Technologies
Cover design: Sheila Tong
Typeset by: TNQ Technologies
Printed in the UK

ISBN 978-1-5297-9859-3
ISBN 978-1-5297-9858-6 (pbk)

Contents

Contents

Series editor's preface

Since the fifth edition of this book the world has changed significantly. The United Kingdom has left the European Union with the economic, political and social ramifications of the act affecting us all and creating greater vulnerability for many. The world has experienced the deadly COVID-19 pandemic leaving strains on our helping professions, social work included, and the continuing issues arising from health concerns, economic and work difficulties among many others. The prosecution of an unjust and brutal war in Ukraine by Putin's Russian forces has led to many seeking refuge in the United Kingdom, while at the same time right-wing ideologues protest against those fleeing into Britain from other conflict and oppressive situations. The intensification of the climate crisis is having deeper and impacts on people made vulnerable by poverty, political alienation and general marginalisation from society. These factors alongside a continuing need for social work services on a daily basis mean this sixth edition of this book timely and important. It is important that we reflect on what is happening around us as social workers, what the experiences of the world mean for us and that we take that reflection into our practice and demand the time to reflect about our practice and about consequences that result from national and international events. Only in this way can we practice as moral, professional social workers.

During my teaching sessions for student social workers and others, I have been struck keenly by the impact that changes permeating our contemporary world have on the perceptions and mental health of participants. The need for quiet as well as active reflection starting from the time of learning onwards is central to the social work mentality. Values and ethics lie at the heart of social work, and social work education, and we address these throughout all the books in the series; however, reflective practitioners actively engage with values and ethics. The positions that we take in terms of values and ethics are, to an extent, determined by context, time and experience, and these are expressed in different ways by students coming into social work education today. Since the turn of this century, we have witnessed shifts and challenges as the marketised neoliberal landscape of politics, economy and social life may attract little comment or contest from some. We have observed the political machinery directing much of statutory social work towards a focus on individuals apart from their environment. However, we have also seen a recent turn to the social in the #MeToo campaign where unquestioned entitlement to women's bodies and psychology is exposed and resisted. We have seen defiance of those perpetuating social injustices that see long-term migrants alongside today's migrants abused and shunned by society, institutions as well as individuals. It is likely that, as a student of social work, you will lay bare and face many previously unquestioned assumptions, which can be very perplexing and uncover needs for learning, support and understanding. This series of books acts as an aid as you make these steps. Each book stands in a long and international tradition of social work that promotes social justice and human rights, introducing you to the importance of sometimes new and difficult concepts, and inculcating the importance of close questioning of yourself as you make your journey towards becoming part of that tradition. The books also act as a beginning step in your preparation to dig deeper, to learn, to reflect and by doing so to protect yourself while serving others.

There are numerous contemporary challenges for the wider world, and for all four countries of the United Kingdom. These include political shifts to the 'popular' Right, a growing antipathy to care and support, and dealing with lies and 'alternative truths' in our daily lives. Alongside this, is the need to address the impact of an increasingly ageing population with its attendant social care needs and working with the financial implications that such a changing demography brings. At the other end of the lifespan the need for high quality childcare, welfare and safeguarding services has been highlighted as society develops and responds to the changing complexion. As demand rises, so do the costs and the unquestioned assumption that new austerity measures are necessary after the disastrous consequences of the imposition of earlier measures continues to create tensions and restrictions in services, policies and expectations.

It is likely that as a social worker you will work with a diverse range of people throughout your career, many of whom have experienced significant, even traumatic, events that require a professional and caring response. As well as working with individuals, however, you may be required to respond to the needs of a particular community disadvantaged by local, national or world events or groups excluded within their local communities because of assumptions made about them.

The importance of high-quality social work education remains if we are adequately to address the complexities of modern life. We should continually strive for excellence in education as this allows us to focus clearly on what knowledge it is useful to engage with when learning to be a social worker. Questioning everything, especially from a position of knowledge, is central to being a social worker.

The books in this series respond to the agendas driven by changes brought about by professional bodies, governments and disciplinary reviews. They aim to build on and offer introductory texts based on up-to-date knowledge and to help communicate this in an accessible way, so preparing the ground for future study and for encouraging good practice as you develop your social work career. Each book is written by educators and practitioners who are passionate about social work and social services and who aim to instil that passion in others.

You will hear the terms 'reflective practice', 'reflexive practice', 'reflection' and 'reflexivity' often throughout your social work education. Unfortunately, these terms are sometimes used without fully exploring, or allowing you to explore, what they mean in practice. The sixth edition of this book introduces you to the concepts of reflection, the place of reflective practice and the processes involved in social work practice. This will help you to set the scene for exploring more specialised areas of social work and providing you with a grounding from which to enhance your learning in practice.

Professor Jonathan Parker

November 2022

About the editors and contributors

Anita Atwal is Associate Professor Interprofessional Working, London South Bank University.

Linda Bell is Honorary Research Fellow, Associate Professor (retired), Dept of Mental Health and Social Work, Middlesex University.

Gill Butler is Emeritus Research Fellow and was formerly Deputy Dean (Learning and Teaching), University of Chichester.

Gill Constable was formerly Lecturer in Social Work, Glasgow Caledonian University.

Denise Harvey is a former Professional Lead for Social Work at LSBU.

Martyn Higgins is Associate Professor Social Work Community and Public Health, London South Bank University.

Sarah Houghton is a Lecturer, School of Social Work and Education, University of Sussex.

Andy Mantell (editor) is Principal Lecturer in the School of Health and Social Care at Anglia Ruskin University London.

Terry Scragg (editor) is an Independent Practice Educator and was former Principal Lecturer in Social Work, University of Chichester.

Chris Smethurst Co-Director of Institute of Education and Social Sciences, University of Chichester.

Catherine Tucher is Senior Social Worker, Child Protection and Court Proceedings Team, Surrey Children's Services.

TRANSFORMING SOCIAL WORK PRACTICE

Since launching in 2003, *Transforming Social Work Practice* has become the market-leading series for social work students. Each book is:

- Affordable
- Written to the Professional Capabilities Framework
- Mapped to the Social Work curriculum
- Practical with clear links between theory and practice

These books use activities and case studies to build critical thinking and reflection skills and will help social work students to develop good practice through learning.

BESTSELLING TEXTBOOKS

7th Edition

Social Work & Mental Health

Malcolm Golightley & Robert Goemans

LM

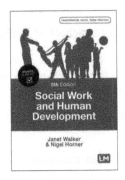

5th Edition

Social Work and Human Development

Janet Walker & Nigel Horner

LM

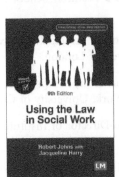

9th Edition

Using the Law in Social Work

Robert Johns with Jacqueline Harry

LM

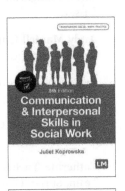

5th Edition

Communication & Interpersonal Skills in Social Work

Juliet Koprowska

LM

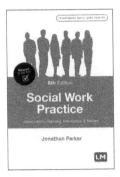

6th Edition

Social Work Practice

Assessment, Planning, Intervention & Review

Jonathan Parker

LM

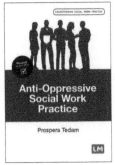

Anti-Oppressive Social Work Practice

Prospera Tedam

LM

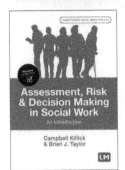

Assessment, Risk & Decision Making in Social Work

An Introduction

Campbell Killick & Brian J. Taylor

LM

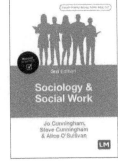

3rd Edition

Sociology & Social Work

Jo Cunningham, Steve Cunningham & Alice O'Sullivan

LM

About the Series Editor

DR JONATHAN PARKER is Professor of Society & Social Welfare at Bournemouth University and Honorary Visiting Professor at University of Stavanger, Norway. He has published widely on social work education, policy, theory for practice, disadvantage, marginalisation and violence, across the world.

Acknowledgements

We would like to thank Kate Keers and Sarah Turpie for their support throughout the completion of this new sixth edition.

Introduction

This book has been written for the student social worker either in your qualifying course, post-qualifying awards and your ASYE (Assessed and Supported Year in Employment), and explores a range of approaches to reflective practice that will be helpful across all stages of your development as a social worker. Experienced and qualified social workers contributing to practice learning will also be able to use this book for consultation, teaching and revision, and to gain an insight into the expectations raised by the qualifying degree in social work. Essentially this book is designed to assist you in developing an understanding of the concept of the reflective practitioner, and in learning how, in conjunction with your practice educator and others, you can take a perspective on your own actions and experiences that have the potential for refining and reframing your practice as a result of these deliberations. Reflection is central to good social work practice, but only if action results from that reflection.

Great emphasis is now placed on developing the skills of reflection at each stage of practice. This has developed over many years in social work and is not only important during your education to become a social worker but is also considered key to continued professional development (CPD). As a profession it increasingly acknowledges the value of lifelong learning as a way of keeping up to date, ensuring that research informs practice and honing skills and values for practice, and it is important to begin the process at the outset of your development. The importance of reflection as one component of professional development is recognised by its inclusion in Social Work England's (2019) Professional standards for social workers.

Book structure

The book starts with a broad exploration of reflective practice drawing on some of the key sources that have informed the development of the concept and some of the processes that can be adopted in reflective practice. This then forms the basis for the following chapters that are concerned with aspects of the development of the reflective practitioner from a range of standpoints. Finally, we explore issues of the management of social work practice and interprofessional leadership in the context of reflection.

Part 1: What is reflective practice?

Chapter 1 explores what is meant by reflective practice and some of the potential outcomes from using this technique. The chapter then examines the roots of the concept of reflective practice, with the work of Dewey and Schön as our starting point, and goes on to discuss its application to practice situations through the use of the reflective cycle. It highlights the importance of reflection in challenging our taken for granted values and assumptions as an essential aspect of anti-discriminatory practice. The chapter concludes with an exploration of some of the ethical challenges posed by reflective practice, recognising that it can provoke anxiety and where it is essential that positive relationships and processes need to be in place for safe and effective reflection to take place.

Chapter 2 builds on the foundations of the previous chapter and provides you with a number of practical ways of getting started in reflecting on your practice, with a series of progressive activities that you can adopt to develop and refine your skills as a reflective practitioner. From the important starting point of creating a space where you can comfortably and safely reflect on your practice, the chapter recognises the value of understanding your personal approach to learning through recognising your preferred learning style and its influence on how you approach the analysis of practice situations. From the use of learning logs through online blogs to narrative analysis, there are a wealth of creative ideas that you can choose from and incorporate into your reflective activities depending on your personal approach to learning.

Chapter 3 recognises that the reflective process involves the emotions. This chapter raises important questions about the role of language in both shaping and reflecting dominant discourses in practice. The importance in social work of understanding and processing emotions is then considered, illustrated with reference to child protection practice. An acknowledgement of the emotional component in practice has long been neglected but is now increasingly recognised as helping practitioners understand some of the contradictions and complexities inherent in social work practice. The concept of emotional intelligence is identified as providing a helpful framework for developing emotionally competent practice. A series of reflective tasks is included to support the development of emotional awareness and regulation, which are considered central to the development of emotional intelligence.

Part 2: Developing the reflective practitioner

Chapter 4 focuses on the use of reflection to enable you to develop personal and professional effectiveness, through extensive use of case examples and exercises to enable you to increase your self-awareness and manage stress. A number of approaches are considered such as writing reflectively, analysis of self-talk and belief systems, and SWOT analysis will help you to develop positive thinking and challenge self-defeating thoughts, drawing on techniques of cognitive behaviour therapy. The aim of the chapter is to enable you to develop ideas about how you can reflect in a purposeful manner, which will enable you to problem-solve and develop personal confidence and professional competence.

Chapter 5 highlights the potential pitfalls when applying reflective practice to work with carers and service users. The evolving professional conception of 'the carer' is examined and contrasted with the lived experience of people providing care. This chapter draws extensively on case studies and research summaries, focusing particularly on the experience of families with Huntington's disease, to enable you to reflect on the importance of the carers' and service users' perspectives, and their participation in social work and the challenging perspective they may bring. The SHARE model is incorporated to reflect on the assessment process. An exploration of knowledge, experience and power in understanding and interpretation is included as well as how to use the reflective process to consider other standpoints.

Chapter 6 explores unsafe practice where a service user or practitioner is at risk of physical, social or emotional harm. The first part of the chapter examines the concept of unsafe practice from a range of perspectives through key national reports which have examined examples of high-profile failures in practice. The second part of the chapter suggests ways in which you can use reflection to explore ways of minimising unsafe practice, with case examples and activities that will help you understand how you can use techniques of reflection to analyse how practices can be improved. Unsafe practice can also extend to the organisations that employ social workers and the chapter will examine some of the organisational systems and processes that can unwittingly increase risks of unsafe practice. Finally, the chapter explores practitioner fears and some strategies for ensuring personal safety.

Chapter 7 discusses gender in social work from a range of perspectives, and how the men and women in social work can be both shaped by socialisation and influenced by others' expectation of gender roles and what are seen as appropriate behaviours for male and female social workers. The chapter explores theories of gender identity and the notion of 'gender fluidity' and the contested views about the origins and influences of gender differences. The chapter also considers issues of emotions in social work and how stereotyped assumptions about the expression of emotions are intimately bound up with notions of gender. In helping you to consider issues of gender identity from a range of perspectives, the chapter provides you with opportunities to explore gender issues from a personal perspective, in the context of the practice settings, and social work training through the use of exercises, case studies and research findings.

Chapter 8 introduces you to reflective learning while on placement, with the role of supervision and your relationship with your practice educator central to this experience. The chapter provides a range of suggestions for adopting reflection to your work on placement, with case studies to illustrate how this can be applied in typical social work situations. The application of the learning cycle is used with an accompanying case study to enable you to understand some of the issues you face when first working with complex cases. The final part of the chapter considers the contribution of social work theories which should become an integral part of your practice, and which will enable you to develop analytic and intuitive skills that provide a degree of certainty when faced with novel and complex situations.

Part 3: Maintaining reflective practice

Chapter 9 introduces you to the world of management, particularly the work of the team manager who is often responsible for your practice and often acts as your supervisor. The chapter explores some of the pressures faced by team managers and the demands placed on them as they manage demands at the front line of the service. The second part of this chapter explores how you can actively manage your relationship with your team manager to ensure that you both develop a mutually satisfying working relationship.

Lastly, this chapter introduces you to a range of techniques that can be used when reflecting on and about practice. The final part of the chapter introduces you to the importance of supervision, consultation and evaluation as opportunities for developing reflective practice.

Finally, Chapter 10 recognises that social work is increasingly practised in an interprofessional context in complex organisational structures, and to work effectively in such teams means social workers need a range of interprofessional skills and a strong professional identity. The chapter provides you with activities that will enable you to identify the effectiveness of team working, including reference to serious case reviews where services failed to ensure effective interprofessional working and a case study highlighting poor joint working. The chapter explores how reflection can be an important part of teams reviewing their performance, with self-reflective activities that you can use while on placement. The chapter challenges you to explore how you can prepare yourself for work in multidisciplinary teams and the skills you need to develop to work collaboratively alongside colleagues from other services.

Learning features

This book is interactive and you are encouraged to work through the book as an active participant, taking responsibility for your learning, in order to increase your knowledge, understanding and ability to apply this learning to practice. You will be expected to reflect creatively on how immediate learning needs can be met in the area of assessment, planning, intervention and review and how your professional learning can be developed in your future career. Case studies throughout the book will help you to examine theories and models of reflective practice. We have devised activities that require you to reflect on experiences, situations and events and help you to review and summarise learning undertaken. In this way your knowledge will become deeply embedded as part of your development. When you come to practise learning in an agency, the work and reflection undertaken here will help you to improve and hone your skills and knowledge. This book will introduce knowledge and learning activities for you as a student social worker concerning the central processes relating to issues of reflective practice in all areas of the discipline. Suggestions for further reading are made at the end of each chapter.

This book has been carefully mapped to Social Work England's (2019) Professional Standards, the Social Work Subject Benchmark Statements (2019) and the 2018 Professional Capabilities Framework for Social Workers in England and will help you to develop the appropriate standards at the right level. These standards are:

1. Professionalism
   Identify and behave as a professional social worker committed to professional development.
2. Values and ethics
   Apply social work ethical principles and values to guide professional practice.

3. Diversity and equality
   Recognise diversity and apply anti-discriminatory and anti-oppressive principles in practice.
4. Rights, justice and economic well-being
   Advance human rights and promote social justice and economic well-being.
5. Knowledge
   Develop and apply relevant knowledge from social work practice and research, social sciences, law, other professional and relevant fields, and from the experience of people who use services.
6. Critical reflection and analysis
   Apply critical reflection and analysis to inform and provide a rationale for professional decision-making.
7. Skills and interventions
   Use judgement, knowledge and authority to intervene with individuals, families and communities to promote independence, provide support, prevent harm and enable progress.
8. Contexts and organisations
   Engage with, inform, and adapt to changing organisational contexts, and the social and policy environments that shape practice. Operate effectively within and contribute to the development of organisations and services, including multi-agency and interprofessional settings.
9. Professional leadership
   Promote the profession and good social work practice. Take responsibility for the professional learning and development of others. Develop personal influence and be part of the collective leadership and impact of the profession.

References to these standards will be made throughout the text and you will find a diagram of the Professional Capability Framework 2018 in Appendix 1.

Part I

What is reflective practice?

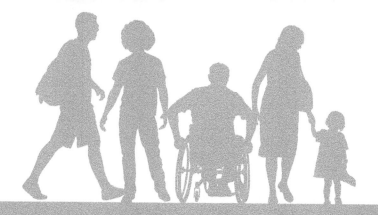

1

Reflective practice revisited

Andy Mantell

(Continued)

4.4 Demonstrate good subject knowledge on key aspects of social work practice and develop knowledge of current issues in society and social policies impacting on social work.

4.5 Contribute to an open and creative learning culture in the workplace to discuss, reflect on and share best practice.

4.6 Reflect on my learning activities and evidence what impact continuing professional development has on the quality of my practice.

4.7 Record my learning and reflection on a regular basis and in accordance with Social Work England's guidance on continuing professional development.

4.8 Reflect on my own values and challenge the impact they have on my practice.

Professional Capabilities Framework (2018)

1. Professionalism
2. Values and ethics
3. Knowledge
4. Critical reflection and analysis

See Appendix 1 for the Professional Capabilities Framework Fan and a description of the nine domains.

Social Work Subject Benchmark Statement (2019)

4.4 qualified social workers, therefore, need to be equipped both to understand, and to work within, this context of contested debate about the nature, scope and purpose of social work, and be able to analyse, adapt to, manage and eventually lead the process of change;

7.3 vii a developed capacity for the critical evaluation of knowledge and evidence from a range of sources.

See Appendix 2 for a detailed description of these standards.

Introduction

This introductory chapter reviews the knowledge of reflective practice which has been developed in social work and allied health professions. We look beyond social work in recognition that we can learn from other professionals, but also that we work with other professionals, and therefore need to appreciate how they make sense of situations (see Chapter 10). This chapter considers how our ideas about critical thinking, reflection and reflexivity have evolved. Reflection, as an aspect of professional judgement, is considered in relation to evidence-informed practice, not as opposing concepts but as integrated aspects of social work practice. This book advocates a strengths perspective (Saleebey,

2012) to social work that emphasises reflective and reflexive practice in building supportive relationships with service users and carers.

What is reflective practice?

Horner (2012), in exploring the question 'What is social work?', considers reflection to be central to good social work practice but only if action results from that reflection. This is what is generally known as reflective practice. He considers that reflecting about, on and in practice needs to be developed during initial social work education and is the key to continuing professional development. Hence, it is a concept that also underpins post-qualifying training.

One way to consider the different qualities required of a competent practitioner is to use a model (framework) such as the *Head, Heart and Hand*. This model was first expounded by Kubler-Ross (1997), but has been adapted by numerous writers, such as Cameron (2005) and Ingram (2013).

The head represents our understanding (including critical thinking and reflection) and knowledge (theories and evidence for understanding a situation and the evidence base of methods for intervening). The heart is about our values, attitudes and feelings. The hand refers to our activities and the skills we employ. Ingram (2013) added 'feet' to the model, which situates our practice, providing the context in which your head, heart and hands come into play.

Activity 1.1

What makes a good social worker?

Using the Head, Heart and Hand model, list what you think are the knowledge, skills and attitudes that social workers need in an area of practice that interests you.

Constable (see Chapter 4) argues that SWOT (Strengths, Weaknesses, Opportunities and Threats) analysis can be applied to reflection as well as tasks. Repeat Activity 1.1 using SWOT analysis to think of where your knowledge, skills and attitudes are currently at. How do you compare to your ideal of the social worker?

Comment

Students and practitioners can be quick to identify their weaknesses, but often do not fully acknowledge their strengths. You may find that it was easier to think about opportunities and threats when thinking of particular situations, for example, facing an angry service user. Try to avoid seeing your strengths and weaknesses as absolute, for example, you may feel that you have particularly good people skills, but this could lead to over-confidence. Conversely, it is easy to think of those areas where we are weak as threats, but they are also opportunities for exploration and growth.

This activity demonstrated the use of reflection to become more self-aware (see Chapter 4). Perhaps one of the hardest areas for practitioners to explore is their heart,

(Continued)

(Continued)

our taken-for-granted attitudes, but also recognising feelings that may not coincide with their perception of a professional. For example, would you see it as okay to cry in front of a service user? Schwartz (1995) provided a powerful account of his experience of being diagnosed with advanced lung cancer (he died later that year). A nurse who was working with him came to see him before he had surgery and 'held my hand and with moist eyes wished me luck. This small gesture was powerful; my apprehension gave away to a much-needed moment of calm' (Schwartz, 1995). While it is dependent on the situation and on you whether you will cry, as Schwartz illustrated, we should never lose sight of our humanity and compassion. Oelofsen (2012) pointed out that 'engaging regular reflection enables practitioners to manage the personal and professional impact' of meeting service users' needs and building our resilience.

Emotional intelligence is a crucial factor in self-awareness that enables us to look after ourselves and empathise with others. At an individual level this requires compassion. Practitioners focus on being compassionate to those they work with, but often neglect compassion for themselves. Mindfulness Based Stress Reduction is a meditative approach, developed by Jon Kabat-Zinn (1992), that raises awareness of how we feel physically, emotionally and cognitively and how these elements are integrated. It is a valuable tool for reducing stress, enabling the practitioner to be more present in the moment rather than ruminating on past events or worrying about future ones. At an organisational level, Schwartz Rounds (Dean, 2017) encourage staff to meet together to raise and explore the emotional challenges of their work, in a safe environment, ultimately building staff resilience. The *Head, Heart, Hand and Feet* model covers the domains of knowledge, skills and attitudes required within preparation for practice. Douglas (2008) has developed a systematic framework for exploring these areas in preparation for contact with service users. Blending the two models produces the following framework:

Feet – The environment/context in which you will be practising; this might include the use of case studies and observations to start acclimatising to the situations that you will face.

Head – Consider (a) relevant legislation (b) relevant policy (c) theory for understanding the situation (d) methods for intervening (e) previous knowledge, held by you, other professionals, the service user and carer (f) a tentative strategy for intervening.

Heart – Explore (a) ethical dilemmas raised by the situation (b) the issues these raise for practice (c) anti-oppressive practice (d) your attitudes to the issues raised in this setting (e) self-awareness and emotional intelligence, acknowledging and responding to how you, your client and their carer feel.

Hands – Identify (a) what skills are required (b) your level of competence and confidence in these skills.

On your course you will be introduced to knowledge about how to practise, using such methods as task-centred, cognitive-behavioural or person-centred approaches. You will be expected to apply these theories, when you are on assessed practice and when you are a qualified practitioner. What also happens during and after qualification, according to Parker (2021), however, is that you also begin to construct a body of informal knowledge, or experiential wisdom from working with people in practice. Reflection and reflective practice help you to integrate theoretical learning, whether formal or informal, into your practice, but also to contextualise and make sense of your practice experiences.

So what is this phenomenon of reflection?

The importance of reflective practice is recognised across health care and allied professions. For example, Rolfe et al. (2001) writing about nursing, Tate and Sills (2004) writing about health professions, and Jennings and Kennedy (1996) writing about education are clear that it is relevant for the development of these professions too. Other writers, including Moon (1999, 2004), take a generic approach that is valid for a range of professional development activities, not least social work teaching and learning. Moon (2004) concludes that reflection is applied to relatively complicated, ill-structured ideas for which there is not an obvious solution and is largely based on the further processing of knowledge and understanding that we already possess. Various models have been developed for structuring reflective practice, but perhaps the simplest is the *What, So What, Now What?* model. This model originally developed by Borton (1970) asks the practitioner to think: What has happened? What does it mean to me? What should I do as a consequence?

Activity 1.2

Think of an interaction that happened recently on your course, either in class or in practice, and analyse it using the What, So What, Now What? model. What was the main outcome for you?

Comment

Thinking back to the Kubler-Ross (1997) model, you may have found that your reflections centred on either your thoughts, feelings or actions or all three domains. Were the outcomes of your reflection the same as any of those identified by Moon (2004) below?

- learning, knowledge and understanding;
- some form of action;
- a process of critical review;
- personal and continuing professional development;
- reflection on the process of learning or personal functioning (meta-cognition);
- the building of theory from observations in practice situations;
- the making of decisions/resolution of uncertainty, the solving of problems, empowerment and emancipation;
- unexpected outcomes (e.g. images, ideas that could be solutions to dilemmas or seen as creative activity);
- emotion (that can be an outcome or can be part of the process);
- clarification and the recognition that there is a need for further reflection.

(Moon, 2004, p84)

One critique of Borton's model from Maclean et al. (2018) is that it does not consider 'Why?'. Consequently, they offer an alternative version: What, Why and How? What is it we are concerned with? Why has it occurred? How can we learn from it or change the situation?

Roots of reflective practice

Writers taking a historical approach to the development of ideas on reflective practice generally go back to the work of educational philosopher John Dewey, writing in the inter-war period (Dewey, 1933, 1938). His view was that people only begin to reflect when there is a problem to be solved (see Moon, above). This is very familiar for social work. Dewey argued that reflection is the continual re-evaluation of personal beliefs, assumptions and ideas in the light of experience and data and the generation of alternative interpretations of those experiences and data. This openness to challenging our beliefs and assumptions can be seen as essential to anti-discriminatory practice, which like reflective practice is not a discrete activity, but an ongoing process to gain more self-awareness through critical self-examination (Kendi, 2019). As Williams (2021) points out, also in relation to anti-racism, the impact of our socialisation and the continued, often seemingly invisible cultural, structural and systemic discrimination that occurs requires ongoing curiosity, imagination and examination to expose. Critical thinking and listening to others is essential if we are to overcome our unconscious bias.

The starting point revisiting the roots of reflective practice, however, began with the work of such adult educationalists as Donald Schön (1983, 1987, 2002) writing about the reflective practitioner, and the work of Steven Brookfield (1987) writing about critical thinking and the associated idea of critical learning. Schön advocated two types of reflection: reflection-on-action and reflection-in-action. *Reflection-on-action* is thinking back on something already done, away from the action, such as the What, So What, Now What? model. The process aims to transform the experience into knowledge, which is different from just thinking about practice, which is merely recall without learning from it.

There are several techniques that can be used to enhance this process of reflection-on-action, for example, talking with others, either one to one or in a small group, writing or re-enacting, with another or in a group. Learning from experience and by experience is an essential element of social work training both in class and practice. Some of these activities for stimulating reflection will be explored in more detail in the following chapter.

Reflection-on-action is a retrospective activity that allows us the benefit of hindsight. However, Søren Kierkegaard famously argued that while life can only be understood backwards, it must be lived forwards. Schön's second type of reflection, *reflection-in-action*, focuses on making sense and acting on our analysis, while events are occurring. *Reflection-on-practice* allows us to learn from our mistakes, but *reflection-in-practice* enables us to learn before our errors become irretrievable. Consequently, this way of practising is more difficult, but an important form of reflection for experienced practitioners.

Logically, it is also important that social workers pause before action to give themselves time to think, plan and hopefully avoid errors. This we can call *reflection-for-action*. Thompson and Thompson (2018) explored this and advised that it can help in anticipating possible difficulties and thus give the social worker a greater sense of confidence and control, with a positive effect on morale and motivation. Use of simulation (role play) can help you to practise how you might respond to particular situations. Chapter 5 explores these three phases of reflection in more detail.

Gibbs's (1988) *Reflective Cycle* is a popular, but more detailed approach similar to the What, So What, Now What model, and while most suited to reflection-on-action, it can be applied to the other phases of reflection.

Stage 1: Description

Describes what has happened. Describing a situation is a skilled task in itself. It requires the production of a concise summary, but in so doing some information may be neglected and other items emphasised. For example, you might include more of the points made by one person than another. So, it is important to be sensitive to bias and confirmation bias (where you may unconsciously select information that supports your pre-existing view or values) impacting upon what sense you make of a situation.

Stage 2: Feelings and thoughts

Considers what we thought and felt at the time. Our mood can act like a lens, colouring or distorting our view of an event. For example, if you are feeling threatened, it might shape your interpretation of the behaviour of the person who concerns you. It is important to be aware that other factors, such as our cultural background and our core views can be behind the emotions we feel, and create another lens through which we interpret the world. For example, dementia if viewed in some cultures negatively, leading to fear and stigma (Farmer and Grant, 2020), but in others understood as a part of the cycle of life and viewed a return to a childlike state (Jacklin and Chiovitte, 2020). From the biomedical perspective, these views may seem absurd, but from their perspective so may the medical model. We need to be able to understand these different perspectives, while also adhering to the legal framework in which we work, our agency's policies and our professional standards (Social Work England, 2020).

Stage 3: Evaluation

Identifies what went well and not so well. This is a subjective decision; each person present may have a different but equally valid evaluation of an event. Consequently, it is important to consider the perspective of all stakeholders, whether present, for example, the service user, or not present, for example, your employing organisation. When considering what went well, evaluate the process and content; you might develop a very good therapeutic alliance with a service user (the process), but not be able to achieve what you had hoped to (the substantive content). It is important to also distinguish between the *output* of your work, for example, an assessment and the *outcome*, what the service user wanted to achieve.

Stage 4: Analysis

This is a more critical exploration of why some things went well or not so well, drawing on experience and the evidence base. This stage encourages a further shift of frame of reference, a stepping back to consider wider knowledge. However, be careful to consider what 'lens' you are reaching for. For example, are you considering literature aimed at change in the individual or change in the family, community or society?

Stage 5: Conclusion

Summarises your learning from the situation. It is better to identify a few key points to focus on rather than every possible point.

Stage 6: Action plan

Without an action plan, the reflection remains an academic exercise. To stand a chance of success, the action plan should be SMART. *Specific* actions are much more achievable than vague aims. The actions should be *measurable*, so that progress can be monitored. They should be *achievable*, so there should be several progressive stages rather than one unrealistic one. When reflecting it can be tempting to be distracted by what others could do better, but reflecting is about you, so you are the person *responsible*, and it should always be written in the first person (Moon, 2004). Finally, any plan must be *timely*, as a plan without a timescale remains an aspiration.

Activity 1.3

Reflect back to a recent practice experience, either simulated on your course or actual, using Gibb's Reflective Cycle, and describe the lens that you used to make sense of what you observed. What feelings were uppermost for you?

Comment

An additional metaphor of the *mirror* may also aid our understanding. The mirror reflects back to us what is going on for us in tricky situations. It also helps us to recognise what we are feeling as well as thinking. A good tutor/mentor/practice teacher/assessor as well as fellow students and service users and carers can facilitate this mirroring process, or clear reflecting back. Don't forget to reflect on the process of receiving feedback; it is all too easy to become defensive, particularly when receiving feedback from someone with more power than you. However, this requires that a degree of trust has been created in that relationship. Jacklin and Chiovitte (2020) recommend nurturing cultural safety, in which there is sensitivity to the impact of institutional and systemic racism. Good feedback can aid learning during an experience as well as afterwards. So, it is relevant for reflection-in-action as well as reflection-on-action.

Depth of learning

What, So What, Now What and Gibbs's (1988) Reflective Cycle illustrate different levels of reflection, but as your knowledge and experience grow so will the depth of your reflection (Moon, 2004). Our early attempts at reflection tend to be descriptive and even that can be a challenge; if, for example, you are not accustomed to examining your emotional responses, then that process can take time.

Johari's window (Luft and Ingham, 1955) is a model that helps us to develop our self-awareness. Imagine the quadrants of a window and that through one is what you and other people know about you. This is called the *arena*, and it is where you should try to practise. Through the second panel is what you know, but others don't know about you. This is a *facade*; it is inauthentic, so you should try to be open and honest. For example, if I am training nurses, I make it clear to them that I am a social worker. In the next panel is what others know and you don't know about yourself. This *blind spot* is not going to be uncovered simply by your reflections; it needs you to listen to the feedback of others. Videoing can also be helpful here, for example, I discovered that I had a tendency to tap my foot when anxious. The final panel is the *unknown*, those aspects of yourself, of which you and others are unaware. This requires undertaking new and novel experiences to uncover. For example, on a ward round I realised that I am squeamish.

Activity 1.4

Think of a time when you were wrong – it might be something you did or a thought or opinion you held. How did you feel?

Comment

Your answer might include embarrassment, guilt, regret and annoyance at yourself. However, those are the feelings that come from realising you are wrong. Before that we are oblivious, in the *blind spot*. We may feel confident, righteous and even annoyed. Consequently, we must always reflect on how open we are to having our thoughts and actions challenged.

As we develop our understanding and knowledge, our reflections become more sophisticated and nuanced. In adult education literature, deep reflection is associated with Mezirow's (1991) concept of perspective transformation. This also resonates with practitioners evolving from novices to experts. The novice is characterised by adherence to taught rules and little discretionary judgement, while the expert is characterised by being guided by principles, an intuitive grasp of situations, based on deep understanding, knowing what is possible, using analytical approaches in novel situations or when new problems occur. The competence model of development (attributed to Maslow) suggests that novices go from unconscious incompetence (not knowing what they don't know) to conscious incompetence (recognising what they need to learn), to conscious competence (being able to actively perform correctly) and finally to unconscious competence, where it becomes second nature. Experience in itself is not sufficient for this transformation, as that can produce passive repetition; it requires reflection and acting on those reflections. Early in this process, watch out for the Dunning-Kruger Effect (1999) – as we gain a little knowledge and skill our confidence may increase beyond our competence and we reach the 'peak of mount stupid', before our confidence drops as we realise how little we actually know. Feedback from others is an essential antidote to our subjective perspective.

The expert can be characterised by implicit and unconscious practice. However, Munro (2011b), in her review of child protection, recognised that social workers use analytic and intuitive reasoning in their work and together these enable the practitioner to make assumptions that result in decisions based on sound judgements. Kahneman (2011) has cautioned that people predominantly use intuitive (or 'system 1') thinking, rather than critical analysis (or 'system 2') thinking. System 1 thinking does have the advantage of being much faster, but it is also much more prone to biases, such as stereotyping and our mood at a particular time. Consequently, practitioners need to use reflection to critically consider their decisions, in terms of their rationale and their emotional state (see Chapter 2). However, in our attempts to be objective we need to recognise the pervasive and important influence of our emotions – we cannot step outside our bodies and nor should we try. We seek an awareness not an absence of emotion.

The Professional Capabilities Framework for England (BASW, 2018) has nine capabilities (domains), divided into three super domains of *purpose*, *practice* and *impact*, which are relevant regardless of your level of experience. They provide a single comprehensive set of expectations of social workers at each stage of their career. The framework also has nine levels, from entry to social work training to the strategic social work level. This book is mostly concerned with your initial qualification and Assessed and Supported Year in Employment (ASYE).

Evidence-based practice and reflective practice

A dominant approach within health and social care is 'evidence-based practice' (EBP), which as the name suggests, advocates using what has been objectively found to be the most effective methods and consequently has also been termed empirical practice (Reid, 1994). From Schön's perspective, this would be a technical/rational perspective, rather than intuitive artistry (Schön, 1987). However, the evidence base only takes us so far. Just because a particular approach worked in one situation does not mean it will work in another, as each situation we deal with is unique. Social work is a messy occupation, which involves perceptions and feelings as well as material facts (Parton, 2001). Consequently, *evidence informed practice* has become the preferred term as it recognises the expertise of the practitioner in determining if a particular method will be suitable for a given situation.

Activity 1.5

The evidence base and the judgement of the practitioner are still not sufficient to determine what approach would be best to use in each situation – what do you think is missing?

Comment

The most essential elements in decision-making are service users and their carers, whom the decisions are about. We are guests (albeit, sometimes unwanted) in service users' and their carers' lives. Consequently, while we may be experts in our field, and conversant in the evidence base, if we do not build relationships with and listen to the perspective of service users and carers, the outcomes of our practice are likely to be poor. We do not practise in isolation and should also draw upon the knowledge and expertise of our supervisors, and colleagues from social work and other professions. Their views inform our professional judgements; the accumulation of our reflections and practice wisdom, in combination with the perspective of service users and their carers, enables us to select the relevant evidence-based practice for a specific situation. We must never forget that 'human relationships are of paramount importance and should be at the heart of good social work practice' (Knott, 2016). Developing a therapeutic relationship with a service user and/or carer has significant value in itself, but it is in sharing our expertise and knowledge that we can enable greater gains to be made – for our clients, and also for us. As a social worker new to a specialist unit for people with Huntington's disease, I read the key texts on this rare neurological condition. They gave me an understanding into how people die from Huntington's disease, but it was the service users and their families that gave me insight into how they live with it.

Reflective and critical thinking

John Dewey (1933, p195), when he coined the term 'reflective thinking', argued that it can 'transform a situation in which there is obscurity, doubt, conflict and disturbance of some sort into a situation that is clear, coherent, settled and harmonious'. This requires reflection to be critical, involving critical thinking and critical self-awareness and leading to ethical practice. According to Paul and Elder (2005) of the Foundation for Critical Thinking, a critical thinker is capable of:

- raising vital questions and problems, clearly and precisely;
- gathering and assessing relevant information, using theories and ideas to interpret it effectively;
- reaching conclusions and solutions, tested against relevant criteria;
- thinking open-mindedly, owning assumptions and consequences;
- communicating effectively.

Note that there is a distinction between analytical thinking which helps us to understand a phenomenon in more depth by using a model that enables us to break something down into its component parts, and critical thinking which enables us to form an objective judgement on something. Rutter and Brown (2019), in their book on critical thinking for social work, explore the intellectual resources that are needed for critical thinking as follows:

- background knowledge;
- critical concepts;
- critical thinking standards;
- strategies;
- habits of mind.

Reading peer-reviewed journal articles can give you examples of how others critically appraise each other's work.

Story telling

If we think back to Dewey's quote, did you just accept it, or did you challenge it? If we take a critical approach, we can realise that while clarity would be an ideal, it often eludes us and may not actually be possible. When we gather information, we are attempting to create a narrative of what has happened and is happening, in which we have become a participant. We need to be careful, that in our quest for clarity we do not misinterpret or ignore 'facts' that do not comply with our emerging interpretation. Fook's (2012) model of reflective practice focuses on deconstructing this story with particular attention to issues of power. Individual narratives are not formed in a vacuum and can be influenced by wider discourses, for example, in mental health the medical model has been the dominant discourse, but more recently, service users have been developing an alternative narrative of recovery and hope that is not dependent on a cure for their condition. Fook's (2007) model attempts to deconstruct and then reconstruct the narrative, in an emancipatory vision. In mental health, there has been a growth in interest in ways that service users can be supported to tell and take control of their story, such as the Tidal model (Barker and Buchanan-Barker, 2012) and Open Dialogue, which focuses on the person exploring their mental distress within their support network (Seikkula and Olsen, 2003).

Students and newly qualified workers can find themselves looking for certainty where none exists. This can lead to an over-reliance on procedural approaches to provide a sense of certainty and reduce anxiety. Procedural approaches and anxiety can both reduce a worker's curiosity (Kashdan, 2007). Philippe Mandin, from the Tavistock Centre, argued: 'Sometimes in social work we can be risk-averse and look for quick answers, but reflective practice is about how to contain your own anxieties and still keep your curiosity about a family situation' (Cooper, 2011). Curiosity is the motivation for our reflections, driving us to understand ourselves, our interprofessional colleagues, service users and carers: 'By being curious, we are open to new ideas, challenges and ways of doing things. This constant seeking of knowledge makes innovation happen' (Oshikanlu, 2014).

A lack of professional curiosity has frequently been cited in serious case reviews, following the deaths of children and adults (Victoria Climbie, Peter Connolly and Steven Hoskins are just three high-profile tragedies). Following Operation Bullfinch, which investigated the child sexual exploitation of 370 children and young people in Oxford over a 15-year period, Bedford (2015, p1) argued 'there was a lack of curiosity across agencies about the visible suffering of the children and the information that did emerge from girls, parents, or carers, or some very worried staff'. Munro (2011b), in her review of child protection, four years earlier, summed it up, by arguing that social workers did not identify that child maltreatment was occurring. They had failed to uncover the real story. There is a dilemma for practitioners as Kirtley (2013, p37) pointed out: 'Young people will only tell if they have been asked. The importance of asking the questions must be emphasised'. However, Bedford cautioned: 'There is a fine line between what staff perceive as an appropriate degree of professional curiosity and what a young person perceives as simply too nosey or intrusive'.

Activity 1.6

'Nobody expects the Spanish Inquisition'

How would you try to address the dilemma of probing for more information, but not seeming nosey?

Comment

Showing an interest in someone and giving them an opportunity to tell their story are key aspects of the therapeutic alliance at the heart of good practice. Techniques such as Socratic questioning, where you ask the person to question themselves, for example, 'Why do you think that led you to do that?', are helpful for building a rapport in which you explore the person's world with them. It is, however, important not to get into asking questions, particularly closed ones (which require single word answers) one after the other, as that can feel inquisitorial.

As we have seen, we may not have the information to develop the perfect response, but Rutter and Brown argue that 'the skills of critical thinking allow the best quality decisions or actions possible for the situations we encounter' (2019, p10).

Ethical issues

The other aspect that seems to be involved in developing the critical reflective practitioner is the awareness of ethical issues or value conflicts and the potential, as there is in any relationship or process, for oppression. Austin et al. (2012, p182) argued that 'identifying the discomfort that some experiences entail is a key element of critical reflection'. Rutter and Brown (2019) make a similar point that the process of critical thinking can be threatening, provoke anxiety and create adverse reactions from other people. It can, however, go beyond that immediate experience to re-activate painful experiences from the past (Taylor, 2000). Rutter and Brown (2019) advise people to seek support if the negative aspects are adversely affecting them. This applies to the educational setting as well as the practice setting. So, the process of critical thinking and thus critical reflection needs support. This is where a tutor in the educational setting and a practice educator/supervisor in the practice setting are crucial. If this support is not forthcoming, then there is the ethical question as to the level to which critical reflection should be encouraged. Recognition of feelings (see above), therefore, is an important part of critical reflection. There is some evidence that men find it harder to engage in reflection than women (Moon, 2004, p93). Gender and social work will be discussed further in Chapter 7.

All experiential learning has an element of risk as the responsibility for the level of engagement passes from the tutor/mentor to the students in learning environments and from the practice educator/assessor in the practice environment. Guidance should be given about the potential for distress, either from the nature of the reflected-upon material or the actual process of reflection.

Ixer makes the important point that:

> Social work has become steeped in demands that students should demonstrate reflection in practice as a learning outcome. The danger this poses to vulnerable learners in the assessment relationship, when assessors' own conceptions of reflection may be poorly formed and may not match those of their students, is worryingly likely to compound the imbalance of power between them ... Until such time as we can state more clearly what it is, we have to accept that there is no theory of reflection that can be adequately assessed.

> (1999, p513)

What is reflexive practice?

Taylor and White define reflexivity as:

> an elusive term often used interchangeably with reflection. It encompasses reflection but also incorporates other features so that it is not just the individualised action of separate practitioners in the manner suggested by reflective practice, rather it is the collective action of an academic discipline or occupational group. For workers in health and welfare it means that they subject knowledge claims and practice to analysis.

> (2000, p206)

So, reflexivity goes further, it is our reflections on our reflective process. Prpic (2005) makes an interesting distinction between three different types of reflexivity: the intra-view, an introspective examination of how our thoughts and feelings influence our reflections; the inter-view, where we engaged with others, for example, through supervision or group discussion; and the trans-view, which considers the collective norms and values that shape the other two views. This model fits well to social work, as it encourages us to be concerned with the wider social and cultural context and, in combination with the other two perspectives, to question our values and assumptions and challenge discrimination. Social workers, as Parton (2001) argued, 'work the social'.

Reflection of itself does not lead to 'good enough' professional practice. It needs to be tested against agreed standards for that profession. It could equally be argued that having a Code of Ethics does not of itself lead to ethical practice. Indeed, those social workers involved in statutory social work have to deal with many ethical issues arising from the increasingly bureaucratic, managerial context in which they are required to practise. The role of the state has changed from one of provider of welfare to those in need, to one of commissioner and regulator. The case could be made that the needs of managers are privileged over the needs of service users and carers. Consequently, the reflective practitioner must place their reflections-on-and-in-and-for-action in the context of economic and social policy.

Ixer (1999) has actually made the case that there is no such thing as reflection. He considers that often uncritical attention has been paid to developing and accessing reflective practice in social work education. He finds definitions of reflection and reflective practice to be problematic and theoretical explanations open to debate: 'We do not know enough about reflection or how intricate and complex cognitive processes can enhance learning to be able to assess it fairly. Much of what is assessed remains speculative and conjectural' (1999, p522).

In a thought-provoking article, Yip (2006) strikes a note of caution about self-reflection in reflective practice. Yip agrees that under appropriate conditions reflection can be constructive and result in self-enhancement. However, the pertinent point is made that under inappropriate conditions it can be highly destructive to a social worker's self-development. The inappropriate conditions may include such things as an oppressive social environment at work/placement which could include a highly critical supervisor, apathetic colleagues and a demanding working environment, which includes a demanding workload. The development of a trusting relationship with the practice educator and the supervisor in the workplace is essential for reflection to take place honestly and openly so that learning and professional practice is enhanced. Disclosure of learning needs and practice difficulties must not be misused so that the student/worker feels undermined and/or exploited. Reflection should not become *gaslighting*, in which events are reconstructed, to problematise the student where there are systemic failings. As stated above, reflection is a powerful process and requires mutual respect by all parties. Perhaps more seriously, reflection may uncover unresolved past traumas from childhood, family and partner relationships. Under these circumstances, where physical and mental health issues are apparent, Yip argues that self-reflection in reflective practice may create more harm than good. The clear message is that appropriate conditions need to be in place for constructive reflection to take place.

Reflection is a very subjective practice. Consequently, we need to be constantly searching for other frames of reference to contextualise and calibrate our reflection to ensure our lenses are not becoming tinted or distorted. When we find contradictory or challenging information, we need to be open to assimilate it into the sense we are making and the actions we are taking. This necessitates an open curiosity or what Buddhists call a 'beginner's mind' to our approach. A question frequently asked of students both verbally and on written work is 'Where is your evidence for that?' If the information is only based on evidence from research, students will be asked to reflect on the research and find meaning relevant to themselves and the practice situation. Thus, we promote the concept of the *informed reflective practitioner* in an uncertain world.

This book is attempting to add to that clarification so that both the process and outcome of reflection can be more clearly taught and assessed.

Chapter summary

There is no doubt that the terminology around reflection, reflexivity and reflective practice is difficult and that some educators and practitioners will favour one interpretation above another. We would argue that an integration of both the reflective and evidence-based approaches to learning and practice is needed and that they are not necessarily mutually exclusive. Social workers need to be informed reflective practitioners. They need to know from research which interventions are most likely to lead to the best outcomes. In other words, 'what works'. Kubler-Ross (1997, p119), however, pointed out that 'knowledge helps, but knowledge alone is not going to help anybody if you do not use your head and your heart and your hands, you are not going to help a single human being'.

Further reading

Healy, K (2022) *Social work theories in context: Creating frameworks for practice* (3rd edn). Basingstoke: Palgrave Macmillan.

McLaughlin, H and Teater, B (2017) *Evidence informed practice for social work*. Milton Keynes: Open University Press.

Moon, J (2004) *A handbook of reflective and experiential learning: Theory and practice*. London: RoutledgeFalmer.

Ruch, G, Turney, D and Ward, A (eds) (2018) *Relationship-based social work: Getting to the heart of practice* (2nd edn). London: Jessica Kingsley.

Rutter, L and Brown, K (2019) *Critical thinking and professional judgment for social work* (5th edn). Exeter: Learning Matters.

Schön, D (2002) From technical rationality to reflection-in-action. In R Harrison, F Reeve, A Hanson and J Clarke (eds), *Supporting lifelong learning. Volume 1: Perspectives on learning*. London: Routledge/Open University.

Yip, K (2006) Self-reflection in reflective practice: A note of caution. *British Journal of Social Work*, 36: 777–788.

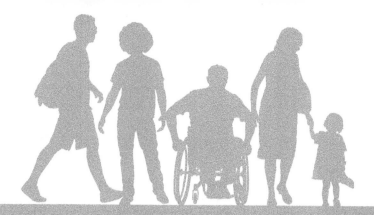

2

Getting started

Martyn Higgins

(Continued)

4.4 Demonstrate good subject knowledge on key aspects of social work practice and develop knowledge of current issues in society and social policies impacting on social work.

4.5 Contribute to an open and creative learning culture in the workplace to discuss, reflect on and share best practice.

4.6 Reflect on my learning activities and evidence what impact continuing professional development has on the quality of my practice.

4.7 Record my learning and reflection on a regular basis and in accordance with Social Work England's guidance on continuing professional development.

4.8 Reflect on my own values and challenge the impact they have on my practice.

Professional Capabilities Framework (2018)

1. Professionalism
2. Knowledge
3. Critical reflection and analysis

See Appendix 1 for the Professional Capabilities Framework Fan and a description of the nine domains.

Social Work Subject Benchmark Statement (2019)

5.3 xii continuous professional development as a reflective, informed and skilled practitioner, including the constructive use of professional supervision;

5.12 ii take into account differences of viewpoint in gathering information and critically assess the reliability and relevance of the information gathered;

5.13 ii analyse and synthesise information gathered, weighing competing evidence and modifying own viewpoint in the light of new information, then relate this information to a particular task, situation or problem;

5.17 ii advance own learning and understanding with a degree of independence and use supervision as a tool to aid professional development.

See Appendix 2 for a detailed description of these standards.

Introduction

This chapter links with the previous chapter and offers some useful and practical ways to develop your skills of reflection. Most social work courses at qualifying and post-qualifying levels will require you to complete reflective pieces of work, which will be assessed. Some may form part of your assessment of the professional practice elements of your course and others will be part of your learning and assessment of university-based elements. Many students find this process of reflection difficult to grasp, but once the process has been developed, it will underpin your learning about the theory and practice of social work while you are students and on into your life as a qualified social worker. So, the earlier you address and value the process of reflection, the better. It will also underpin your continuing professional development as a social worker, which is a requirement for continuing registration. When you continue into post-qualifying studies, you will also be required to enhance your reflective capabilities. In terms of interprofessional work, most other professions with whom you will work, such as the health professions and teaching, also value the process of reflection as part of their professional and post-professional education and training.

The framework for this chapter starts with understanding how we learn and some models of learning from experience. The reflective practitioner is a worker who can use experience and theory to guide and inform practice. Reflection involves being open-minded, carefully thinking things through; it can be a source of constant learning rather than a rigid, routinised approach to practice (Munro, 2011b; Thompson, 2015).

Getting started on any activity is for some of us the hardest part. However, once we have got going, we wonder what all the fuss was about. The avoidance of getting started is known as displacement activity. Instead of getting on with the required activity, we do all sorts of other things, like having a cup of coffee, putting a load into the washing machine and then having another cup of coffee and so on. We call it the 'I'll just' syndrome. We say to ourselves, 'I'll just take the dog for a walk' or 'I'll just have a bath', etc. Extreme displacement can find us doing those things that we would avoid doing in normal circumstances, such as cleaning the oven or sorting out the mess in the garage. We can all experience blocks to reflection and so to learning. A useful early activity is to reflect on experiences that have enhanced or blocked learning.

Activity 2.1

Make a list of three good learning experiences and three learning experiences that could be improved. What happened that helped your learning and what happened that blocked your learning? Where possible share the results of this activity with a colleague on the course, your tutor and/or practice educator.

Comment

This activity provides a solid foundation for beginning the process of learning how to learn and reflecting on what helps you learn. This will be a continuing theme throughout this chapter. It is sometimes helpful to realise that you are not the only person who finds that learning can be both enhancing and difficult. It is useful to share our previous experiences of learning. It is also important for those who are employed to facilitate our learning, both academic and from practice, to be aware of what we find helpful to that process. Finally, it is up to each of us to begin to take responsibility for our own learning and to try to deal with or avoid those experiences that block our

(Continued)

(Continued)

learning. It is important to see your learning as an appreciative enquiry whereby your focus is on what you can learn from your experience and build upon the learning as part of your professional development. An appreciative enquiry approach reflects on what we have learnt rather than on what went wrong (Rawles, 2016).

Case study

In completing this activity, Susan, a year one student, realised that there had been several times during a lecture when she found it hard to listen, take notes and understand what she was hearing. She always had to go away and spend time reading over her notes and still felt she did not fully understand. On reflection, she recognised that if she had prior access to the lecture notes she would learn better. So, she approached the lecturer and asked if it was possible to have the lecture notes before the session. The lecturer agreed to post the lecture notes on the intranet a few days before each lecture. Susan then found that with the opportunity to read ahead, she was able to participate more fully in any discussion. Many of the other students were also grateful to Susan for making this request.

Reflective space

The idea of a reflective space is an important one for us. By this we mean both a physical space and the time to spend in it. A reflective space requires organisation and negotiation. Some of your social work courses will have negotiated this for you so far as your academic work is concerned. Study time will hopefully have been timetabled and space in university learning resource centres is there to be used. Of course, some of your own time will be needed too. Ideally, on placement, a desk and regular supervision will form part of placement agreement meetings/contracts so that a reflective space is available there too, although this may not always be possible. It is important that the same negotiation and organisation occurs in your domestic life if you are to benefit from reflective activities. The level and amount of negotiation will vary according to your circumstances. If you are living in shared accommodation such as a shared student house, or with a partner and/or children, then it is very important to make your needs known and agreed. We recognise that a reflective space may sometimes be part of another activity such as having a bath or a shower, doing household tasks, waiting for a bus or a train. These sorts of spaces can be used productively and are often free of potential learning blocks that can be evoked by sitting at a desk. It helps us to realise how often we do, in fact, engage in reflection. Some of these activities may be seen as part of a ritual that marks the beginning of a reflective process.

It is probably more challenging to secure a reflective space from work on post-qualifying social work courses, but it is worth the effort to negotiate time and space from your line manager as it will be in your agency's interests that you enhance your learning and practice capabilities as a post-qualified practitioner.

Activity 2.2

Experiment with finding something that helps you to enter a different space to begin your reflection, for example, a few minutes with your eyes closed, deep breathing, arranging your space to suit yourself, having a cup of tea or wearing a particular item of clothing.

Comment

This activity will help you to put on your 'thinking cap'. Over time you will find what works best for you. This may change depending on your mood, time of day and what you want to accomplish.

Experiential learning and the learning cycle

Most social work courses will use experiential learning techniques such as role play and simulation. So, what are the components of learning by and from experience? Goldstein (2001, p65) says experiential learning is:

> expressed in reflective thought and action, in confidence about one's wisdom tested by experience and shaped by a mind that is open to new and possibly contradictory knowledge.

Reflection has a key role in experiential learning or in enabling experiential learning. On your qualifying social work course, over half of the course is spent in professional practice and quite a high proportion of university learning and teaching will also employ teaching methods that seek to value the experience you bring with you and to create new/ simulated experiences. Skills laboratories will facilitate experiential learning. Generally, such laboratories will have audio-visual equipment so that skills of effective communication can be recorded and reflected upon. A good starting point is with an audio tape.

Activity 2.3

Using a recorder, begin by reading a short paragraph from a book. Once you have got the settings right, record your response to the following questions and try to be as relaxed and conversational as possible:

(Continued)

(Continued)

- What did I enjoy most on the course today?
- What learning stood out for me?
- What did I find uncomfortable or difficult?

Comment

You may find that some important learning on the course does not happen in class but as a result of an informal interaction or incident that you were part of. Reflection on situations can help you to learn how you respond and how you might wish you had responded. As you become more confident in using recordings, you can then try recording a more conversational exchange with another student.

Models of learning

A major model of learning that you may encounter is the *Kolb Learning Cycle*. Kolb's (1984) Learning Cycle includes the following concepts:

- concrete experience;
- observations and reflections;
- formation of abstract concepts and generalisations;
- testing the implications of concepts in new situations.

Kolb makes the case that to be effective learners, the above four kinds of ability are needed, which match the four stages of the learning cycle, namely concrete experiencing of a situation, reflective observation, abstract conceptualisation and active experimentation. The key message we can see from Kolb's model is that learning is more than just obtaining information. Learning is experiential and reflective. As learners we test out theories and observations in our practice. This testing out in practice and reflection on our practice gives us the opportunity to develop our knowledge and understanding based on our professional experience. Experiential learning is a kind of active experiment whereby we can learn from the results of our experimentation (Goldstein, 2001).

Learning styles

Following on from Kolb's learning cycle, a number of self-evaluation questionnaires have been developed to help you explore what 'type' of learner you are. They tend to form part of study skills programmes, and most social work courses will include this aspect of helping their students understand their preferences, styles and habits. Cottrell (2010) summarises and includes some of these questionnaires which students may like to access. Honey and Mumford (2006) may provide a helpful way to reflect on what best helps you learn. Their terminology is similar to that of Kolb, as follows:

Activists prefer to work in an intuitive, flexible and spontaneous way, generating ideas and trying out new things. They usually have lots to say and contribute. They like to learn from experience, such as through problem-based learning, working in groups, workshops, discussion and teamwork.

Reflectors prefer to watch and reflect, gathering data and taking time to consider all the options and alternatives before making a decision. They prefer to learn through lectures, project work and working alone.

Theorists prefer to learn by going through things thoroughly and logically, step by step with clear guidelines, and have to feel they have learnt solidly before they apply what they know. They prefer to learn from books, problem-based learning and discussion.

Pragmatists prefer to learn by 'trying things out' to see if they work, just getting on with it, getting to the point. They like to be practical and realistic. They prefer to learn on work-based projects and practical applications.

However, the use of Honey and Mumford needs to be used with some caution. There is evidence the Honey and Mumford has limited efficacy (Caple and Martin, 1994). If used, Honey and Mumford may be best applied as one of a number of approaches available.

There are other models and approaches to learning styles. For example, you may want to have a look at the Visual, Aural, Read/write and Kinesthetic model (VARK) discussed in Fleming and Baume (2006). It is important to see these approaches as just some of the tools that can help you reflect on what helps you learn in a variety of settings (Cottrell, 2010).

Activity 2.4

Look at the learning preferences as described above and decide which type best describes you and whether the associated way of learning matches your preferences.

Comment

You may have recognised that you prefer learning in a particular way and that may be a good starting point for you. You will need, however, to develop the other styles as most teachers will have a preference for teaching according to a particular style, although good teachers will vary their methods so that all students can be engaged in the learning. Honey and Mumford (2006) offer a list of suggested exercises that will help you develop the full range of learning styles and thus become more competent learners.

Case study

Swaati, a very confident active student, always volunteered for role play and other experiential activities in class. However, she gradually realised that other students

(Continued)

(Continued)

were learning more from the activity than she was. After completing a learning style questionnaire, she recognised that her reflector style needed some development. Consequently, she began to pay more attention to recording thoughts and feelings and taking part in the post-activity discussion. She then began to make more sense of the theoretical material given out by the tutor and to make more sense of her learning from practice. In this way she had completed the learning cycle. She realised that she did not need to lead in role play and could learn by observing and listening to others.

What follows in this chapter are some of the activities that may be used on your social work course, in the order that they are generally experienced. These activities may vary as we recognise that they can operate at different depths of learning.

Personal development planning (PDP)

All university students are being encouraged/required to undertake some form of PDP self-evaluation, and Cottrell (2010) is very helpful in this respect. Many social work courses have used self-evaluation techniques for several years based on the premise that you need to know yourself before you try to know and work with other people in any deep or meaningful way. As stated above, Cottrell advocates starting early on reflection as part of a lifelong skill. She considers that the process of reflection has a number of basic steps as follows:

- small regular bites;
- be specific;
- aim at improvement;
- focus on yourself;
- use prompts;
- critical rather than descriptive writing;
- have a purpose;
- find the right questions;
- review.

Thompson builds on these basic steps by suggesting that reflective practice combines both a focus on practice and the use of theory to make sense of practice dilemmas. Moving on from basic reflection, social work reflection involves (Thompson, 2015):

- drawing selectively and appropriately on our professional knowledge base, using both formal and informal knowledge;
- integrating theory and practice, rather than looking to theory to provide 'ready-made' answers;
- drawing on the vast professional knowledge base available to us;
- making use of available research, particularly in relation to the evaluation of outcomes (what is often referred to as 'evidence-based practice');

- thinking on our feet and being prepared to be imaginative and creative;
- being prepared to learn from experience by reflecting on it;
- being open to new ideas and approaches.

Learning logs or journals

One of the most common ways of developing the reflective practice used on social work courses is the use of learning logs or learning journals, so we will make this an early activity for getting started. Subsequent chapters also refer to this important activity. We use the term 'learning journal' although we appreciate that a variety of terminology may be used. The use of reflective journals is not restricted to professional courses, and we have heard of their use on such diverse undergraduate degrees as theology and media studies. There is a wide range of ways to structure a learning or reflective log. Cottrell (2010) suggests you:

1. note down all aspects of an experience;
2. keep a daily or weekly diary on a particular theme;
3. share your thoughts with others through a blog;
4. record all the information you consider significant about your learning. This could include:

   - your feelings about a learning experience;
   - class discussions;
   - thoughts about your learning styles and how they help you learn;
   - ideas that come from your studies;
   - how your studies relate to placement experience;
   - relevance of theory learnt in class to practice;
   - what you are learning about yourself through your interactions with others;
   - tips and strategies, you are learning;
   - what you are learning about managing your emotions;
   - things you find difficult;
   - sources of inspiration.

You may have already discovered that some of your reflections might be difficult, possibly painful or upsetting. You may have tried to block or censor these reflections. It is important to acknowledge that we all sometimes avoid reflecting on difficult or uncomfortable events. However, learning to reflect on painful experiences and learn from them is a core skill we develop over time as social workers (Ferguson, 2018). Supportive supervision from your manager and colleagues is one very good tool to help you reflect.

Guidance about the writing of journals may vary. On social work courses, journals may be required to follow a particular structure or they may be totally unstructured. Our experience is that students prefer structured guidance in the initial stages but then develop their own style and structure. Essentially, journals start off being rather descriptive but may quite quickly move to being more critically analytical about an event. Once the essential elements of a situation are described, then this can be followed by some form of self-evaluation of personal experience, strengths, qualities and skills. Sometimes journals themselves are assessed, or selections from the journal are included in the form of a journal analysis. This means that the students can remove those sections that are more private. They may, however, be shared in a tutorial or practice supervision.

Cottrell (2010) makes the important point that keeping a reflective journal can be very challenging, especially being motivated to making regular entries. It requires determination, good planning and a far-sighted approach. Being convinced of the value of the journal is paramount.

Activity 2.5

On your own: Spend about 10–15 minutes composing a message to a previous teacher or tutor, giving them positive feedback about how you experienced them in that role. Include your feelings and any outcomes of this experience, for example, you inspired me to read Jane Austen, to think about working with people, etc.

With another student: Swap letters with your partner and take it in turns to role play being the recipient of the letter and meeting the writer to discuss it.

Comment

This activity builds on Activity 2.1 and enables you to be more concrete and specific about a previous learning experience and leads you to explore the consequences and implications for future learning. You could take this further by reflecting on the role play in your journal.

Online reflection

Rafferty and Steyaert (2007) explore the fact that we live in a digital society which has significantly changed the information landscape, affecting every aspect of our lives. The current wave of technological innovation is part of the context in which social work students, practitioners and service users and carers operate. What follows are some basic ideas about this.

A blog can be used by students to write reflectively about their learning experiences and can provide a continuous record of a student's activities, progress and development.

A blog is an abbreviation of 'web **log**' and is designed as a web space that can be written to, published and viewed online. Blogs can be written about a wide variety of subjects and can also include audio (podcasting), video (vlog) and photos (photoblog), as well as blogs on mobiles and tablets.

The online blog is purely a tool which enables people to publish directly to a web space which is usually personal, but it could also be set up as a group space if preferred. Typically, users register with a blog and then, as they log in, their passwords identify them to the blog. Users will be able to view their most recent entry to their blogs first and older entries are archived.

Blogs can be set up using commercially available spaces that use a hosting website, for example, Blogger.com, or a restricted website where users must be pre-registered, such as a university blog. Blogs can also be customised to meet the requirements of users, for example, blog entries might automatically trigger emails to supporting tutors to inform them that a new log entry has been published.

The advantage of writing reflectively online means that students can access their online logs or journals from any computer with internet access. If permissions are set up, students may choose to publish their reflective blogs to tutors, peers or a worldwide audience.

Reflective blog entries can be structured to provide responses to set questions or left more open. Tutors or peers can provide formative feedback to blog entries that students can then respond back to and set goals for their future learning. The blog can eventually form part or all of a summative assessment, providing evidence of learning achievements.

Online practice has been transformed since COVID-19. Current social work literature offers an overview of the significant impact of the move to working online. For example, emerging evidence of the impact of COVID can be seen in emerging evidence on the impact of working digitally with children in child protection (Anna Freud Centre, 2020, available at https://www.annafreud.org/coronavirus-support/our-research/). Students may find it helpful to reflect on the following questions (Talor-Beswick, 2021):

1. How has the pandemic altered your own use of digital tools professionally and personally?
2. Why is digital criticality important for social work in the future?

Activity 2.6

Search the web and read some online blogs where people have reflected upon their learning. Look at how people reflect upon their learning and the style of language they use.

Register for your own online blog (for example at Blogger.com) or your university blog and post up your next learning reflections to your blog. If desired, email the web address to your tutor or peer and ask for some constructive feedback.

Comment

The exercise should provide good insight into the variety of ways blogs can be presented, and you should also recognise that the language used is often less formal. When writing a blog, remember that the last entry is always viewed first.

Peer feedback can be extremely beneficial, and without involving the tutor it can be seen as less threatening by participants. Interestingly, peers who provide feedback can also learn through participation in the process to appreciate the value of creating constructive criticism, enabling students to become more critical and perceptive about their own learning (McConnell, 2006).

A final point about writing reflectively, particularly in journals and blogs, is that it is different from academic writing in the essential sense that it is written in the first person and not the third person. This may cause some students initial problems as they will have been encouraged in other writing to adhere to academic conventions. Writing about Open University students, Rai (2006) notes that expectations for reflective journal writing seemed to contradict the usual academic conventions. She concludes that guidance for reflective writing such as journals needs to be made explicit so that students are clear about the alternative conventions for reflective writing, such as writing in the first person about the self, about feelings and about skill development, whether this is for learning and/or assessment. We would encourage you to carefully share your learning using social networking as part of your ongoing professional development.

Skills laboratory work

Used sensitively and competently, skills laboratory work can greatly enhance student reflection on their performance, particularly in communication and interview skills. The students undertake interview-type scenarios and are filmed doing so. These scenarios can either be previously prepared or they can arise from the students' own practice situations, such as might have been selected for presentation of a critical incident for analysis. Thus, a more visual form of reflection is encouraged.

The resulting feedback acts as a *mirror*, as outlined in Chapter 1. You may find that having your skills recorded for analysis is a frightening experience to begin with but eventually you will come to appreciate the learning that can be achieved by this form of reflection and analysis. Learning to give feedback to fellow students is a good skill to learn, as it is an important social work skill. The use of audio-visual recording methods helps to provide evidence to support the feedback. It also allows the student to reflect on the skills they have demonstrated in the recording and be given guidance either from fellow students or tutors on how they can enhance their performance in future. The aim of all feedback is to encourage reflection on practice and provide ideas for improvement of performance.

Activity 2.7

The importance of feedback in the reflective process cannot be overestimated, so work in pairs on the following tasks:

* Share with your partner some verbal or written feedback that you have recently been given about your skills, either from a skills laboratory workshop or from a practice educator's observation of practice.
* Share how you responded to the feedback. For example, were the comments unexpected, and did you agree or disagree with them? What feelings were raised for you from the feedback?
* What steps will you take to improve your performance?
* Your partner should give their response to what has been shared, including comments on any anti-oppressive issues.

(Continued)

Exchange roles and repeat the exercise.

Comment

This exercise requires good listening skills, trust, respect and courage to share in a supportive space and to receive honest feedback. Try not to become complicit with your partner but to give praise where appropriate and also ideas for improvement, such as helpful resources including readings, web pages, people who might help, etc.

Case study

John was very anxious about being filmed in the skills laboratory and did all he could to avoid the experience. Eventually, however, he was encouraged to take part in a listening exercise in the laboratory. Despite being nervous, the feedback he received from both students and staff was very encouraging. They told him that he appeared calm and confident, he made good eye contact, his body language clearly showed that he was listening and his responses were thoughtful. He also learned that his voice was very quiet and he needed to develop his tone of voice and volume.

Non-verbal techniques

Much of what we have written in this chapter has been about verbal and written approaches to getting started in reflection. However, there are a number of non-verbal techniques that some students may find helpful in getting started. Others may find them less helpful. Some can be integrated with the verbal and written approaches.

Many students find these approaches to reflection both challenging and fun. They can be also used with service users for whom written and verbal approaches are difficult. Generally, they come under what is termed 'right-brain activities' as follows:

- using aesthetic approaches such as drawing, sculpting, making collages, making or listening to music, composing a poem;
- graphical exercises such as drawing life lines or route maps;
- projective techniques such as photographs, pictures, film clips, audio clips;
- relaxation with guided fantasies;
- drama, including forum theatre techniques, role plays and simulations;
- concept mapping and organograms;
- using metaphor.

Activity 2.8

Draw, paint or make a collage from old magazines as a metaphor for your own entry into social work. This can be done either with a partner or in a small group.

Comment

Using varied materials and approaches can release energy and encourage reflection in diverse ways. It can provide an opportunity for fun and creativity and also provide further insight into the process of reflection and the ways in which other students learn and develop.

Asking good questions

By making this a short separate section in this chapter, we are emphasising the point that to be asked a good question either as a student or as a service user can be life-enhancing and may promote deeper reflection. You will probably spend some time on your course developing effective communication skills, and asking good questions is worth the effort. Unfortunately, in social work practice many questions are bureaucratically designed in the form of assessment forms and questionnaires. Nevertheless, the ability to ask and be asked good questions enables deep reflection to take place. When we are asked a good question, it seems to demand a thoughtful answer. Freud (1988, p110) says that asking good questions could have a liberating effect. She views good questions as gifts rather than intrusive assaults.

It is how a question is asked as well as what is asked that can make a good question. Open questions, such as those using the 5WH formula, are helpful. Who, What, When, Where, Why and How questions tend to suit thinkers who like to work in a logical, ordered or controlled way and appreciate some external direction. This is good to begin with but then it may be advisable to move on quickly to open reflection, to go with the flow, let go and be relatively unstructured, promoting free writing and thinking.

Using Socratic questioning can help you develop a reflective approach to the use of questions. The philosopher Socrates developed the model to test what our assumptions were and whether there was justification for our beliefs. Socratic questioning is based on principles such as (Ferreira and Ferreira, 2015):

- Respond to all answers with a further question that will call upon you to develop their thinking in a fuller and deeper way.
- Seek to understand the ultimate foundations for what is said or believed and follow the implications of those foundations through further questions.
- Treat all assertions as a connecting point to further thoughts.
- Treat all thoughts as in need of development (starting with your own thoughts).

- Recognise that any thought can only fully exist in a network of connected thoughts – pursue those connections.
- Recognise that all questions presuppose prior questions and all thinking presupposes prior thinking.

Activity 2.9

What is the best question that you have been asked on your social work course? Why was it a good question? Have you asked the same question of other people? What was the response?

Comment

We hope that the answer to this activity is that you have been asked good questions and that they made you stop and think. According to Freud (1988), asking real questions means that you stand a chance of getting real answers, which may be upsetting, painful or disturbing, so you need to be able to bear the answers.

Critical incident analysis

The process of using critical incident analysis with social work students has been used for many years (Crisp et al., 2005). Tutor groups meeting on a weekly or bi-weekly basis, during recall days from assessed practice placements, may ask students to present to the group an analysis of an incident from their practice placement. Some students find the term 'critical' difficult to begin with, assuming that it means something negative. This is certainly not the case, as seen below. The presentation usually includes:

- a brief description of the incident;
- an exploration of why the incident had a particular impact on you: what made it critical;
- an examination of which theoretical concepts informed your response and intervention;
- reflection on what has been learned from the incident and how it might inform future practice.

With the presentation, which is assessed, students submit a brief report of the incident. Following feedback on both the presentation and the report, the student is then required to submit a longer evaluation of the critical incident, also for assessment. This takes the learning from the incident further and places it in a broader social context, exploring issues of discrimination, inequality and oppression.

So, what constitutes a critical incident? Our view is that it must be an incident that relates to an aspect of the student's own practice, and it is their own actions in response to the incident that are reflected upon. It cannot be an incident in which they were an observer, however interesting that might be. A critical incident is one that causes us to think and reflect, which leads to learning about ourselves and others (individual and organisations) or about processes. Most incidents are not at all dramatic or obvious but commonplace events that occur routinely in social work education and/or professional practice. They may include any of the following situations:

- when you felt you had done something well;
- when you had made the wrong decision;
- when something went better than expected;
- when you lacked confidence;
- when you made a mistake;
- when you really enjoyed working with someone or a group;
- when you had a feeling of pressure;
- when you found it difficult to accept or value a service user(s);
- when you felt unsupported;
- when you were worried about a service user(s);
- when you took a risk and it paid/didn't pay off.

Activity 2.10

Select an incident from your practice and use the above framework to reflect on and analyse the incident. This is a useful exercise to complete in pairs in the first instance.

Comment

What sort of incident did you select for analysis? Was it dramatic or commonplace? It is important that you are aware that the term 'critical' does not necessarily mean dramatic or negative.

It is very likely that you will be asked to undertake something like this on your course, with the analysis of the critical incident being used for either formative or summative assessment. For most students, completing these in groups is an important element of learning from reflection (reflection-on-action), from our own and that of others.

Narrative analysis

As suggested in Chapter 1, social work practice is often complex and messy and reflections on practice frequently endorse this. It is important, therefore, to try and reflect on your reflections, and this we are calling narrative analysis. This is probably a section of the chapter that may be more relevant for post-qualifying students, especially those who are training to become practice educators and/or supervisors.

Many of us find meaning in our lives from the stories or narratives that we ourselves tell or hear about ourselves, our families and friends and others. Story is taken to mean the actual events, while narrative is the recounting of the story. Taylor (2006, p193) says that we grasp our lives in narrative – it enables us to make sense, to pattern the events of our lives. She adopts a dialogical approach to narrative, involving a narrator and an audience, attending to the interactive/performance aspects of narrative rather than its formal properties. She goes on to make the important point that in social work education reflective accounts in the form of journals, diaries, etc. tend to be taken as 'what really happened' in any situation, whereas it should be recognised that narrators select, order and report events in particular ways for particular effects. This may be particularly the case when reflective accounts or commentaries are being assessed. Students will try and structure their journals to meet the requirements for a pass grade and write what they think the marker wants to read. In Taylor's analysis they are performing two closely connected identities, one as the competent and caring professional and the other as competent reflector, forming a composite identity as the 'reflective practitioner' (Taylor, 2006). Of course, this is what this book is attempting to promote and so are social work courses that value the reflective approach, but it needs to be authentic and genuine and not 'just for the sake of'.

The aim of a narrative is to persuade the listener or reader that the story is true and that the author is to be believed. It is important that in telling the story we trust what the narrator is telling us. Both the narrator and the story need to ring true. Sometimes what helps in narration is the inclusion of actual dialogue, as this aids authenticity. In persuading the listener/reader of the veracity of the story, the inclusion of reflections on practice will help so that the narrative is not just a descriptive account but something that promotes deeper learning about the professional identity of the social worker and their view of the world of the service user. Students writing narratives and staff responsible for their assessment need to bear this in mind as they undertake their respective difficult and responsible tasks. Narratives can be seen to be a type of 'life story', often used in adoption. Narratives in this sense are developmental, telling the story of both social work students' professional development and the life story of service users (Higgins et al., 2015; Higgins, 2016). A case could be made that such narratives should not be used for assessment but rather for formative development. We consider that assessment is part of learning and that sensitive assessment, carefully carried out and moderated, is worth the time and effort.

Activity 2.11

Reflect on all the activities that we have asked you to do in this chapter and in pairs identify themes/patterns that have emerged from your narratives and share them with your partner. Alternatively, if you are in placement or post-qualifying, reflect on a story that you have been told by a service user or carer for its authenticity and veracity.

Comment

This kind of reflection draws upon many of the skills already mentioned in this chapter such as observation and critical incident analysis. It is a profound part of your development as a professional.

Blocks to learning

We have so far in this chapter looked at how we can start to learn to reflect effectively and professionally as social workers. Sometimes, however, there can be what we call 'blocks to learning' when previous or existing learning experiences hinder or adversely affect successful learning. Blocks to learning can be seen to consist of three types (adapted from Horwath and Morrison, 1999): personal, professional and placement/organisation.

Personal blocks come about when our own personal experiences affect negatively our opportunities to learn. As children and young people we may have felt that we were not bright or clever enough to succeed academically. Existing personal circumstances may hinder our learning. This could be due to health problems, financial difficulties or learning issues such as dyslexia. Using some of the models of learning discussed above can provide ways for you to reflect on what helps you learn and how to address those personal learning needs. In Susan's case study, Susan identified what was hindering her learning and sought support from her lecturer. Universities provide a wide range of learning support from specialised equipment to extra time for essays and exams. Taking advantage of these provisions will help facilitate your learning. Activity 2.3 in this chapter provides a technique to help you reflect on what you learnt in class and identify what went well and what you found difficult or uncomfortable. Cottrell (2010) has written a useful chapter on how to 'start with yourself' as a way to learn to identify your strengths and developmental needs as a learner. Narrative analysis discussed above can also help you explore and consider your own learning needs and abilities.

Professional blocks occur in your professional practice while you are a student and when you become a qualified social worker. Social work is a profession that experiences frequent changes. What this means is that social work students and qualified practitioners must engage with dilemmas, unpredictability and conflicting professional requirements and expectations (Higgins, 2013). Having a core sense of your own professional values and the reasons why you want to become and remain a social worker is the essential first step in managing change. Using learning logs and critical incident analysis can encourage and strengthen your ability to reflect on your values and how you are affected by the challenges of change. Cottrell (2010) provides further tools to explore how to manage change.

Whether you are on placement or in qualified practice, the culture of your agency has a major impact on you personally and your practice. Senge (2006) emphasises the importance of organisations needing to be learning organisations. In terms of your relationship with your practice educator/supervisor, you can use teaching tools to explore together your learning approaches and how you can best work together given your preferred learning styles. However, your ability to influence the organisation's learning can be more problematic. Developing a trusting and engaged relationship with your practice educator or supervisor is crucial and making use of learning tools such as Honey and Mumford is an excellent first step. A critical analysis can also help to broaden out your incident to include the organisational context and factors. With your practice educator or supervisor, you can work together over a period of weeks to explore the role of the organisation with a critical incident analysis. Regular seminars, critical incident groups and effective use of online reflection can also encourage a learning culture within the organisation.

Colonisation and the impact on learning

Negative experiences can impact on Black students and their learning. Challenging racism and linking colonization to the Black Lives Movement can help teachers and students reflect on and challenge implicit and explicit racism in the white dominated academy (Moore and Simango, 2021).

Chapter summary

In this chapter, we have introduced you to a number of ways of getting started in reflecting on your practice and learning how to learn. All the activities are practical and each one builds on the previous activities, helping you to develop your reflective skills. We have set the scene for you about how adults learn and why reflective practice is worth the effort. We have also discussed a wide range of ways in which your reflections will be central to your learning and practice as a social worker. Some of the ideas we have presented will appeal more than others and this itself is worthy of reflection, but we hope that you will enjoy getting started and learning more about yourself as a reflective practitioner. It is important to know what works for you and what you need to develop.

Further reading

For a good general overview of the practical skills of reflection, theory and their application to social work practice, the following are recommended.

Caple, J and Martin, P (1994) Reflections of two pragmatists: A critique of Honey and Mumford's learning styles. *Industrial and Commercial Training*, 26(1).

Cottrell, S (2010) *Skills for success: The personal development planning handbook* (2nd edn). Basingstoke: Palgrave Macmillan.

Thompson, N (2015) *Understanding social work: Preparing for practice* (4th edn). London: Palgrave.

3

Reflecting on emotion in social work

Gill Butler

Achieving a social work degree

This chapter will help you to meet the current Social Work England Professional Standards (2019), develop capabilities from the Professional Capabilities Framework (2018) and introduce you to the Social Work Benchmark Statement (2019). The following are of particular relevance to this chapter:

Social Work England Professional Standards (2019)

4.2 Use supervision and feedback to critically reflect on, and identify my learning needs, including how I use research and evidence to inform my practice.
4.3 Keep my practice up to date and record how I use research, theories and frameworks to inform my practice and my professional judgement.
4.4 Demonstrate good subject knowledge on key aspects of social work practice and develop knowledge of current issues in society and social policies impacting on social work.

(Continued)

4.5 Contribute to an open and creative learning culture in the workplace to discuss, reflect on and share best practice.

4.6 Reflect on my learning activities and evidence what impact continuing professional development has on the quality of my practice.

4.7 Record my learning and reflection on a regular basis and in accordance with Social Work England's guidance on continuing professional development.

4.8 Reflect on my own values and challenge the impact they have on my practice.

Professional Capabilities Framework (2018)

- 1. Professionalism
- 2. Values and ethics
- 3. Diversity and equality
- 5. Knowledge
- 6. Critical reflection and analysis
- 7. Intervention and skills
- 9. Professional leadership

See Appendix 1 for the Professional Capabilities Framework Fan and a description of the nine domains.

Social Work Subject Benchmark Statement (2019)

5.1.5 The nature of social work practice

5.5 Problem-solving skills

5.8 Skills in personal and professional development

See Appendix 2 for a detailed description of these standards.

Activity 3.1

Never let your emotions cloud your judgement.

Before you read this chapter, think about this popular saying and the following quotations. Consider which most accurately reflects your views.

Nothing disturbs feeling . . . so much as thinking: emotion remains the other side of reason.

(Giddens, 1992, p200)

(Continued)

(Continued)

Emotions are sometimes unavoidable.

(Observer newspaper 22.11.15)

Thinking devoid of emotional knowledge is as problematic as emotion devoid of thought.

(Morrison, 2007, p256)

Comment

These quotations raise some of the critical issues that this chapter will help you to consider. The first two typify comments that juxtapose emotion and reason. Society and the organisations that we work in are informed by this way of thinking: we need to consider what impact this has on us personally and on our social work practice. The third, taken from a debate about whether it was acceptable for journalists and judges to display their emotions, recognises the existence of emotion, but sees it as a personal issue that needs to be managed, rather than as something that may make a contribution to our understanding. Lastly, the quotation from Morrison reflects the perspective that will be argued for within this chapter, that emotions are not something that can be set aside in the interests of greater efficiency and professionalism, but rather that they are a crucial source of information, both about ourselves and others. Social work practice frequently operates in difficult contexts which arouse strong emotions, both in those using services and in those providing them. Hence, understanding and working with feelings and emotions is vital, if we are to make sense of the complicated, sometimes frightening, emotionally charged situations that social workers are faced with.

Introduction

We will begin this chapter by drawing on the developing field of neurobiology to gain an understanding of why emotions exist and where they come from. Increased understanding of emotions and the way in which the brain works challenges earlier views of emotion as the antithesis of reason. It requires a fundamental reappraisal of prevalent thinking about the contribution of emotions to thinking, understanding and reasoning, which is highly relevant to professional social work practice. The impact on social work practice of approaches which devalued or disregarded the contribution of emotion will then be explored by considering some of the difficulties associated with the language of social work, which is heavily influenced by managerialism. As Munro (2011b) recognises, this cloaks the reality of social work practice in which the need to be able to understand and process our own and others' emotions is central to many of the interactions that take place. As we will see, the absence of such an understanding may be associated with notable failures in social work, where workers have been unable to think about the significance of the emotional dimension, so have been unable to recognise what was happening. The ability to recognise, name and process emotions will enable you to express yourself more effectively, so improving your practice and increasing your emotional resilience. Structured approaches to reflection and the development of emotional intelligence are explored as helpful ways forward.

By the end of this chapter, you will have an increased understanding of:

- the nature and purpose of emotion;
- the significance of language in constructing social work practice;
- the impact of emotion on social work practice;
- the concept of emotional intelligence;
- your own and others' emotional responses;
- the role of reflection in developing emotionally intelligent practice;
- emotion as a source of information.

What are emotions and where do they come from?

Research summary

Emotions always arise within particular social and cultural contexts, which shape how they may be expressed. This has contributed to difficulties in trying to understand them, leading some to suggest that they are best understood as 'as nebulous umbrella concepts' (Dore, 2016). However, the development of neurobiology has enabled a much clearer understanding. Emotions were once thought to come from a particular part of the brain, but it is now recognised that they can be found throughout the entire brain (Siegel, 2015, p147). As they engage all aspects of the brain, they have the power to disrupt thought (McLannahan, 2004). Hence, if you try to read this chapter when you are upset, worried or exhausted, you may read the words in front of you, but struggle to think about their meaning, as your ability to think is being disrupted by your feelings. Emotions begin as changes in the flows of energy throughout the brain and the body, causing changes in our state of integration. We may not be conscious of this changed state, but it has an important function in readying us for action, telling us that we need to pay attention and be alert. We may feel unsettled in a way that we cannot define. Siegel (2015) explains that the value system of the brain then appraises this information (a process involving cognition) so that we decide what the stimulus means: is it good or bad, is it safe, or a threat? This may be accompanied by physiological responses which may arise rapidly in response to certain stimuli, but may only last a short time in the absence of the trigger (when the person making you angry leaves the room, your anger subsides). If we reflect, we are usually able to identify the trigger.

(Continued)

(Continued)

Next there is a process of differentiation, as identifiable emotions, often referred to as feelings, emerge from the altered state of mind. While there is some debate about how many basic emotions there are, most would include:

happiness/joy;
sadness;
anger;
fear;
surprise;
anticipation;
disgust.

Other emotions such as envy, shame and gratitude may be seen as stemming from various combinations of these. Feelings are usually conscious and have an object – for example, a person who has made you angry. They are, thus, evaluative and form part of the process of making moral judgements (he has made you angry because you are upset by his treatment of his partner) and so reveal our values (Keinemans, 2015). Howe (2013, p48) explains that within the brain there are complex links, as information sharing taking place across many areas. He summarises research by Eisenburg and Eggum, explaining that the brain responds rapidly and intuitively to information received through emotions, but more slowly to information received by the thinking 'rational' cortical area of the brain.

Moods do not usually have an object; they are less intense, longer-lasting affective states that may affect the way we view things. Often we may be unclear about what has caused a mood as they are more muted than emotions. They may, therefore, have a less immediate impact on our responses, but may still affect our perceptions and judgement.

The purpose of emotion

Emotions can serve an important purpose in alerting us to the potential need to alter our goals. Originally, this may have been to ensure survival, hence the importance of very rapid emotional responses designed to ensure safety (McLannahan, 2004). Porges (2009) has developed a theory that in addition to the primitive, *reactive* fight, flight or freeze responses to threats, there is a more highly evolved way of ensuring safety, namely a *receptive* emotional response, which activates the *social engagement system*. He suggests that this is the one that we generally use: if we can see someone is becoming annoyed, we may first try to calm their anger or apologise. If this does not work, we may then resort to the fight or flight response. If the social engagement response works, the flow of energy giving rise to the emotion subsides, allowing us to return to a state of integration. Sometimes we call these responses *gut feelings* or *instinct*.

Comment

As social workers, it is important to recognise the function of our emotions in alerting us to situations that we need to pay particular attention to. We need to listen carefully to those niggly feelings that we can't quite place. Emotion can provide us with access to information about ourselves and about others, which we may otherwise not be conscious of. With careful reflection we may be able to process what we are feeling, so gaining greater insight into the lives of those we are working with. We can then make conscious use of feelings, in order to better understand and manage our responses.

Emotions and rationality

From the time of Greek philosophers such as Plato until the present day, reason has dominated the development of Western philosophical thinking as the basis for deter-mining what is good (Hugman, 2005; Turner and Stets, 2005). The dominance of rational thought creates particular difficulties in relation to recognising the contribution of emotion to understanding. These difficulties are compounded by thinking in a way that is described as *dualistic* (Bock and James, 1992). By that we mean that we think in terms of either/or, for example, Black or white, good or bad. We also tend to think in terms of one state being preferable to the other; this is known as *asymmetric dualism*. The positive qualities of one imply that the other is negative, or less desirable. This way of thinking can unconsciously limit our ability to appreciate difference. As a result, rather than seeing emotion as part of cognition and logical thought, it is defined in opposition to reason, as unreliable and subjective (Hugman, 2005, p48). Williams and Bendelow (1998) argue that as part of this tradition, reason has been associated with masculinity and public life, whereas emotion has been associated with women and relegated to private life. Hence, working with emotions is an area that has been largely invisible, undertaken primarily by women and conflated with notions of women's 'natural' caring role (Smethurst, 2004).

Feeling rules

While emotions arise within the mind and body from a response to stimuli, our feelings are expressed within specific cultural contexts that convey expectations about what people are supposed to feel in particular situations. These are known as *feeling rules* (Garey et al., 2011). So, for example, it may be expected that people who are attending a funeral will look sad, but that open displays of crying and grief will be limited to close friends and family. Cultural expectations about how men and women should behave may be different, putting particular pressure on those who do not conform to the expected norms of behaviour. In some cultures in the East, the *feeling rules* require that any expression of negative emotions such as frustration or irritation are avoided.

Activity 3.2

Can you identify the feeling rules in your current or last workplace?
How did these expectations affect you?
How did they affect the service users with whom you work?
What happened if people did not conform to these expectations?

Comment

We may feel embarrassed by talking about our feelings, particularly at work, as we may think that expression of emotion should be confined to our private lives, or we may worry that we may be seen as irrational. At a personal, professional and organisational level, the unspoken rules and expectations about the role of emotion within professional life will vary, so in some contexts, it may be permissible to talk about feelings, while in others it may be far more difficult.

Ingram (2015) argues for the importance of recognising the place of emotion within professional practice. He conducted research with social work practitioners that explored their views about emotion and their practice. This highlighted a reluctance to record or write about their feelings and variability in their experience of feeling safe to express their emotions, particularly within the context of supervision. Interestingly, this research does not consider whether gender impacts on attitudes towards working with and expressing emotion. While there may be some changes in relation to gendered expectations about the expression of feelings, the impact of these arguably still needs careful consideration, as illustrated by research into men's suicides. In 2019, 4,268 men committed suicide, and this figure constituted 75 per cent of all suicides in that year (Campaign Against Living Miserably, CALM). Of 2,000 men interviewed for a survey commissioned by CALM, 43 per cent said that they did not seek help because they did not want to talk about their feelings or felt ashamed, and 49 per cent said that they did not want to worry people. Issues relating to identity and gender continue to need attention and will be discussed further in Chapter 7.

What does the language of social work tell us about the place of emotion in social work practice?

Until relatively recently, little attention has been paid to the significance of language as both reflecting and shaping notions of effective social work practice (Gregory and Holloway, 2005). However, through writing and talking, practitioners and academics demonstrate what they are preoccupied with and believe to be important. The language used in legislation, policy and management has the power to shape practice in a top-down way, whereas user and carer movements have exerted power from the bottom, by challenging the labels applied to them by professionals. This is discussed further in Chapter 5. The changing nature of social work and attitudes towards emotion are thus revealed through the language that is used.

A historical perspective

Gregory and Holloway (2005) outline stages in the development of social work. They describe the initial phase as a moral enterprise arising from the work of the social reformers at the end of the nineteenth century. They believed that impoverishment was caused by moral weakness, so they endeavoured to reform the morals of those who were in need, regardless of how they might feel about this! A good example of the language which reflects their concerns can be found in this list from the NSPCC in 1901, which identifies the following child-abusing types:

the devil-may-care and idler;
the drunkard;
the married and unfaithful;
the married and estranged;
the unmarried;
the tramp;
the better and gambler;
the speculator in child life insurance;
the avaricious and greedy.

This paternalistic, reformist approach broadly persisted until the 1950s when therapeutic psycho-social approaches gained in popularity. Here the aim was to treat people, who were defined as clients, with a focus on the individual and interpersonal relationships. The work of Biestek (1961) was highly influential. He identified seven principles which he considered essential to effective practice. Of these the first two focus directly on the emotional component of practice, while the other five pay attention to the nature of the 'client/worker' relationship:

- purposeful expression of feelings;
- controlled emotional involvement;
- individualisation;
- acceptance;
- non-judgemental attitude;
- client self-determination;
- confidentiality.

In the 1970s, the Marxist analysis presented by radical social workers endeavoured to challenge the individualistic focus of therapeutic social work, locating problems within the context of structural inequality, hence the focus shifted away from the quality of individual relationships. The overall aim of radical social work was to empower people to change the system that oppressed them. Bailey and Brake (1975, pp57–58) highlight the importance of:

education (development of critical consciousness);
systems linking;
counter-systems building.

However, alongside this, treatment-based problem-solving approaches continued to form the basis for mainstream social work practice.

In the 1980s, the language used began to shift again to focus on the tasks that were expected of social workers. Confidence in social work was at a low ebb, which opened the door for increasing bureaucratisation and the steady rise of managerialism. Language from this period reflects the emphasis on following procedures, achieving outcomes, evidence-based practice and key performance indicators as a way to address perceived failures in practice. There was an emphasis on technical proficiency and empirical data as the essential platform for competent performance of the tasks required of social workers. The limitations of this approach were demonstrated in the 2002 National Occupational Standards (NOS) for social work. Ostensibly they provided a framework for developing the competence required of a 'beginning social worker' and a model representing the holistic nature of social work practice. However, by framing this entirely in terms of values, roles and tasks, the affective or 'third dimension' of practice is invisible. There were no references to feelings, emotions or indeed reflection, but 17 references to managing. There was a similar absence of references to emotion and feeling in the subject benchmark statement.

In a climate where the defensive adherence to procedures has been seen as a vital mechanism to ensure survival and avoid the possibility of blame or criticism, it is arguably difficult for social work to maintain a focus on the significance of relationships and feelings. The Munro Review (2011b, p6) identifies the concern of social workers to *do the right thing, rather than doing things right*. In a critical political and media environment, it is unsurprising that technical rationality was more attractive to an emerging profession seeking to gain status alongside established professional groups. The Review was accompanied by a growing recognition within the social work profession that knowledge, skills and rational thought are insufficient to help us properly understand complex situations. Nor do they equip us to respond effectively, when faced with powerful emotions, such as grief, fear, anger and hostility, which can overwhelm both service users and practitioners (Wilson et al., 2008; Ruch et al., 2010; Ferguson, 2011; Trevithick, 2014).

These concerns have been accompanied by a resurgence in interest in *relationship-based practice* which builds on earlier psycho-dynamic approaches to practice, but also includes a recognition of the impact of structural issues and diversity. The language of *relationship-based practice* highlights the importance of recognising that people are not simply rational beings and that the emotions of both service users and practitioners are central to social work practice (Wilson et al., 2008). Trevithick (2016) argues that this approach is consistent with radical approaches to social work. She emphasises the need to locate relationships within the power structures and social systems that shape people's lives.

Alongside the renewed interest in relationship-based practice, the language of the current Professional Capabilities Framework (2018) also provides a significant change of emphasis by moving away from the detailed technical prescription of the NOS. In identifying the need for social workers to develop emotional resilience in order to manage the emotional impact of practice, there is an explicit recognition that social work is often an emotionally charged activity. Thus, within the profession, there is a readiness to consider the implications of increased understandings of the working of the brain and of the purpose of emotion. However, the neoliberal policy context, austerity, staff shortages and the challenges of the pandemic provide a harsh and challenging landscape for those seeking to move away from the reductionist technical competency-based approaches of the end of the twentieth century.

The impact of emotion on practice

Firstly, we will look at research that focuses on the emotional impact of social work on a personal level. We will then focus on the impact that this can have on professional practice.

Research summary

In 2018, Lavee and Strier conducted research focusing on the emotional experience of frontline social workers in Israel who were working with families in poverty. The context was one of decreasing resources and a neoliberal political discourse, which resonates strongly with the experiences faced by social workers in the United Kingdom. The participants emphasised 'their workload and the never-ending routine of attempting to meet the increasing needs of their impoverished clients'. They developed a model (Figure 3.1) which provides a useful framework for reflecting on the emotional impact of social work practice.

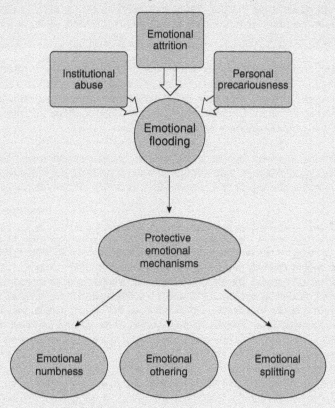

Figure 3.1 Emotional flooding

The model identifies three main elements that contributed to the emotional overload, which they term 'flooding':

Institutional abuse: Workers described feelings of helplessness, battling within their organisation to work effectively, but without adequate resources.

(Continued)

(Continued)

Emotional attrition: being overwhelmed by intense emotions, feeling like a walking dishrag.

Personal precariousness: anxiety, fearful for their own safety, concern for their own lives and those of their families.

The process of being overwhelmed led workers to develop the following protective emotional defence mechanisms:

- **Emotional numbness** and **denial**: becoming inured to their clients suffering, to protect against being overcome by the suffering and unbearable sadness of the children (Ferguson, 2021):
- **Emotional 'othering'**: enables distancing and so reduces personal precariousness.
- **Emotional splitting**: drawing distinctions between service users as deserving or undeserving to lessen contradictions between social work ethics and neoliberal policies.

The highly charged environments that invariably surround social work practice in the United Kingdom mean that our protective emotional defence mechanisms are aroused. Recent examples of this can be seen in the early reflections on the deaths in 2020 of Star Hobson and Arthur Labinjo-Hughes. Ferguson (2021) suggests that the emotional impact of the parents may have been a critical issue:

> It is clear that they were frighteningly strategic in their abuse of Arthur and no doubt in concealing it.' Moreover that: 'Organisational support (was) not available to help them recognise the impact of fear and anxiety and their distorted thinking.

> (Ferguson, 2021)

The issues relevant in the enquiry into the death of Victoria Climbie in 2000 thus continue to be highly relevant (Laming Report, 2003; Ferguson, 2005; Foster, 2005; Rustin, 2005). The enquiry carefully details the many missed opportunities to recognise the tragic circumstances of Victoria's life. Resource issues, poor interprofessional communication, inexperience, failures in accountability and poor management are seen as the major reasons for the failure to protect Victoria. However, the enquiry fails to move from the relatively superficial, albeit meticulous presentation of the data to an in-depth exploration of why, on this as well as on notable previous occasions; despite working very hard, practitioners were unable to attribute meaning to what they were seeing and to recognise the deep distress of the child. This was illustrated by the comment of one social worker who had said that Victoria looked like an advert for Action Aid.

It is argued that this state of seeing but not seeing, knowing and not knowing needs to be understood from a psychoanalytic perspective (Cooper and Lousada, 2005).

We can then begin to understand that the difficulties may be seen as defence mechanisms operating to protect the workers. If we have become numb and deny what we see and what we feel, then we are unable to acknowledge the true horror of the situation, which feels unbearable. It, therefore, removed the need for workers to take action to protect Victoria, so protecting themselves from a potentially very frightening experience, given the power of her aunt (Ferguson, 2005). Cooper and

(Continued)

Lousada (2005) explore the pervasiveness of these defensive mechanisms in relation to the wider development of social policy and organisational practice. The Laming enquiry failed to recognise the presence of defence mechanisms operating to protect practitioners from emotions which could be overwhelming.

The research summarised above provides helpful reference points for reflecting on the impact of emotional flooding and illustrate the difficulties for practitioners faced with overwhelming, deeply distressing and frightening situations, which may result in the worker being unable to act, because the feelings aroused are suppressed, unbearable and, therefore, denied. We may dismiss our fears and anxieties as irrational feelings, to be kept private.

Activity 3.3

Reflect on the model explained in the above Research Summary box.
In your current practice environment, have you experienced/observed any of the elements that contribute to emotional overload?
What protective defence mechanisms have you used/observed others to use?
What impact may these have personally?
What impact may these have on practice?

Feelings may also be denied because we are not confident about the important role of feelings as an invaluable source of information, for some of the reasons outlined above. Munro provides a very clear explanation of the complexity of the sources of information that social workers need to pay attention to:

the conscious mind is paying attention to the purpose of the visit; at an intuitive level they are forming a picture of the child and family and sensing the dynamics in the room, noting evidence of anger, confusion, or anxiety. This feeds into their conscious awareness and shapes the way the interview progresses. Their own emotional reaction is one source of information.

(2011a, p35)

The possible impacts and risks created by the arousal of our emotions can be seen in the case study below. In this situation feelings of loss are evoked and avoided.

Case study

Vivienne is a student who came to Britain from Zimbabwe five years ago. She has audio-recorded an interview in preparation for an assignment where she will be required

(Continued)

(Continued)

to analyse her communication skills. The recording is played back in the tutorial group, which provides Vivienne with an opportunity to receive feedback from the group. The interviewee was seeking asylum. When she started to speak about her sadness in relation to home and members of her family who were left behind, the student interviewer responded by asking her about her financial difficulties and benefits. When asked by her tutor why she had done this, her initial response was that she had changed the subject because she did not want to upset the interviewee.

Activity 3.4

Write down a list of feelings that the interviewee was conveying to the interviewer.

- How might the interviewer have felt as she listened to this?
- Why?
- What effect might changing the subject have had on the interviewee?

Comment

In the previous section, we have considered some examples that demonstrate the difficulties that can arise when practitioners are unable or unwilling to recognise the feelings of others. As we have seen, we may do this in some situations to protect ourselves from those feelings and to remove the need to respond to the situation. However, it is likely that this will not only lead to us failing to recognise issues, but will also contribute to stress and burn-out. In other situations that are less threatening, we may still lack confidence and so fail to pay sufficient attention to the emotional dimension of the interaction. As a result, our responses are not fully attuned to the needs of the service user and may be experienced as unhelpful or inappropriate, as in the example of Vivienne.

The absence of a language to identify the significance of the emotional component of practice exacerbates the problem. If, as suggested earlier, emotion is contrasted with reason, we may not recognise the value of exploring the emotional component of practice and of paying close attention to the affective elements of communication and systematically analysing feelings.

In the next sections, we will attempt to address these difficulties by exploring the language of feelings and emotions in more depth. We will then draw on the work of Solway developed by Goleman (1996) and constructs from psychoanalytic theory to help us to understand and work with feelings and emotions more effectively.

Talking about emotion and feelings

In the first moments that we experience an emotion, any attempt at expressing it verbally may seem impossible. As we start to appraise the emotion and it emerges as a conscious feeling, we can then try to find words that express it. While there are hundreds of words that we can use to discuss emotion, in practice our vocabularies tend to be restricted. The following activity is designed to help you to develop greater fluency in the language of emotion.

Activity 3.5

This activity would be best completed with a partner.

1. Write down a list of as many words to describe feelings that you can think of.
   - Underline the feeling words that you use regularly.
   - Share this list with your partner. Notice similarities and differences. Explore possible reasons for this (for example, culture, gender, age).
2. *Make another list of the emotions that you have felt in the last two days.*
   - Try to identify the triggers that caused you to feel these emotions.
   - Identify what you were doing at the time when you felt each emotion.
   - Consider the strength of the emotional responses that you have listed. Were they mild, moderate or intense?
3. How far do you consider that your feelings conformed to expectations about what was appropriate?

Comment

Our fluency in identifying, expressing and evaluating feelings will have an impact on our ability to process them and, therefore, to develop resilience, as well as enhancing our ability to support others in expressing their feelings.

Putting emotions to work

We now know that in order to make sense of a situation, activity across the whole brain is required. We, therefore, need to identify and reflect on how we feel as our emotions may add a crucial dimension to our understanding. As Munro (2011a), drawing on the work of Hammond, explains, we *need to see logical and intuitive thinking on a cognitive continuum* (p37). We also know that emotion is closely linked to motivation, so what we feel will influence our actions. You may know that you need to have written 1,000 words by the end of the day in order to have your essay completed on time, but if you feel upset by something you may be unable to motivate yourself to do this, although rationally you know that you should. However, if you associate completing essays on time with previous experiences of success (you got 80 per cent last time!), you are more likely to be able to motivate yourself to persevere than if your previous experiences were of failure.

A good understanding of the relationship between emotion, cognition and actions will enable us to harness our emotions in order to act more appropriately and achieve our goals.

Case study

It is Friday afternoon, and I am planning to make sure my case records are up to date, as I will not be in until Wednesday next week.

I have been working with a woman who is thought to have some degree of learning difficulty. She is pregnant and is the mother of two small children. They were referred to social services by the health visitor, who has concerns about her ability to cope with a third child and about the developmental progress of the children. She says that the mother avoids contact and is dismissive. The case is seen as low priority (Children Act 1989 section 17) and appropriate for a student.

Over the last fortnight during the course of two visits, she tells me that her partner does not think this third baby is his. On the second occasion, she was tearful and mentions that her partner came home the other night rather the worse for wear. She hesitates, then assures me he is very good with his kids and that she can cope without any help. The children are appropriately dressed and have some toys. They are very quiet and seem undemanding and rather subdued.

Somehow by the end of the afternoon, I realise I have barely started writing up my case records.

Activity 3.6

Working in pairs, identify a situation where you have not done what you think you should have done.

Take a sheet of paper and write three headings: *Intended action, What I actually did, Feelings at the time*. Complete the columns with reference to the situation that you have identified. An example of what this might look like in relation to the situation described above is provided in Figure 3.2.

Intended action	What I actually did	Feelings at the time
Write up case notes from the visits in order to discuss them with my manager next week.	Had a cup of tea, chatted to a colleague about plans for the weekend; made some phone calls to set up some non-urgent visits.	Unsettled. Rather low. Worried, but not sure about what.

Figure 3.2 Example of a process recording

Discuss with your partner the relationship between your thoughts about what you plan to do, your feelings and your actions.

Consider how it might help/hinder you if you are more aware of the relationship between your thoughts, actions and feelings.

Could you use this model in supervision?

Emotion and critical thinking

There is increasing recognition of the role of emotion in critical thinking and deep learning. Moon (2005) identifies an approach that *includes emotional as well as cognitive and whole person functioning* (p7). Clearly, the ability to think critically is essential for social workers, but the importance of emotion in this process is not always recognised. Sometimes there is a mistaken belief that we must just concentrate on the facts.

Research summary

Ruch (2005) found in her research that it was possible to categorise reflective practitioners into two broad groupings of either technical or holistically oriented practitioners. She found that the former tended to concentrate on practical issues and were principally concerned with reviewing what had happened and how it had happened in order to improve their practice. The holistic practitioners included these aspects of reflection, but in addition considered why things had or had not happened. She found that the holistic practitioners paid greater attention to emotional processes and were more aware of the importance of self-awareness. This facilitated responsive, relationship-based approaches to practice. As a result they were also more able to tolerate uncertainty and risk.

Emotional intelligence

The concept of emotional intelligence is based on recognition that our emotions are integral to our thought processes. They bring colour and shape to our thoughts and may determine what we say and what we do. Emotional intelligence entails being able to recognise what you are feeling, so that it informs your understanding and enables you to act appropriately. Such a definition suggests that emotional literacy could be key in helping practitioners in the emotional minefields of practice, where the ability to be able to accurately identify our own feelings and those of others, in order to be able to act appropriately is crucial. The relevance and value of emotional intelligence in social work practice is confirmed by Ingram (2013, p994), who has demonstrated that there are very close links between what service users want from practitioners, the core values of social work and the key elements of emotional intelligence.

The emotionally intelligent person is thus able to sense, understand and use emotions in order to improve their own effectiveness and their relationships with others (www.6seconds.org). While there are mixed views about the nature of emotional intelligence, the value of some of the work on emotional intelligence and the claims made in relation to its success in improving effectiveness can provide a helpful framework for developing emotional literacy.

Self-awareness

Goleman's (1998) work on emotional intelligence recognises emotional self-awareness as an essential first stage of using emotion effectively. He drew a distinction between characteristics of emotional competence in relation to:

- **Self:** personal or *intrapersonal* competence, and
- Interactions with **others**, social or *interpersonal* competence.

The model below (Figure 3.3) provides a framework for understanding the development of competent emotionally intelligent behaviours. As we develop greater awareness, we can begin to regulate our behaviour in order to be more effective, both intrapersonally and interpersonally, socially.

Core emotional competences	In relation to self (Intrapersonal EI)	In relation to others (Interpersonal EI)
Recognition	I can Identify my emotions	I cani dentify others' emotions
Understanding	I understand my emotions	I understand others' emotions
Expression	I express my emotions appropriately	I listen to others' emotions
Regulation	I regulate my emotions	I can help others regulate their emotions
Use	I use my emotions effectively	I use others' emotions to achieve better outcomes

Figure 3.3 Dimensions of self-awareness

Source: Geneva Profile of Emotional Competence www.eiconsortium.org with permission.

The reflective activities suggested earlier in this chapter are designed to help with the first stage of emotionally competent practice, by developing your ability to notice, and then to accurately name and identify an expanded range of emotions. Through conscious reflection we can develop our awareness and understanding of our feelings and what has triggered them. We can then start to focus on the feelings of others, noticing and reflecting on their meaning. In Chapter 1, you were introduced to Prpic's (2005) model of reflexivity, which used similar language (intra-view and inter-view), but also included an additional term, trans-view, to consider the influence of our values and culture. This provides an interesting lens for considering how our emotions are affected by our background, in terms of what emotions are permitted and prohibited and what are viewed as appropriate ways to express them. One way of doing this is by exploring our responses to particular triggers in small groups. Visual stimuli such as photographs or excerpts from television programmes, documentaries and films can be used for this purpose as they encourage emotionally direct writing. It may also be useful to consciously imagine how characters feel, a technique that Howe (2013, p172) identifies and that has been used to help aggressors to develop empathy with victims. The following activity combines this approach with the technique of guided reflection using a framework of *cue questions* (Wilson et al., 2008, p22).

Activity 3.7

Work with a partner or in small groups.
    Watch a five- to ten-minute extract from a film or television programme (programmes such as *Super Nanny* available on YouTube provide useful material). Do not take any notes, just observe. Afterwards write down:

- *what you saw – do this as a free-flowing narrative;*
- *what you felt when you were watching it;*
- *the feelings, as you perceived them, of the actors;*
- *your feelings now as you write this up – include any other memories, thoughts or feelings that were stirred by this process and record them.*

    Share your responses with your partner and discuss the similarities and differences in your observations and the feelings that this experience evoked.

Comment

This activity will help you to be more aware of your own emotional responses. It will also demonstrate how subjective your observations are. No two people will feel or see exactly the same things in any situation. Often there are different opinions and feelings about the same event. This exercise may help us to be more open-minded and less judgemental about how each of us perceives the world. Observations are influenced by our previous experience as well as by our personal identity which includes our class, gender, age, disability, ethnicity and sexuality.

Child observation

Some social work courses include the opportunity to undertake a series of observations of an infant or young child, using an adaptation of a method originally developed for training child psychoanalysts and pioneered at the Tavistock Clinic. Students are asked to write up their observations in a similar way to that suggested above and then to present them to a small seminar group. This can be a helpful way of developing our self-awareness, particularly in relation to understanding where feelings may be coming from, as memories of our own previous experiences of being parented and/or parenting are often stirred by this process. Trowell and Miles suggest that:

social workers need to be capable of taking an observational stance to give themselves the possibility of objectivity in coming to their conclusions. The observational stance requires them to be aware of the environment, the verbal and non-verbal interaction; to be aware of their own responses as a source of invaluable data, provided that they are aware of what comes from them and what comes from their clients; and to develop the capacity to integrate these and give themselves time to think before arriving at a judgement or making a decision.

(1996, p125)

The ability to use our emotional responses as a source of information may enrich our practice greatly and enable us to understand the meaning of some of the difficult and painful situations that we may be faced with. However, the need to be aware of what comes from us, and what comes from others, is critical. Good supervision is clearly essential, as is an understanding of the processes of transference and counter-transference.

Transference

Sometimes when we say something to someone we are taken aback by their response, which seems to us to have been out of all proportion or unrelated to what we have said. If we are surprised in this way, it is useful to consider whether transference may have taken place.

The concept of transference was first identified by Freud, who noticed that not only were his patients' reactions sometimes unrelated to anything that was taking place in their relationship with him, they also had fantasies about him that bore no relation to reality (Conner, 2001). From this, he developed a theory that their responses might be triggered by a memory of an earlier experience, which unconsciously then determined their feelings and responses in the present relationship with him. This phenomenon is consistent with the research noted by Goleman (1998), leading to his conclusion that the emotional mind may react to the present as though it were the past. Transference reactions may be positive or negative. I may, for example, assume that someone who enjoys a particular food that reminds me of my father, of whom I have fond memories, is a kind and patient person, when in fact there is no evidence to support this assumption.

Case study

Linda is a student plagued by fear of failure and feels unable to talk about this, either to her tutor, who she knows has been very supportive to other students, or in the tutor group that she has been part of for two years. This is a supportive group and other students in it often gain support from each other by sharing problems and exchanging ideas. She has obtained good results on the course so far, but believes that somehow this must just be luck, which is bound to change soon. Linda is convinced that the other members of her tutor group will make fun of her if she discusses her anxieties and that

(Continued)

she will be exposed as being stupid. As a child she was expected by her parents to get on with things without asking for help. She was bullied at school and did poorly in her GCSE examinations. Her school teachers seemed uninterested in her.

Counter-transference

This is a related concept, where the practitioner's own (repressed) feelings are unconsciously placed on the client/service user. The counter-transference may derive form earlier unresolved experiences in the practitioner's life. For example, I may find myself wondering why I am finding it hard to work with someone who reminds me of someone I knew and disliked as a teenager, who happens to have the same name. Or, if we return to the example of Linda, her tutor may start to wonder if she has the ability to help her, and wonders if Linda will ever make any progress.

Counter-transference can be problematic, leading to over-identification and collusion, or conversely to a misplaced negative reaction and avoidance. However, if recognised and held within appropriate boundaries, it can also be very helpful in providing the motivation to care and illuminating issues in the present helping relationship (Lowe, 2016).

Activity 3.8

Identify an interaction on placement where you are left thinking, 'Why did they react like that?' How can you use your understanding of transference to further your understanding of interactions with service users and colleagues?

Regulation and action: emotionally intelligent practice

The reflective activities so far have helped us to notice what is happening in relation to our own feelings and those of others, so that we are more personally and socially aware, congruent and empathic. We can then move on to consider how we can use this awareness to regulate or channel our energy and act in such a way that we have harnessed the insight that we have gained. This can help us to behave in ways that are socially skilled and assist in managing emotion in our relationships with others. Again, reflection can provide a pathway to achieving this. In the next case study, the social worker uses reflection to ensure that he communicates effectively and works in a collaborative rather than a confrontational way.

Case study

Dave, a social worker in a busy community learning disability team, is checking his emails. He has five minutes before he needs to leave to go to a case conference involving a service user he has been working with. He is anticipating that it will be difficult as the child care team are extremely critical of her parenting. Dave feels they have failed to provide adequate support and are patronising towards her. He opens an email from the manager of a local day centre headed URGENT. The email is personally critical and demands an immediate response from Dave as he has not completed all the details on a referral form that he recently sent through. The email further states that they will not deal with the referral until he has done so. Dave knows it will be difficult to find these details and considers that the referral needed urgent action. He notices that it has been copied to his manager. He is tempted to reply angrily, but instead prints out the email, in order to reflect before he responds. Later Dave reads the email again and (using a similar framework of cue questions to that suggested for Activity 3.7) writes down:

- what was happening when he received the email;
- how he felt when he received the email;
- what he thought the manager might have been feeling when she sent the email;
- what he feels now;
- how he might channel his feelings to use them constructively;
- what actions might be helpful to ensure that his long-term goals are achieved.

He was then able to respond appropriately to the email, recognising that they were both under pressure; his need was to ensure that a service was provided, but she needed the additional information in order to deliver an appropriate service.

It can also be helpful when reflecting to consider the impact of your feelings on your:

- communication with others;
- energy levels;
- ability to complete routine tasks;
- ability to make decisions.

Comment

The impact of emotion on the achievement of goals can be very positive, so it is useful to take time to reflect on both positive and apparently negative experiences. The particular value of writing about difficult experiences and our feelings about them has been highlighted in research studies by Pennebaker (2007) that have found that people who had been made redundant who were required to write about this on four consecutive days for 15 minutes a day were more likely to succeed in finding another job, as they were able to process their anger, achieve insight and channel their actions to achieve their new goals. In a similar study, improvements were also found in people's physical well-being, as measured through their immune systems (Pennebaker, 1997). Research with trainee social workers by Grant and Kinman (2012) has found that emotional intelligence, empathy and reflective ability are important predictors of emotional resilience, hence the development of these competencies is useful not only for our practice, but also in helping to ensure our own well-being.

Chapter summary

Developments in neuroscience support the need to pay serious attention to emotions. Siegel argues that emotional activity 'pervades all mental functions' (Siegel, 2015, p184). Perhaps a bolder claim should be made, because as discussed earlier in the chapter, the arousal of our emotions has a physiological impact: emotions arise from changes in the flows of energy in the brain **and** the body. Hitherto social work reflective practice activities have focused primarily on mental processes, reflection on information that we have received from many different sources, our thoughts about our thoughts, *head stuff*. This chapter argues for a more holistic approach to reflection and an appreciation of the role and impact of emotion on ourselves and our practice.

Conscious awareness of the emotions present is needed if we are to understand the impact on ourselves and the meaning of a situation. Without a careful analysis of the emotional dimension of practice, there is a risk that we become physically and emotionally exhausted, information is missed and reasoning is diminished. We need to see emotion and reason as complementary rather than opposing states of awareness.

Historically, however, emotion has been seen as hindering rational thought. It is perhaps, therefore, not surprising that as social work has struggled to gain recognition as a profession it has had a somewhat ambivalent approach to recognising the centrality of emotions to effective practice. The prevailing managerialist approaches, stressing technical competence and marginalising the importance of building and sustaining effective relationships, have been shown to be inadequate to deal with the complex situations that social workers need to deal with, where what is going on is often charged with emotions and barely within conscious understanding.

It is essential that we recognise, understand and express our own emotions – intra-personal competence. We also need to recognise, understand and work with the emotional communication of those whom we are working with – interpersonal competence. The development of emotional intelligence through reflection on emotion may hold the key to enabling you to do this and will help you to be resilient. The reflective exercises outlined above and in Chapter 1 will help you with this. Failure to recognise this dimension of practice may at the least be seen to miss the point and at worst may result in an inability to understand the meaning of important information. It is, therefore, essential that your reflection includes this third dimension of reflection on emotion. The importance of good supervision in supporting this process will be discussed further in Chapter 9.

Further reading

Clouston, TJ (2015) *Challenging stress, burnout and rust-out: Finding balance in busy lives.* London: JKP.

Cooper, A and Lousada, J (2005) *Borderline welfare: Feeling and fear of feeling in modern welfare.* London: Karnac.
    Coming from a psychodynamic perspective the authors explore in much greater depth the significance of defence mechanisms that operate to protect society from certain forms of feeling. The impact of this on policy and practice is explored and includes an excellent analysis of the Laming report.

Goleman, D (2004) *Emotional intelligence and working with emotional intelligence.* London: Bloomsbury.
A good introduction to emotional intelligence for those who would like to explore this further.

Ingram, R (2015) *Understanding emotions in social work.* Maidenhead: Open University Press.
    This new text provides a welcome and comprehensive overview of emotions in social work and draws on research with social work practitioners, undertaken by the author.

Cova, F, Garcia, F, Oyanadel, C, Villagran, L, Páez, D and Inostroza, C (2019) Adaptive reflection on negative emotional experiences. *Frontiers in Psychology.* https://doi.org/10.3389/fpsyg.2019.01943.
Mackenzie, C (2002) Critical reflection, self-knowledge, and the emotions. *Philosophical Explorations,* 5(3): 186–206. DOI: 10.1080/10002002108538732.
Sargeant, J, Mann, K, Sinclair, D, der Vleuten, CV and Metsemakers, J (2006) Understanding the influence of emotions and reflection upon multi-source feedback acceptance and use. *Advances in Health Sciences Education,* 13(3): 275–288.

Useful websites

www.eiconsortium.org
Useful website with examples of research into a range of approaches to developing emotional intelligence.

Part II

Developing the reflective practitioner

Part II

Developing the reflective practitioner

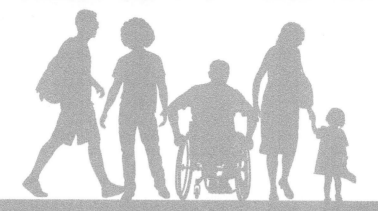

4

Reflection as a catalyst in the development of personal and professional effectiveness

Gill Constable

Achieving a social work degree

This chapter will help you to meet the current Social Work England Professional Standards (2019), develop capabilities from the Professional Capabilities Framework (2018) and introduce you to the Social Work Benchmark Statement (2019). The following are of particular relevance to this chapter:

Social Work England Professional Standards (2019)

4.2 Use supervision and feedback to critically reflect on, and identify my learning needs, including how I use research and evidence to inform my practice.
4.3 Keep my practice up to date and record how I use research, theories and frameworks to inform my practice and my professional judgement.

(Continued)

(Continued)

4.4 Demonstrate good subject knowledge on key aspects of social work practice and develop knowledge of current issues in society and social policies impacting on social work.
4.5 Contribute to an open and creative learning culture in the workplace to discuss, reflect on and share best practice.
4.6 Reflect on my learning activities and evidence what impact continuing professional development has on the quality of my practice.
4.7 Record my learning and reflection on a regular basis and in accordance with Social Work England's guidance on continuing professional development.
4.8 Reflect on my own values and challenge the impact they have on my practice.

Professional Capabilities Framework for Social Work (2018)

1. Professionalism
3. Diversity and equality
6. Critical reflection and analysis

See Appendix 1 for the Professional Capabilities Framework Fan and a description of the nine domains.

Social Work Subject Benchmark Statement (2019):

5.8 Ability to reflect on and learn from the exercise of skills in order to build professional identity.
6.2 i. Awareness raising, skills and knowledge acquisition.
     ii. Conceptual understanding.
     iii. Practice Skills and experience.
     iv. Reflection on performance.

See Appendix 2 for a detailed description of these standards.

Introduction

This chapter will focus on the use of reflection to develop personal and professional effectiveness. The process of reflection will be underpinned by the development of critical thinking skills in addition to approaches derived from cognitive and behavioural theories, including Ellis and Dryden's (2007) ABC theory found within Rational Emotive Behaviour Therapy.

Social work is a profession with reported higher levels of stress-related ill health, such as musculoskeletal disorders, depression and anxiety, than other occupational groups (Health and Safety Executive, 2017). It is important, then, that we do not neglect the opportunity to develop our emotional resilience, as this will impact on our attitude and behaviour towards service users and carers, as well as the quality of our life. These approaches can be shared with users and carers to help them manage stressful and difficult experiences.

The chapter will begin by giving some definitions and explanations of what is meant by reflection. An exploration will then take place into what cognitive and behavioural theories are, and how they can be applied with particular reference to patterns of thinking and behaviour that are disempowering. A number of approaches will be discussed, such as:

- defining critical thinking skills;
- thoughts and belief systems;
- developing self-acceptance.

The chapter will follow Suzy, a student social worker, on her assessed practice placement. Suzy developed her capacity to reflect, which helped her to manage herself when working with complex and stressful situations. Suzy's progress through her placement will be structured around the framework she used in her reflective journal.

Throughout the chapter, there will be several exercises for you to do that will enable you to understand how the theory and the methods arising from it can be put into use.

What do we understand by reflection?

A definition of reflection in terms of social work practice was discussed in Chapter 1. If we now return to this, Horner (2012) suggests that reflection is a prerequisite to being an effective social worker, as it requires an approach that questions our thoughts, experiences and actions. We can learn from experience and enhance our knowledge and skills. The important point is that through reflection we can *change* how we think, feel and behave, as our understanding of ourselves is deepened. This enables us to build on our strengths and engage in a process of continuous learning (SCIE, 2022, online). Reflection is certainly not about mulling over things, or ruminating in an unhelpful manner, rather it is an active process of improving our practice.

Where do we start?

Assessment is a core activity in social work and requires the development of critical thinking skills, which Cottrell (2017, p2) defines as a process that incorporates:

- having the ability to recognise other people's viewpoints and their reasons for maintaining this perspective;
- being able to evaluate the evidence to support a particular view;
- having the capacity to compare and contrast different arguments;

- being able to consider issues in some depth, not just accepting superficial explanations;
- having the skill to notice when arguments are used to support a particular position that appear sound but are in fact erroneous;
- being able to reflect in a structured manner;
- having the capacity to bring together different factors and come to a conclusion;
- being able to present a well-evidenced argument that is credible to other people.

Cottrell suggests that sometimes our emotional responses can impact in an unhelpful way on our capacity to think critically. Therefore, if we learn how to recognise and manage our emotions, for example: if we are aware that certain situations will affect us, we can better understand why we feel a particular way, and we can learn how to manage these feelings through thinking about them objectively. The experience of Josh, a student social worker, illustrates this.

Case study

As part of Josh's first practice placement, he was allocated the role of link social worker with the local infant school. On his first visit it was raining heavily outside. The deputy headteacher greeted him warmly and showed him around the school. When they went through the cloakroom where all the children's wet coats hung, Josh became suddenly anxious. He felt confused about his feelings and hoped that the deputy headteacher did not notice his discomfort. It was as if he was five years old again. Josh had been bullied by three older boys in the cloakroom, which was some distance from the classrooms. He always tried to avoid using it, but when it was raining his teacher told him to hang his coat up. It was the smell of the wet coats that brought the memory back of something that occurred 14 years earlier.

Can you recall an incident when you were taken aback by a strong emotional response that you were not expecting? Did you find that understanding where these emotions came from enabled you to be more in control, even if the feelings were uncomfortable?

To assist us to reflect, it can be helpful to develop a framework that we can use. Before we turn to a framework for a reflective journal, we will consider what research suggests about the usefulness of writing to support reflection.

Research summary

Research has demonstrated that writing about experiences is beneficial (Pennebaker et al. cited by Nicolson et al., 2006; Bolton, 2014). Think of a recent interaction with a service user or carer. Use this template to reflect back on what took place. Does your experience confirm this research? If so, what were the benefits of using a structured approach to aid reflection? Are there other questions that you would like to include?

Structure for a reflective journal

Stage 1: Reflect or think about an issue or concern that you have. This should be done in an unstructured manner to capture your thoughts spontaneously.

Stage 2: Analyse what you have written and ask yourself the following questions:

- What is going on here?
- What assumptions am I making?
- What does this tell me about my beliefs?
- Are there other ways of looking at this?

Be precise and specific in your analysis – paraphrase the key points. If you read your journal over a number of entries, are there any themes emerging?

Stage 3: Action – answer the following questions:

- What action could I take?
- How can I learn from this?
- Would I respond differently if this occurs again?
- What does this tell me about the beliefs that I hold about myself?

To be a reflective practitioner, we need to develop self-awareness and recognise how we impact on other people through our attitudes and behaviour, while being conscious of what triggers particular thoughts and emotions in us. Josh recognised that his emotional discomfort was due to an unhappy memory. Because he knew this Josh was able to manage his emotional reaction rationally. We will look at an exercise to develop self-awareness before we move on to the reflective journal template.

Developing self-awareness

There are a number of approaches that can be used to assess ourselves in terms of our personality traits and preferred learning style, which supports our self-awareness. Strengths, Weaknesses, Opportunities and Threats (SWOT) analysis is a technique that is often used in organisations and teams to obtain a position statement of how the organisation or team are functioning. Nonetheless, this is an effective technique to use on ourselves.

Suzy is a social work student who completed a SWOT analysis (Figure 4.1) to share with her practice educator Nasreen at her placement in a children and family centre. Suzy has been able to identify her strengths, and give a balanced assessment of her learning needs, without overly dwelling on what she perceives as her deficits. Strengths-based approaches focus on what people can do, and the resources that they have access to within themselves and their social networks. It recognises that people are the experts in their own lives and have autonomy. We need to recognise our strengths, skills, knowledge and experience, and to implement this approach with service users and carers, so that our practice is hopeful, supportive and encouraging (Gilbert, 2009, p299; SCIE, 2022, online). Nasreen and Suzy were able to develop an action plan for the

Strengths	Weakness
I'm friendly and find it easy to get on with people. I enjoy being with children. I want to support parents to care for their children, so that their life together is happier. I am committed to working as a social worker, and motivated to learn and develop. I always work hard. I care about people and social justice.	I have a tendency to worry and experience stress (the risk of harm has been identified as a factor for most of the children I will be working with). I am unsure if I will be able to manage emotionally in this placement. I get very upset when children are not treated affectionately. I want people to like me; sometimes social workers have to make very difficult decisions, such as recommending that children be separated from their families. At times I take myself and life a bit too seriously – I need to remember to have a sense of humour!
Opportunities	Threats
To learn new skills and develop knowledge. Practise the skills and implement the theories learned on my social work course at university. Tackle my weaknesses (above) and threats (opposite)!	Find that I can't cope with the work due to being upset and getting very stressed. My fear of failure. I don't have a lot of confidence in situations of conflict. I set very high standards for myself, maybe they are not always realistic.

Figure 4.1 Suzy's SWOT analysis at the start of her placement in a children and family centre

placement so Suzy's learning needs could be met, and opportunities were identified for her to demonstrate competencies in social work practice.

Activity 4.1

Complete a SWOT analysis of yourself. It is important to be honest in the same way that Suzy has been. We will return to your SWOT analysis after Activity 4.2.

Comment

When tackling this exercise, use the template of four boxes. Do not try to do it in a logical sequence unless this is easiest for you. You may find that what feels like a potential threat is also an opportunity, and so needs to go into both boxes. When completing the strengths box, acknowledge what you can do, what you know, what you have done in the past. Through understanding what your strengths are, you can transfer these skills when faced with new challenges. In this way you are building your

(Continued)

confidence and resilience. When completing the strengths box, use the following prompts (Thomas, 2005, pp79–82):

* What strengths have you demonstrated in education/voluntary work/employment?
* What strengths do you show in your personal life?
* What strengths do you use at difficult times?

If we continue to follow Suzy in her placement, we can see how she used the self-knowledge gained from the SWOT analysis in her thoughts following an incident at the children and family centre, which she recorded in her reflective journal. Suzy used the template that we considered earlier.

Case study

This is an example of a journal entry that Suzy took to supervision.

I was sitting with Katie (19 years old) and her daughter Amy, nine months, who was on her lap. Amy spilt her drink over her and Katie.

Katie got very angry really quickly and shouted at Amy. 'You f****** dirty cow – you've messed up your new dress. Get the f**** off me'.

She then roughly put Amy on the floor. Amy started to cry and this made Katie even more angry. She told her to 'shut the f**** up'.

I watched and I froze. I was very frightened. Katie's anger was so quick. I hate myself for being frightened.

I'm pathetic, useless and weak. I can't cope. I just sat and watched.

Colleen (staff) heard the shouting and came in. She picked Amy up and gave her a cuddle and sat near Katie. She asked Katie what had happened. Katie said that Lee (her boyfriend) has been seeing her best friend, and Amy spilling her drink was the last straw.

Colleen listened to Katie and when she had calmed down, she asked Katie what effect she thought that her outburst had had on Amy. Colleen was relaxed and non-judgemental in her manner, and this helped Katie to be open about her feelings and think about her behaviour.

Finally, Katie took Amy from Colleen and told Amy that she was sorry that she had taken her anger out on her. Colleen discussed with Katie age-appropriate behaviour and children do mess their clothes up. She offered to help Katie learn how to manage her frustration and angry feelings.

Following this incident, I became aware that I had a headache, and my shoulders felt sore where I had tensed them. I also felt really down.

Suzy's use of the reflective journal template

When I analysed this, I became aware of how I behave under stress and what I tell myself. This is a summary of the key learning points for me.

(Continued)

(Continued)

- *I froze with fear.*
- *I was frightened (although at no time did, I feel threatened).*
- *I thought, 'I hate myself for not protecting or comforting Amy'.*
- *I told myself, 'I am pathetic, useless and weak'.*
- *I remember thinking, 'I can't cope'.*
- *My shoulders and neck felt sore, and I had a headache.*
- *When I now think about the incident, I feel sad.*

Action

1. *To get better management of my thoughts and feelings, and to discuss with Nasreen ways that I can begin to do this.*
2. *To discuss with Nasreen offering to work jointly with Colleen to support Katie to understand Amy's needs and manage her angry feelings (Colleen will be a good role model.).*

Activity 4.2

Now let us return to you, and the SWOT analysis that you completed earlier.

- What did your SWOT analysis reveal about you?
- What are your strengths?
- How might you build on them, and could this impact on areas that you have identified as weaknesses?

Comment

Start to write a reflective journal using the structure outlined above. Think about actions that you could take to solve any challenges that you have. You might want to take a notebook with you and jot down thoughts and observations that you have during the day. Then explore them, and identify what you have learnt in more detail in your reflective journal. This can be shared with your practice educator during supervision.

Action planning

In the same way that an assessment of service users or carers enables social workers to develop a care plan to meet people's needs (Parker, 2021), so the self-assessment that Suzy has completed through the SWOT analysis, reflective journal and supervision with Nasreen heightened her self-awareness and identified specific learning needs. They identified self-management in relation to stress as one of Suzy's priorities. Together they reformulated this into a positive goal that focuses on what Suzy wants – to be personally effective in her practice – rather than emphasising what she does not want – excessive stress. This is the action plan that has been produced. Part of the plan is for Suzy to pass on her learning to service users and carers, so they can better manage stressful feelings and thoughts, and remain calm rather than lose control, as Katie did with her sudden outburst at Amy.

Suzy's action plan

Student Social Worker: Suzy Fitzgerald
Practice Educator: Nasreen Khan

Aims

- *This action plan seeks to enhance Suzy's personal effectiveness as a student social worker at Southside Children and Family Centre.*

Objectives

- *To support Suzy to develop strategies and approaches that enable her to reduce unhelpful stress that impacts on her work within the centre, especially in relation to conflict.*
- *For Suzy to use her own self-development to support children and parents at the centre to manage stressful and unhelpful thoughts, feelings and behaviours.*
- *For Suzy to develop her capacity to take personal responsibility for her own continuous professional development and become a reflective practitioner.*

Actions

- *Suzy to write a reflective journal using the agreed structure and bring a journal extract to supervision every week for discussion.*
- *Suzy to do some research into the fight, flight or freeze theory for discussion in supervision. (This will be linked to university work.)*
- *Suzy to reflect on the use of cognitive and behavioural theories in terms of herself. (This will be linked to university work.)*
- *Nasreen to give Suzy information about breathing, neck and shoulder exercises.*
- *The learning from the above to be taught to service users and carers focusing initially on joint work between Suzy and Colleen with Katie.*

Outcomes

- *The learning that Suzy achieves in terms of the management of her own responses to stress can be used with families at the centre, many of whom experience significant stress.*

Review

- *The action plan will be discussed at supervision each week in terms of progress.*
- *A full review will take place in six weeks' time.*

(Continued)

(Continued)

The action plan requires Suzy to research into particular theories such as fight, flight or freeze, as well as learning physical exercises to manage stress (Mind, 2022, online). The cumulative effect of stress, over many years, has serious consequences for people's health and well-being.

Approaches that can help us manage our stress

As well as developing an understanding of the fight, flight or freeze theory, Suzy needs to become aware of her thoughts, and assess what these tell her about the beliefs she holds about herself. We will also consider the role that cognitive and behavioural theories can play.

Fight, flight or freeze theory

The fight, flight or freeze theory describes a physiological response to situations where we believe ourselves to be in danger. Our minds think that we are about to be attacked and our bodies tense ready to attack the perceived aggressor, run away or become immobilised. These reactions date back to prehistoric times when human beings had to respond to many physical threats in the same way that animals do. The difficulty is that we can respond to situations in an automatic physiological manner that is disproportionate to the threat that we are experiencing.

If we return to Suzy's reflective journal, she has written:

- I froze with fear.
- I was frightened (although at no time did, I feel threatened).
- I have become aware of how often my shoulders and neck feel sore, and I often get headaches.
- When I think about the incident, I feel sad.

In this situation, Suzy's automatic physiological response was to sense danger, and she became unable to move rather like the proverbial frightened rabbit that stops in the middle of the road, as a car approaches rather than run to safety. Suzy's body has tensed especially around her shoulders and neck, which has probably resulted in her getting a headache.

If Suzy had slowed her breathing, lowered her shoulders and her thoughts had been encouraging and reassuring, this may have prevented the intensity and duration of her reaction. This is not to minimise the incident; to witness a small child being subjected to an unexpected and aggressive outburst is distressing. Suzy's response to Amy shows her empathy, which Howe (2013, p9) defines as being able to see and feel as another person does, so we can better understand them. Suzy felt Amy's fear, and did not know how best to respond to protect her. Through observing and modelling her behaviour on that of Colleen, Suzy will develop ways of working in an assured manner that protects children, while providing insight and support to parents to manage their frustrations without oppressing and harming their children.

Cognitive behaviour therapy

During the 1960s, Aaron T. Beck developed cognitive behaviour therapy, which was directed towards assisting people to solve their difficulties through restructuring their thought processes. Beck trained as a psychotherapist and found that traditional psychodynamic interventions took people back to early experiences where they gained insights into the possible causes of their difficulties, but did not enable them to necessarily overcome them. Beck developed an approach that was fixed in the present and that challenged thinking errors and behaviour.

CBT uses two approaches: cognitive strategies that enable us to learn to recognise our thoughts, beliefs and attitudes, which impede our well-being. These are reframed so that they can be challenged and more productive and supportive ways of thinking can be developed. The other approach is strategies, which change our behaviour, which in turn changes how we think and feel. This is achieved by learning how to effectively problem solve, setting goals, using social support, engaging in activities and finding ways of relaxing (Edelman, 2006, p3; Myles and Shafran, 2015, pp14–26).

Thinking about our thoughts

We are constantly thinking about our daily lives: work, family, friends, problems, obligations, commitments, tasks, which may form in our minds as words, images or memories. A powerful thought may be accompanied by a strong feeling. Hence: '... thoughts are clues to understanding moods' (Greenberger and Padesky, 2016, p50). We saw in the above example Katie's change of mood, and outburst was triggered by her thinking about her boyfriend and best friend.

Sometimes our thoughts are positive and helpful, while at other times they are destructive and problematic. If we start to pay attention to our thoughts, we will be able to identify patterns of thinking, and what causes them. Negative thoughts build on each other and create a 'downward spiral', which has 'emotional amplifiers' that increase the intensity of the negativity (Gilbert, 2009, p100). This cycle needs to be interrupted by becoming aware of our thinking, and rather than blaming and criticising ourselves as Suzy has done, to acknowledge the thought, but to recognise what we think may not be true.

Mindfulness is the practice of focusing on the present moment, while noticing and accepting thoughts and feelings without judgement. It has been incorporated into CBT, as a helpful practice that enables you to observe your patterns of thought, memories and images, and your response to them. The aim is to create a calm state of mind, as you realise that you can observe your thoughts objectively without having to respond to them. Often, we are preoccupied with worries and anxieties about the past or the future rather than experiencing the present.

We need to notice how we react physically in tense situations, so we can move and stretch to reduce the muscles becoming rigid, and sore. Breathing exercises are physically and mentally relaxing and create calmness. They can be done wherever we are. However, sometimes our body will alert us to genuine risks, and these messages should not to be ignored. There are many resources available to assist in the development of mindfulness (Greenberger and Padesky, 2016, p241; nhs.uk/mental-health).

Thinking errors

Ways of thinking are developed through the course of our lives. Negative or unhelpful thoughts are interpretations, which CBT terms, as thinking errors or distortions. These are some common thinking errors (Branch and Wilson, 2010, p43).

- Catastrophizing: anticipating the worst outcome which creates fearfulness.
- All or nothing thinking: extreme thinking with no room for uncertainty and ambiguity.
- Mind reading: jumping to conclusions without any evidence.
- Over-generalising: using words such as 'always' and 'never' on the basis of a single incident.
- Labelling: using negative language to describe self or others.
- Mental-filtering: discounting the positive and focusing on the negative.
- Emotional reasoning: relying on feelings rather than examining the facts.
- Personalising: blaming ourselves for another person's behaviour or feelings without looking at other factors.
- Fortune telling: predicting the future instead of waiting to see what happens.
- Disqualifying the positive: taking no account of constructive factors, or turning a beneficial aspect into a negative.
- Demanding: using words such as 'should', 'must', 'ought' and 'have to' thereby making rigid rules for ourselves, other people or the world.
- Low tolerance or frustration: telling ourselves that something is intolerable when in fact it is bearable, and worth tolerating to achieve our outcome.

Activity 4.3

Can you recognise any of these thinking errors? Are you aware of times when you are most susceptible to them? Try this exercise next time this occurs:

1. Catch the negative thought
2. Spot the thinking error
3. Acknowledge a strength you have that challenges the thinking error
4. Replace the negative thought with an alternative constructive thought

(Alexander et al., 2014, Henley and Newman, 2014, p104)

> (Continued)
>
> **Comment**
>
> Thoughts impact on our moods, such as suddenly being irritated because you have remembered a task that you have to do, or feeling excited when you think of an anticipated pleasurable event such as going on holiday. Building on this self-knowledge will help you to better manage your state of mind, support your well-being and resilience.

Beliefs

Beliefs may or may not have any objective truth; they are quite simply what we believe to be true. In childhood we develop beliefs that are so profound and entrenched that we do not express them to ourselves or others (Beck, 2011). They are ideas that we have formulated through our past experiences that develop into beliefs about ourselves, other people and society, and underpin our automatic thoughts.

Beliefs enable us to navigate our way through life, but along the way we can acquire inflexible, rigid and damaging beliefs that are destructive to ourselves and others. If a child is told on a regular basis that they are thoughtless and ungrateful, or unfavourably compared to a sibling, how do you imagine this may influence their beliefs about themselves, other people and the world when they reach adolescence?

If we return to Suzy, we can see that her thoughts are negative and unsupportive:

- I hate myself.
- I am pathetic, useless and weak.
- I can't cope.

These statements are rigid, permanent and pervasive. They suggest that Suzy is *always* pathetic, useless, weak and unable to cope in *all* situations and at *all* times. This is factually untrue and has impacted on her self-esteem and confidence. It has affected her mood. Suzy wrote in her reflective journal how she feels sad when she thinks about the incident with Katie and Amy. This reinforces her beliefs about herself; we can see how these thoughts are problematic and in fact increase her stress, and impact on her feelings, behaviour and physiology. This can be expressed in a diagram (adapted from Beck, 2011) as seen in Figure 4.2.

Rational emotive behaviour therapy

Albert Ellis (1957) developed this therapeutic intervention which emphasises that people need to have a purpose and goals to achieve if their lives are to be satisfying. This can be

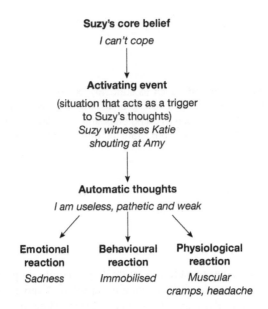

Figure 4.2 Suzy's response to Katie's treatment of Amy

undermined by our thinking that prevents people achieving their goals. Ellis developed the ABC schema as a tool to challenge unhelpful beliefs and thoughts. It operates as follows:

A = Adversity – the situation that triggered the belief.
B = Belief – the person holds.
C = Consequence – the emotional, behavioural and physiological impact of the belief.

We often think that an event (adversity) happens, and this causes us to feel or behave in a particular way. In fact, it is our belief about the cause of the event that makes us feel and behave as we do. This is an example of how the approach works.

Case study

Dara has completed her BA Social Work and has applied for a vacancy in the team where she had her final placement. She is very confident that she will be offered a permanent job, as her practice educator was positive about her performance.

Dara contacts her personal tutor Abedi at university following the interview and tells her: 'I am devastated, Abedi. I didn't get the job. I don't understand. I feel really bad. It's shattered my confidence'.

Abedi meets with Dara, and they agree to structure their discussion around the ABC approach at Abedi's suggestion.

(Continued)

Adversity – Dara is not offered the post in the Community Mental Team where she had her last practice placement as a student.

Consequence – Dara explains that she feels very upset and thinks that maybe the team do not like her, and that her practice is poor.

Abedi points out that Dara has gone from the situation of not being offered the job to the consequences. In other words, Dara thinks she feels distressed because she did not get the job. In fact, it is Dara's beliefs about not getting the job that has caused her to feel low in spirit. Abedi asks her to explain what goes through her mind when she thinks about not being offered the job.

Dara says: 'I feel I am rubbish. I was OK as a student but they won't employ me. Maybe they don't like me, but I liked them. It was a great placement'.

Abedi repeats back to Dara what she has said: 'I feel I am rubbish'. Abedi writes down the following with Dara:

Adversity

I have not been offered a job in the team where I had my last placement.

Belief

I am rubbish.

Consequences

I feel defeated and discouraged.

Seligman (2002, p93) has added Disputation and Energisation to the ABC approach. Disputation is about asking robust questions and challenging our thoughts. What evidence is there that what we think or feel is based on fact, and is true? Are there other reasons to explain what has happened? Abedi suggests Dara should put forward arguments that dispute her belief that she is rubbish. Dara could do this by imagining a lawyer arguing her case for her. Constructive challenge in itself can give us energy, hope and a sense that we have choices and a way forward can be found. This enabled Dara to recognise her strengths, challenge her negative thinking and set herself some tasks.

Disputation

Dara was able to think of her achievements and strengths.

- I have achieved my BA Social Work, and I am now qualified.
- I work hard. This can be evidenced by the tutors' comments on my dissertation.
- Feedback from the service users' group that I developed in my last placement about my role as the group facilitator was very positive.
- The manager in the hospice where I had my first placement told me that the multi-disciplinary team had so enjoyed having a social work student on placement, which they would like to take another student from this university.

(Continued)

(Continued)

Abedi advises Dara that telling herself that she is 'rubbish' was an example of unhelpful thinking. In addition, Dara had an interpretation of the situation where she blamed herself, personalised the situation and mind-read the interviewing panel. For example, Dara assumed that maybe they did not like her. Abedi suggested that Dara should question her unhelpful thoughts, and recognise just because she thinks something it does not make it true. She needed to develop a balanced, compassionate and supportive attitude towards herself, and adopt an encouraging and smoothing internal voice, rather than berate herself.

They then moved on to consider some options that Dara could pursue to learn from the experience, and plan for the future.

Energisation

- I will contact the chair of the interviewing panel and ask for feedback as to why I was not offered the job.
- I will take notes from this conversation and use this as a basis of an action plan. (I know that I did not sufficiently address issues about equalities in the case study, and that I could have shown more awareness about the impact of policy on local mental health services.)
- I will meet with the careers officer in the university and ask for some support in preparing for interviews.
- I will work hard on developing helpful and encouraging thinking habits. This is important for me personally, but also in my work with service users and carers.

Returning to the children and family centre, we will see how Colleen and Suzy worked with Katie using this approach.

Case study

Katie has been attending the children and family centre for three weeks. During that time, she has been able to discuss with Colleen and Suzy her sense of hopelessness and her expectation that Amy will be removed from her care. She has spoken about being angry with the whole world, and suspects that this is linked to the death of her mother three years ago. She knows that sometimes she speaks harshly to Amy, and then feels guilty afterwards. Using the ABC approach, they worked through with Katie the incident where Amy had spilt her drink. This is set out as a conversation between Katie and Colleen (see Figure 4.3).

From Colleen's conversation with Katie, we can see the impact that unfounded beliefs and unhelpful thinking can have emotionally, behaviourally and physiologically for Katie and, importantly, for Amy too. For Katie and Suzy, the process of reflecting and having the opportunity to talk through their insights is necessary for Katie to develop into a consistently caring parent and for Suzy as a social worker.

Adversity	Colleen	Katie, what was going through your mind before Amy spilt her drink?
	Katie	I had this picture of Lee with Sarah, who is meant to be my best friend, going out together. I thought about Mum and about how lonely I am.
Belief	Colleen	Tell me more about your lonely feelings, Katie.
	Katie	Mum was 38 when she died. I often think if she had really loved me she wouldn't have died. I know it's daft because she died of cancer. Amy's father never bothered with me and now Lee has gone.
	Colleen	Katie, are you saying that you feel unloved and no one will ever love you?
	Katie	I suppose I am.
Consequences	Katie	I get stressed out and angry about stupid things that don't matter like Amy messing her clothes up.
Disputation	Colleen	Katie, it must be hard for you to cope with the belief that you are unlovable. Even if it were true it's important that you accept yourself. Another way of thinking about this is: 'I'm my own person and I can love myself, so I will always be loved. This will make me more attractive to other people, as I will feel good about myself'.
Energisation	Colleen	Katie, do you think it would help to start to notice what goes through your mind when you are upset, or feel down? Bad moods don't just happen – there is always something that causes them. Then you can start to challenge some of those self-beliefs you have. I can show you some breathing exercises and ways of relaxing physically, as that will help too. The other thing is that we have links with the college. We could look to see if there is a course that you might be interested in. It would enable you to make new friends.
	Katie	I am already starting to think more about things. I want to be good to Amy. You are right – I have always managed on my own. I would like you to teach me how to relax. I think I've been low for so long it's got to be a habit, but I feel much better now. It helps to talk about things – you help me to see things from a different point of view.

Figure 4.3 Katie and Colleen's conversation

Activity 4.4

Think of a situation that has caused you anxiety and upset. Analyse it using the ABC approach. Reflect on your understanding of the situation now. What have you learned about your beliefs?

(Continued)

(Continued)

Comment

The ABC approach is very effective in enabling us to gain new insights into problems and assists us to challenge interpretations and beliefs that cause us difficulties. It is essential to remember that it is not the actual event that often causes us distress, but our reaction to it. If you recall, Josh became panicky when he smelt the wet coats in the cloakroom. It triggered a memory of being bullied by other children. In reality, Josh was now an adult and in no danger from ever being bullied again in an infant school cloakroom.

Critique of the theory

Milner, Myers and O'Byrne (2015) state that cognitive and behavioural theory are focused on change at an individual level rather than taking account of societal inequalities. In addition, the structured approach of the intervention can feel mechanistic and prescriptive, locating the difficulty in the person, rather than taking account of their social environment and experiences. Katie's situation is not understood, for example, from a feminist perspective. This would place emphasis on her as a lone parent operating within a patriarchal social system that expects her to assume care of Amy without similar requirements of Amy's father. In other words, if she had deserted Amy as her father had, this would be viewed more severely because Katie is a woman and mother. It can of course be argued that by supporting Katie to develop the ability to accept herself, she will be able to dispute unhelpful self-beliefs, which will enhance her well-being and empower her.

Being a reflective practitioner

To summarise, Suzy's development as a reflective social worker has been assisted by the following approaches that are supporting her professional and personal development.

- Through the SWOT analysis she has assessed her strengths and areas for development.
- Suzy is keeping a structured reflective journal.
- Suzy is working on developing supportive and encouraging ways of thinking by monitoring her thoughts, and questioning her interpretations and beliefs. She is learning more about cognitive behaviour theory and the ABC technique by using these concepts on herself, as part of the process of reflection, which is deepening her self-knowledge.
- Suzy is co-working with Collen, an experienced member of staff. She is developing her practice by using Coleen as a professional role model.

- Finally, Suzy is committed to integrating her learning into her practice and sharing this knowledge and skills in her work with service users and carers.

These activities and approaches will be reviewed and evaluated with her practice educator, but it is important that Suzy takes personal responsibility for her own learning and development.

Chapter summary

In this chapter, we have explored the use of self-assessment as a vehicle to start to develop reflective practice. Cognitive and behavioural theories have been the dominant theoretical perspective examined with an emphasis on its practical application for service users, carers and social workers. It is necessary to consider what approaches work for us prior to utilising them in practice. Our commitment and optimism in our capacity to support people in the process of development and change lie in being able to reflect on our own beliefs, motivations and actions, and the development of helpful and encouraging thinking habits. Once we believe in our capacity to change and develop, we can then help others to do so too. To put this simply, effective social workers believe that there is always something they can do, to help people to regain control of their lives.

Further reading

Myles, P and Shafran, R (2015) *The CBT handbook*. Robinson, TX: Great Britain.
   This is a self-help book, which is accessible, comprehensive and helpful, which is available in public libraries. It is part of the National Reading Well Books on Prescription Scheme for England delivered by the Reading Agency and the Chief Librarians with funding from the Arts Council. More information about the scheme and other publications can be found at: www.readingagency.org.uk/readingwell.

Useful websites

There are a number of websites that provide free and accessible information including CBT tools, relaxation exercises, case studies and videos. Set down below are two such websites, which have links to other useful organisations.
   NHS Mental Health: at www.nhs.uk/mental-health/self-help/guides-tools-and-activities.

   MIND: at www.mind.org.uk/information-support.

5

The importance of the perspective of carers and service users

Andy Mantell

Achieving a social work degree

This chapter will help you to meet the current Social Work England Professional Standards (2019), develop capabilities from the Professional Capabilities Framework (2018) and introduce you to the Social Work Benchmark Statement (2019). The following are of particular relevance to this chapter:

Social Work England Professional Standards (2019)

1.1 Value each person as an individual, recognising their strengths and abilities.
1.2 Respect and promote the human rights, views, wishes and feelings of the people I work with, balancing rights and risks and enabling access to advice, advocacy, support and services.
1.3 Work in partnership with people to promote their well-being and achieve the best outcomes, recognising them as experts in their own lives.

(Continued)

4.4 Demonstrate good subject knowledge on key aspects of social work practice and develop knowledge of current issues in society and social policies impacting social work.

4.5 Contribute to an open and creative learning culture in the workplace to discuss, reflect on and share best practices.

4.8 Reflect on my own values and challenge the impact they have on my practice.

Professional Capabilities Framework (2018):

2. Values and ethics
3. Diversity and equality
4. Critical reflection and analysis
5. Skills and interventions

See Appendix 1 for the Professional Capabilities Framework Fan and a description of the nine domains.

Social Work Subject Benchmark Statement (2019):

5.15 v engage appropriately with the life experiences of service users, to understand accurately their viewpoint, overcome personal prejudices and respond appropriately to a range of complex personal and interpersonal situations.

5.16 i involve users of social work services in ways that increase their resources, capacity and power to influence factors affecting their lives.

5.16 vii operate within a framework of multiple accountabilities (for examples, to agencies, the public, services users, carers and others).

See Appendix 2 for a detailed description of these standards.

Introduction

This chapter will explore reflective practice, with a particular emphasis on the importance of integrating the perspectives of carers and service users. This is an important part of your social work training, consequently, the chapter starts by uncovering how the language we use to refer to people is not neutral and has a subjective impact which can affect our expectations of that relationship.

The experiences of families of people with Huntington's disease are drawn upon to highlight the competing expectations of social work intervention, which can be held by families, disabled people and practitioners. The chapter concludes with an exploration of how these expectations can influence the social worker's reflections on the nature and outcomes of their practice.

Huntington's disease is a rare neuro-degenerative condition, which carries a 50 per cent possibility of inheritance from an affected parent. Familial 'carers' can be faced with managing cognitive, motor and behavioural disorders, while uncertain about their own at-risk status. Onset usually occurs from the late thirties to the mid-fifties and life expectancy is approximately 15–20 years.

Telling a story

Assessment, like reflection (Chapter 1), can be viewed as piecing together a story. In the process of constructing that narrative, you are making sense of complex situations and your role within those circumstances. In social work this is not simply a contemplative narrative; social sciences seek to understand social phenomena, but social work also seeks to intervene (Johnsson and Svensson, 2004). Your reflection is therefore purposeful: a critical praxis (Rolfe et al., 2010), an ongoing process of improving your actions and decision-making in practice. It is through the repeated critical consideration of the evidence, applying theories and methods and listening to the expertise of other professionals, service users and carers, that our knowledge base evolves over time. Knowledge is consequently the distillation of our best understanding and practice, accumulated over time. Knowledge is the culmination of an ongoing process of development rather than a product we simply use (Fook, 2016). Reflection 'keeps us honest', enabling us to uncover our entrenched biases or those that insidiously arise over time. Curiosity is an essential driver for this process, keeping us searching for better answers, in the lifelong acquisition of knowledge.

Social work intervention has been divided by Parker and Bradley (2020) into four stages: Assessment, Planning, Intervention and Review/Evaluation (ASPIRE). This is not a mechanistic approach, concerned with an expert ticking off each of these stages, but rather it is concerned with 'people not processes' (Skills for Care, 2012); attentive to their interactions, building relationships and the outcomes service users and carers want to achieve. As Maya Angelou (2003, p3, after Buehner, 1991, cited in Quote Investigator, 2014) said 'people will forget what you said, people will forget what you did, but people will never forget how you made them feel'. Consequently, these stages have been expanded here to illuminate the accompanying reflective process using Schön's (1983) seminal work. In addition to reflection-in-action, i.e. your thinking at the time, and reflection-on-action, i.e. your thinking afterwards (Johnsson and Svensson, 2004), reflection-for-action (Thompson and Thompson, 2008) is highlighted as essential. In so doing, this chapter seeks to contribute to addressing the challenge of translating theory into practical, effective and empowering solutions for service users (Corey, 2020).

'Reflection' can be viewed as a 'generic term for those intellectual and affective activities in which individuals engage to explore their experiences in order to lead to new understandings and appreciations' (Boud and Knight, 1996, p19). Schön (1983) considered this process as 'partially beyond conscious articulation', but it is contended here that reflection and reflexivity (reflection on our reflective process) is a lifelong journey to uncover your motivations for actions in order to consciously influence and justify your practice. As such, reflective practice is an iterative activity, which must be experienced rather than abstractly taught.

Naming the characters

The language that we employ to tell a story shapes the images that are evoked and interpretations that are engendered. The main protagonists in this story are called 'carers' and 'service users'. An essential element of reflective practice is to have *a* 'continuous critical dialogue concerning the language we use, deconstructing it and unearthing the assumptions behind its usage' (McLaughlin, 2009, p1114).

Activity 5.1

What's in a name?

Write down what the terms 'carers' and 'service users' mean to you.
Write down what these terms imply to you.
Write down your expectations of a carer.
Write down your expectations of a service user.

Now think of a time when you received care from another person. Did you think of that person as a carer and yourself as an actual or potential service user?

Comment

'Carer' is a relational term, in that to be a carer there must be a 'cared-for' person. This oversimplifies the relationship, and denies the carer's weakness and the cared-for person's strength. It ignores the complexity and richness of relationships (Schofield et al., 1998). We actually need to think about care in the wider context of the relationship within which it occurs (Morris, 1993).

Research summary

Morris (1993) found that disabled people receiving care from a family member referred to them as 'mother', etc. They talked about their relationships, not about their carers (Morris, 1993, p154). In a qualitative study of carers for people with Huntington's disease, Mantell (2010) found that relatives in the early stages of providing care initially used the same terms, but over time the relationship could change to become dominated by care. In these circumstances, spouses valued and felt empowered by viewing themselves as carers.

The term 'carer' was hardly used before the 1970s, but since then the carers' movement has striven for recognition and support for familial carers. The Independent Living Movement, however, questioned the assumption that care should come from the family, arguing that disabled people should be able to manage their own care and employ personal assistants (Morris, 1993). Their campaign has come to partial fruition in the personalisation agenda and the Care Act 2014. Under this Act, carers are now eligible for an assessment in their own right. However, carers, perhaps partly due to unfounded but real feelings of guilt or failure, are often reluctant to seek support until they are in crisis. So, we need to remain mindful that carers can find themselves trying to assert their needs at the point when they feel least able (Mantell, 2010). Simply put, their voice may not be very loud, or they may not tell their story as clearly and calmly as they might wish.

Caring can imply emotional care (Thomas, 1993), i.e. caring about someone (Parker, 1981), and instrumental care (Thomas, 1993), i.e. caring for them (Parker, 1981). The tendency to view these different aspects as synonymous means that a family member's inability to provide physical care may be misconstrued as a negative reflection of their emotional relationship. Family, friends, neighbours and professionals also imbued with this perspective may put additional pressure upon family members to care.

Case study

Presumptions of care

Martha, aged 22, had a volatile relationship with her mother and had followed her sister's example in leaving home as soon as possible. She was, however, concerned that her mother was neglecting herself, and despite arranging for her to attend a day centre and have a care worker, the situation continued to deteriorate. Martha and her elder sister were invited to a meeting at the day centre and were confronted by the spectacle of their mother being asked to perform tests in front of them to demonstrate that she was not well. As Martha pointed out, she was well aware that her mother was not well and did not need to be 'embarrassed' in this way.

Martha was then informed that her mother had Huntington's disease and: 'Oh, by the way, it is hereditary.' While recovering from this shock the sisters were asked which one of them would look after their mother. Neither was in the position to look after their mother, nor did they have the quality of relationship where they would want to provide that care.

Comment

Such expectations owe more to the enduring myth of the prevalence of the 'Oxo' family than the diverse reality of relationships. Presumptions of care within relationships place considerable pressure upon family members to provide care. Consequently, we must be sensitive to our own and the service user's family's cultural expectations around care and crucially the wishes of the family. It is all too easy to become focused on your own and/or your agency's agenda and achieve your desired outcomes taking little account of the ambivalent or conflictual feelings that can exist within families.

Care is a gendered concept; it is associated with female traits and consequently, the expectation of familial care is primarily one of female care. Qureshi and Simons (1987) in their 'hierarchy of obligation' identified how spouses were more likely to provide care than other family members; the next most likely were adult children; same-household members were more likely to care than non-household members; and women are more likely to care than men.

When consideration is given to the person's ability rather than an obligation to care, the focus tends to be on the burden of care. Emphasis is placed on how to improve their capacity to provide instrumental care, through, for example, training. This risks professionalising the carer to the detriment of their relationship. Care shifts from being an element of that relationship to defining it. Nolan (2001) argued that mutuality – that is, reciprocity in the relationship between the carer and service user – is a better determinant of a person's capacity to care than the burden of care. Focusing on mutuality would identify if a primary motivator for caring not only still exists, but also raises the ethical issue of whether people should be expected to provide care if their relationship has changed.

If the term 'carer' speaks of a relationship with a person receiving care, the terms we use for those we provide a service to help to define that relationship. The term 'client' was widely used in the 1960s, 1970s and 1980s, and is still widely used internationally (McDonald, 2006). However, in the United Kingdom, while hinting at early aspirations to therapeutic relationships, it became associated with dependency (McLaughlin, 2009) and was viewed as stigmatising. It has since been replaced by a range of terms that are more enlightening about the evolution of social care in the United Kingdom than the individuals they are ascribed to.

Activity 5.2

Who are you calling a ******?

The language we use can cause offence. What name would you prefer to be called: 'client', 'consumer', 'customer', 'service user', 'person who uses services' or 'expert by experience'?
   Can you think of a better term?

Comment

Each term reflects a different relationship with the individual. The terms 'consumer' and 'customer' indicate progressive shifts towards the marketisation of social care (McLaughlin, 2009, p1104); social workers became care managers and clients became the consumers of their wares, before transforming into customers in a mixed market of state, private and independent services. Social workers have been shifting towards a brokerage role, but they have also remained gatekeepers to resources (Clements, 2011). These terms do not accurately encompass the range of interactions between social workers and the public. It seems a particularly inappropriate reference to apply to the statutory aspects of the social worker's role, for example, care proceedings on a young person.

The phrase 'service user' developed from the drive to involve those who use services in their development. 'People who use services' conforms to the People First Movement's eponymous doctrine of not losing sight of the person but is unwieldy and risks being reduced to the even more dehumanising acronym PWUS (people who uses services). These phrases can reduce a person's rich social identities to the services they use (McLaughlin, 2009) and consequently perpetuate the view of them as a dependent, rather than empowered. As a term, it still fails to adequately reflect the subtleties of the social worker's involvement with people, instead, perhaps tellingly, focusing on the resource outcome of involvement.

A more recent term that has become widely endorsed is 'experts by experience'; this has the benefit of also including those who were ineligible for services and those who refused services (McLaughlin, 2009). Derived from the disability movement, it encourages a shift from deficit models, in which people who use services are problematised and their views neglected in favour of the expertise of the professional, to strengths-based approaches (Saleebey, 2012), in which they are recognised to have knowledge and expertise too. This name does have its limitations, as the nature and length of experience are variable and experience does not always equate to expertise. Furthermore, the privileging of a person's account due to their experiences is not always desirable, for example, the view of a person who abuses children that he does not need intervention (McLaughlin, 2009). However, this term is reflective of social work's concern with 'supporting self-agency and change' (Parton and O'Byrne, 2000, p44) which has evolved 'from a long tradition of anti-oppressive practice' (Sharland and Taylor, 2006, p508). This viewpoint has gained wider acceptance in recent social care policy, for example, in the personalisation agenda. A more subtle variation is 'people with lived experience' and this is used in the latest version of Social Work England's (2019) professional standards. This does not assume expertise but does acknowledge the importance of understanding and responding to 'their lived experience and meanings' (Sharland and Taylor, 2006, p508).

The term 'people with lived experience' is used here to refer to service users and carers collectively, whilst the terms 'service user' and 'carer' are retained for references to that specific group. Service users are not viewed as passive recipients, but active agents in their lives and in the shaping of the services they may receive (Shaping Our Lives National User Network, cited in SCIE, 2004). However, it must be remembered that the meanings attached to any term are not static; they are dynamic and contested and evolve over time and reveal the power in relationships (McLaughlin, 2009). They may initially hold limited or no meaning to those with whom we work yet can be a crucial label for accessing services. As professionals, we must be cautious of our power to label and the access to services labels can confer. We must also remain vigilant to the expectations of roles and behaviour that can accompany labels (Becker, 1963).

Research summary

Steven Hoskin, a 38-year-old man with learning disabilities, 'was forced to swallow a lethal dose of paracetamol, was hauled around his bedsit by a dog lead and burned with cigarettes. Then he was frog marched to the viaduct from where he fell more than

(Continued)

30 metres to his death after Bullock kicked him in the face and stood on his hands' (Valios, 2011). Hoskin had been receiving two hours a week of help from Cornwall Council Adult Services but cancelled it after Darren Stewart and Sarah Bullock moved into his bedsit. The Serious Case Review (now a Safeguarding Adults Review, under the Care Act 2014) found that 'Steven's "choice" to terminate contact with adult social care was not investigated or explored with him, or other key agencies involved in his care, even though such choices may compound a person's "vulnerability"; may be made on the basis of inadequate or inappropriate information; or result from the exercise of inappropriate coercion from third parties' (Valios, 2011). It was recommended that where any life-transforming decisions by a known 'vulnerable adult' occur, this should result in assessments of a person's decision-making capacity.

Since he was no longer receiving services, Steven was not deemed to be a 'vulnerable adult'. If he had been, then interventions may have prevented his tragic death at the hands of those he thought were his friends. Consequently, in the Care Act 2014 safeguarding now applies to those who have a need for Care and Support (whether or not the local authority is meeting any of those needs), are experiencing or at risk of abuse or neglect, and as a result of their care and support needs, the adult is unable to protect themselves from either the risk of or the experience of abuse or neglect. Consequently, safeguarding support is now available to a much broader group of people and they no longer need to be labelled as 'vulnerable'. This was a problematic label, as it focused on the individual as being at risk of abuse, potentially pathologising them, rather than considering wider social and environmental factors (Mantell, 2011). Interestingly, the term 'vulnerable' is still applied to children and the concept of 'vulnerability' is still used by the police (Manners, 2020).

Governing variables

Schön (1983) identified that practice is framed by a range of governing variables, which act as limiting factors upon your practice. Legislation, the policies and procedures of employers, instructions from managers, regulating bodies, codes of practice, ethical codes, and the practitioner's own values and ethics all set the parameters within which your interventions occur. In order to empower and engender trust from service users and carers, it is essential to be open and honest about what you can do, but also to challenge limiting factors where necessary.

Pre-assessment

Before you undertake a visit, you will need to gather as much information as possible. This is an initial step towards understanding what is going on, a first tentative exploration of the story, reflection-for-action (Thompson and Thompson, 2008). It is as much hypothetical as fact, questions to be tested when the visit occurs. It is a telling of the anticipated story that is likely to be clouded by governing variables, such as procedures, and your previous experiences of similar situations. As such, we need to be particularly wary of possible prejudice, such as stereotyping influencing our thinking. We must be careful not to become too wedded to this pre-assessment; otherwise, this tentative hypothesis becomes unquestionable facts, risking confirmation bias (where all future information is interpreted in terms of those initial assumptions). Pre-assessment enables you to identify which of your skills and knowledge may be applicable and/or need developing as well as potential weaknesses in past practice you will need to guard against. You are therefore reflecting on the potential limitations of the transferability of skills and knowledge from a previous practice to this new situation (Gould, 2004). What skills and knowledge do you need to develop and what mistakes do you need to avoid? It requires sensitivity to the attitudes and emotions that the situation you are entering elicits from you. These factors are interconnected, for example, you may feel anxious because you are not confident that you have the necessary skills. This forms part of your ongoing reflective process in which you question how emotionally and practically prepared you to feel for the unique challenges that you will face.

Huntington's disease is illustrative of numerous rare conditions where workers may lack knowledge and understanding. Mantell (2006) found that carers and service users reported professionals adopting several different strategies to address their lack of knowledge. Some proactively sought information or relied on the carers' knowledge. This could add to the responsibilities of carers and leave them anxious that there may be key information that they do not know. Other professionals tried to hide their lack of knowledge behind overt displays of being an expert or relying on their usual procedures, leaving carers angry and frustrated (Mantell, 2006). Refusal to acknowledge their lack of knowledge undermined carers' confidence in professionals. Concerningly, a lack of understanding of a condition can leave professionals susceptible to and unable to challenge wider cultural interpretations of conditions that potentially stigmatise and isolate the person (Farmer and Grant, 2020). In social work, we are often in the situation of only holding partial knowledge and must be sensitive to its applicability and potential impact in any given situation. We must also be mindful that even when we reach the point of being experts in a given field, it does not make us an expert on that person's unique circumstances and we must be sensitive to not imposing what we think is best instead of actively listening to them.

Pre-plan and identify strategies

Pre-planning incorporates a further aspect of reflection-for-action and involves considering various scenarios and corresponding strategies to manage them. When I was a student social worker in a rural team I was asked by a general practitioner (GP) to assess a person for attending a day centre. I could not drive and it took me two hours to get there, by which time it was snowing heavily. I knocked and introduced myself and said that I understood that he was interested in daycare. He replied 'no' and slammed the door shut. After several more unsuccessful attempts to engage him, I travelled the two hours back. I had gone armed with details of a range of day centres, but it had never occurred to me that I would receive such a blunt response. When I contacted the GP, he informed me that he had not discussed daycare with the person, but just thought it might be a good idea.

Napoleon's battle plan was reputedly, to turn up and see what happens. This highlights the importance of not being hidebound by pre-planning but instead staying flexible and responsive. Pre-plans are at best hypotheses to be tested and agreed with the carer(s) and service user. The expert model is particularly at risk of elevating the importance of the professionals' plans or ignoring the views and feelings of the carer(s) and service users. Heavily bureaucratic organisations can also have a similar impact, skewing the practitioners' focus to the requirements of the agency's systems at the expense of the service users' or carers' concerns; as a nurse once told me: *hitting the target, but missing the point.*

Planning and identifying strategies is primarily an organic process evolving within interactions with agencies, service users and carers. Interventions need to be negotiated rather than pre-ordained if service users and carers are to be empowered. This requires that we advocate for their perspective and where appropriate involve advocates for them, particularly if they lack capacity or have difficulty participating in the process.

Case study

Making informed decisions

Cathy (all names have been changed to preserve confidentiality), aged 34, tested negative to carrying the Huntington's disease gene. She had a younger brother who committed suicide (before being aware of the family history of Huntington's disease). Cathy provided care for her mother who had Huntington's disease. She lived in a separate home but following a fall, her mother was admitted to hospital and deemed unable to care for herself or live alone any more. In her early fifties, her mother was admitted to a care home for older people. Cathy did not consider that either she or her mother was fully consulted in the process:

No, they didn't give me a choice at all. They just said you know we're sticking her in there, because they've got room. No, they didn't ask my opinion, and you know, all I mean, I was relieved I just thought you know thank God for that. And it didn't occur to me to ask any questions like, did they know anything about Huntington's or anything like that.

(Mantell, 2006, p146)

Activity 5.3

(Care) home from home

What good practice steps do you think should be taken to enable a person to enter a care home?

(Continued)

(Continued)

   Why do you think that in some situations, such as Cathy's, this good practice does not occur?
   What do you think could be done to remedy these difficulties?

Comment

As well as highlighting the importance of engaging with service users and their carers to provide informed choices, Cathy's experiences also demonstrate how the level of choice for specialist provisions can be limited in crisis situations. Proactive planning, such as developing care pathways, is essential to facilitating real choices for people.

Reflection-for-action (Thompson and Thompson (2008) or preparation for contact (Douglas, 2008), can be seen as a second stage for students, following on from their preparation for the practice module, which more broadly helps students to explore and prepare for the challenges they may face in practice (see Chapter 1, for Douglas's framework on preparation for contact).

Assessment/intervention

Just seeing someone influences their situation. It may, for example, elicit guilt at their behaviour, relief and validation or high expectations that the situation will change (Mantell, 2006). Reflection-in-action forms an integral part of the assessment. A comparison occurs between your expectation of the situation and the actual situation. This adjustment enables a better approximation of the people with lived experiences and perspectives to evolve. The assessment may, for example, identify more pressing needs to be met than those previously anticipated. Practitioners have to remain sensitive to avoid our assumptions limiting our interpretations of situations and denying individuals the space to express their feelings.

Power and assessment

The primary aims of assessment are to find out the stories of those involved in the situation: risk factors, concerns, strengths and what those involved wish to happen. Maclean et al. (2018) have developed SHARE, a reflective model for social work practice, which can be applied to a range of phenomena, from theory to anti-discriminatory practice, but which applies particularly well to assessment. The acronym stands for Seeing, Hearing, Acting, Reading and Evaluating. Once the assessment is complete it becomes SHARED, as we form a decision.

Seeing – what do we observe? This may be the environment the person is in, their body language, and their interactions with others, including us. We must be mindful that: 'We don't see things as they are, we see them as we are' (Anais Nin, cited in Maclean et al., 2018, p97). Our background, our prejudices, our privileges, our mood and what is pre-occupying us, can all influence what we see and the significance we assign to it.

Hearing – What are we hearing? More crucially who are we hearing that from, and whose account are we listening to? Active listening, ensuring you are really understanding what the person has said is a crucial social work skill (Mantell, 2013). As Maclean et al. (2018) point out, we must be aware and sensitive to the input of all our senses and their impact on our emotions, not just sight and sound. For example, if you go into a house and smell a strong smell of excrement, that is likely to elicit an emotional response from you. Emotions can trigger instinctive thinking, which is fast, but more susceptible to stereo-typing, rather than more considered critical thinking (Kahneman, 2011).

Action – What actions are the service user and carer taking, what actions have others taking what actions are different stakeholders keen for you to take? Empowerment is at the core of social work practice, so we should be aiming towards actions by the service user and their family and support network. We increasingly work as part of interdis-ciplinary teams and must coordinate our actions with theirs to avoid repetition and disjointed support. Social workers can experience indirect pressure from media coverage, for example, of child protection, but also direct pressure from the relatives of the child or from managers. This can produce risk adverse, defensive practice. When assessing a situation it can sometimes become quickly apparent that immediate action is required, but in other situations we must be careful not to be cajoled or coerced into potentially rash action before the facts are gathered.

Reading – Much of the reading will have occurred in the pre-assessment phase, as the books and articles we read will help to shape our understanding of the situation (theories) and the interventions (models) we might apply. Prior to visiting you will have read the case notes and reports from the interdisciplinary team on the situation. However, after your first visit you may need to do further reading, for example, a service user may mention a condition that you do not know much about. Some exploratory reading can help you gain an overview, but be cautious with this information and its source, it is easy to misunderstand and to gain incorrect information. Instead ensure you use credible sources, speak with the service user and their family (with their permission) about how they are affected and speak with the relevant members of the interdisci-plinary team. Reading is not just about what you read, but what you write down for others. Think carefully about what you write down, ensuring it is clear, concise and coherent and avoiding subjective, emotive and judgemental language.

Evaluate – The outcome of the assessment will be a coherent, informed and evi-denced sense of what is happening. It will identify the concerns that different stake-holders have, but also the strengths of the service user and their family and their wishes. The points that are identified will also be influenced by the remit of the agency you work for and any statutory requirements. Whilst evaluation is the outcome of the assessment, we also need to evaluate our intervention (see below).

Using the language of this model, we are trying to encourage service users and carers to share their 'SHARE'. The better the rapport that can be established with those involved, the more forthcoming and comprehensive the SHARE and our understanding of their story is likely to be. However, the power imbalance between service users, carers and practitioners can inhibit them.

Activity 5.4

What are the sources of the power imbalance between the practitioner and service user or carer? List as many as you can.

Comment

The power imbalances can be broadly divided into the following:

What you represent to them. This will relate to their previous knowledge of social workers. This may be formed by good or bad previous experiences of social workers and/or the public perception of them. I was surprised on a recent visit to Los Angeles to see social work students wearing T-shirts proclaiming their profession. Sadly, this is unlikely to happen in the United Kingdom, where press vilification of social workers shows no sign of declining.

As a social worker, you also represent authority and this may trigger their feeling towards all figures of authority. This is known as transference and it is possible for us to respond in kind or counter-transference. These may not necessarily be negative response, but the false expectations then raised can nevertheless be damaging (Lefevre, 2018).

How you look can also trigger transference. You may remind them of their best friend, worst enemy, mother, daughter, etc. The same applies to you, however, so we must be alert to how we are responding to a person to ensure that we are responding to them and not what they represent to us.

Experiences of organisational, systemic, and direct racism may leave people from black and minority ethnic (BAME) groups reluctant to approach services and suspicious of any contact they receive. Consequently, Jacklin and Chiovitte (2020, p254) argue for the need to create cultural safety – sensitivity to the person's lived experiences, the barriers that they face and 'seeing and reflecting on culture instead of ignoring it'.

Why they think/hope you are there. It is worth remembering that they may not share your understanding of why you are there. I once visited a disabled man, who lived in an isolated cottage, and we had our initial conversation through the door (note, not through the letterbox, as that is not safe). He thought the social worker's role was to 'take people away'.

If you are there in a statutory capacity, for example for a mental health assessment or child protection investigation, then they may be hostile, resistant or duplicitous, for example, demonstrating disguised compliance (Woolmore, 2014) where they seem to be co-operating but are not. Each can limit, disguise or alter the story that is available to you.

They may alternatively think of you in terms of the gatekeeper for a service they desperately require. This can often give workers a power they do not feel or raise unrealistic expectations.

Where you meet and in what circumstances. Very often when we meet people they are in crisis. This can lead to a narrowing of the focus of their concern. Often it is valuable to let them explore that before broadening the discussion.

Meeting in their house can help them to feel more at ease, but if they are aggressive then meeting in an office is safer. If they are attending a meeting, while this may be intended to be inclusive it can also be intimidating.

(Continued)

It is important to recognise the power difference and be clear about when you may have to do something a person may not want. For example, saying about the limitations of confidentiality at your first visit may make the person more distant from you, but if at a later point, you have to share information and they had not been aware this would happen they will be disempowered and feel betrayed.

If a person feels powerless or threatened, then they may try to claim power by being intimidating, aggressive or violent. It is important to respond assertively if someone is intimidating, but if they become aggressive or violent withdraw immediately and contact your manager.

The emerging story is formed from what we know in advance – what we are told by the service user, carer and professionals involved – but also from what we see, feel, smell and the emotions that are invoked in us (see Chapter 3). We have to be wary of the power imbalance between the accounts of those who are more articulate, assertive and/or have higher social status than others. This is particularly so when working with young children or adults who may have low self-esteem and/or communication difficulties. It also highlights discrepancies and inconsistencies in a situation, which your professional curiosity should prompt you to explore further. This is particularly important where the service user is reluctant to have contact.

Activity 5.5

Jon Dunicliff, the coordinator of Cornwall's Safeguarding Adults Unit, when speaking about Steven Hoskin's situation, said: 'If someone says they don't want a service, you need to look behind that' (Valios, 2011). A similar sentiment was raised in relation to the Serious Case Review into the sexual abuse of 59 young people in Oxford, by groups of men. As well as recommending a more careful assessment of capacity, the review criticised police and social workers for a lack of professional curiosity (Oxfordshire Safeguarding Children Board, 2015).

Whether you are a student or practitioner, you are busy, and with the pressures upon social care it is likely you will become busier. How do you remain curious?

Comment

Professional curiosity prompts reflective practice. UK National Institute for Clinical Excellence (2021) argues it is about not taking information at face value but scrutinising it further. It is also about listening to your gut reaction, that physical feeling that there is something not quite right. It requires that we are actively listening and making sense of what we are told. This can be more difficult when we are pressured, but without it, we are just going through the motions.

Plan and identify strategies

The core activity of planning and identifying strategies requires reflection-in-action to maintain the necessary level of sensitivity to the preferences of all those involved. The exchange model of assessment (Smale et al., 1993) recognises these differences and encourages the exchange of information and negotiation towards consensus on outcomes.

Planning entails thinking about the future, which can be extremely empowering for some carers and service users, enabling them to gain a sense of control. However, for others, particularly families with degenerative diseases, planning means facing the future, which exposes their future loss. Consequently, some carers, such as Tara, who cared for her husband, who had Huntington's disease, prefer to focus on the here and now:

I'd been a great believer, in fact, through Nigel's illness, I take one day at a time. I don't like, I can't think of the future, I don't like to think what the future may hold. I take one day at a time, I get up and just try and get through the day, if it's been a good day, good, and if it's been a bad day, then tomorrow might be better ... And that's how really, I've coped with it.

(Mantell, 2006, p215)

Activity 5.6

Looking to the future

What would be important to talk about with service users and their carers in such circumstances?

How would you feel about having such a conversation? Would there be any topics that you would be nervous or uncomfortable about discussing, such as reduced sexual intimacy or death?

Comment

Your professional and personal perspectives can significantly influence how you explore the future with a service user or carer. What is significant to you may not be as significant to them, or it may hold a much greater significance. The dominance of the medical model can lead professionals to focus on the pathology of a condition, whereas carers focus on the individual affected by the condition recognising their history, their character, their interests and their meaning to the carer. Cultural taboos for example, around death or feeling rules (see Chapter 3) or around expressing emotions, can inhibit the service user, the carer and the professional from exploring painful but often necessary issues.

Meetings – 'not about me without me'?

The disability movement coined the phrase 'not about me without me' as a retort to professionals' exclusion of them from processes that were purportedly about them.

Including service users and carers in meetings is the default approach expected in the guidance to the Care Act 2014 (Department of Health, 2022) and is implicit in the principle of working in partnership with families under the Children Act 1989. The eminent Judge Mumby (cited in Lawson et al., 2014) has argued that failing to involve a person in their safeguarding planning under the Care Act could also be a breach of Article 8, the right to a private life under the Human Rights Act 1998.

Case study

Henry is a 28-year-old man who has had a traumatic brain injury as the result of a road traffic incident. He now uses a wheelchair for mobility; he requires two people to help him transfer and has a right-sided weakness in his leg and arm. He has slurred speech and word-finding difficulties. He has significant cognitive difficulties, including finding it hard to concentrate, and he is easily distracted. His short-term memory is poor and he finds planning difficult. His moods are volatile and he is impulsive. His partner, Molly, would like him to return to their first-floor rented flat. His parents would like him to come home to them. Staff in the independent rehabilitation unit where he has been for the last eight months recommend that he stays there for another three months, and the Clinical Care Group who were funding his placement were reluctant to fund further.

Activity 5.7

What would you do to involve Henry in his future care planning?

Comment

It is easy to pay lip service to involve people instead of giving careful consideration to how that can best be achieved. It was decided that there needed to be a meeting of all the people involved to try to resolve the issues. However, if Henry had attended the meeting he would have found it overwhelming and distracting, even if he had only attended part of it, and the speech and language therapist considered that he would not understand the key information. Consequently, the speech and language therapist and I met with him before and near the end of the meeting. It was important that this was in his room, away from distractions and where he felt safe, as he was anxious about what would happen. Information was shared in simple short sentences and he was given concrete options to choose from, rather than abstract concepts (such as, 'What would you like to happen?'). He wanted to live with Molly and a plan was developed in the meeting towards that goal. We then checked with him that that was okay, before ending the meeting. This approach could be seen as disempowering, but for Henry, it enabled him to take part in the process in a meaningful way. The starting point must be to work towards the outcome the person wants. When working with a child or adult who lacks capacity they should still be involved as much as they can and want, with a focus on their best interest.

In mental health services, approaches such as Open Dialogue (Seikkula and Olsen, 2003) have emerged which emphasise the importance of enabling service users to tell and explore their own narratives and determine solutions to their problems. As Olson et al. (2014) argued, dialogue enables service users to be heard, taken seriously and develop agency.

Open Dialogue is based on systemic family therapy and psychodynamic psychotherapy and focuses on establishing a social network that facilitates the development of dialogue between the service user and those who are important to them. The significance attached to dialogue is such that the creation of dialogue is the primary goal rather than change within the family. This may seem too 'woolly' to be used with those experiencing acute psychotic episodes, but it has been found to be so effective in Lapland that it is the preferred approach for mental health services there and is now being piloted in the United Kingdom. The meetings aim to enable the service user to find the language to make sense of their psychosis; consequently, the sooner the meetings can be held to enable them to reflect upon their experiences the better. It is not in opposition to the biomedical model, but it does challenge the historical perspective that dismissed the perspective of those who were psychotic as 'mad' and that they would not benefit from talk therapy. There is a different emphasis on medication, so it is used as a last resort and for the briefest period required, rather than as the standard procedure. Open Dialogue promotes polyphony; hearing multiple voices – these include outer polyphony, the voices of those around you, and inner polyphony, expressing your own perspective and experiences in different ways. It is from these different perspectives rather than consensus that new insights are gained. This same perspective of being able to simultaneously hold and explore different voices equally applies to reflective practice. Working towards the outcomes a person wants can be particularly difficult where we have a statutory duty. This raises two issues; our interaction with people who may not want us there and our adherence to a legislative imperative, both of which can undermine our assessments.

Case study

Ayeesha Jane Smith, known as 'AJ', was 21 months old when she was stabbed to death, by her mother, despite having had contact with social services since before she was born. The Serious Case Review found that social workers and medical staff did not ask sufficient questions.

Activity 5.8

Why do you think social workers might not have asked sufficient questions?

Comment

There are many factors that can inhibit our curiosity. These can vary from systemic issues, such as a lack of time and high caseloads, to cultural ones ('don't go looking for

(Continued)

work'), to personal concerns such as anxiety, that you might be out of your depth. As mentioned above, it can be curtailed by a carer's aggressive, resistant or duplicitous behaviour. Revell and Burton (2016) argued that professional curiosity can also be curbed by the rule of optimism (Dingwall et al., 1983), in which cultural relativism leads to the significance of the concern being minimised, for example, neglect in a poverty-stricken area, whilst parental attachments are over-emphasised as protective factors.

Bull (2013) warned that social workers have a tendency to approach legislation from either a technical perspective, concerned with a detailed understanding of the law; a procedural perspective, matching needs to resources; or with a focus on how rights are supported or eroded by legislation. There are some similarities (if some blurring) between these three approaches and three forms of reflection identified by Taylor (2010). Drawing on the work of Habermas (1972), Taylor identified technical reflection as empirically based, focused on systematic and objective approaches, for example, evidence-based practice. Practical reflections are concerned with our interactions and our expectations of interactions. Consequently, our language, as demonstrated above, is a crucial factor in our interpretations of interactions. Finally, emancipatory reflection is concerned with power in interactions and trying to liberate people from constraints, for example, the expert model, situating knowledge and solutions in the hands of the practitioner. A focus on technical and procedural approaches risks the service user or carer perspective becoming peripheral to our actions. However, ignoring these constraining factors could lead to unlawful actions and/or conflict with your employer. As Bull (2013) argued in relation to the legislative approaches, a pragmatic blend of the three forms needs to be developed by each practitioner. Alternatively, seen through the filter of Schön's (1983) learning cycle, each of the three paradigms, within each of the two models, can be seen to be incremental in a journey from single-to double-loop learning. Novice workers tend to focus initially on 'getting it right' – on grasping technical legislation, procedures and ways of interacting effectively. Once these concerns are addressed they may feel better equipped to argue against governing variables, towards a rights/emancipatory approach. However, during their novice period, their colleagues should be particularly attentive to their fresh eyes on 'business as usual' and receptive to the challenge they can raise to entrenched practices.

Intervention/assessment

As you shift your focus towards intervention, an ongoing element of assessment is essential. This includes a process of testing those pre-interview hypotheses that still appear applicable and also the generation and testing of new hypotheses. This process of reflection-in-action is concerned with ensuring that the understanding gained is and remains the best possible.

Reflection-in-action (see Chapter 1) is also focused on the process. How are you interacting and understanding each other? What subtexts are occurring? This requires sensitivity to self as well as to the others present, because communication may be at a non-verbal level. For example, a service user who was depressed spoke to me in a calm quiet manner, but I felt uncomfortable; I was becoming tense. I realised that I was mirroring his tension, which was incongruent with his speech. Mirroring, i.e. my unconscious copying of his tension, is a psychoanalytical concept that can help you to understand your interactions. They also highlight the origin of reflective practice in social work, as derived from its therapeutic tradition.

An important area of reflection is on the extent to which we are empowering the individual to take control and implement change as opposed to us intervening. This is where our original assessment comes to fruition. If we have taken a deficit approach then the individual is likely to be looking to you for solutions and also to hold responsibility for what happens, whereas a strengths-based approach (Saleebey, 2012) is more likely to have built their confidence and identified ways in which they have tackled similar problems before.

Reflection must also become outcome-oriented. Is the intervention still heading in the direction of the agreed objectives? If not, why not? Does it need to be redirected? Or do different objectives need to be identified?

Outcome

The outcome of an intervention triggers reflection-on-action. This again focuses on the comparison of the outcome achieved with the outcome sought and the consideration of the process. Was it effective? Could it be improved?

A clear distinction needs to be drawn between output and outcome. This is perhaps best explained using the cake analogy (Cook and Miller, 2012). If you imagine making a cake, then the input is the ingredients (or resources) used. Cooking (or activity) is the process, the cake (or service) is the output and the smile on a child's face (or impact on the individual) is the outcome. In reviewing our intervention, we must be careful to consider each aspect. It is important not to confuse output and outcome; for example, after being refused a package of care, a carer was told that the assessment *was* the service. The assessment process can be beneficial in itself if the social worker maintains a therapeutic rather than a bureaucratic focus.

If we revisit the earlier analogy of a story, Local Authority Social Service Departments have invariably been concerned with tales of needs and risks and how to meet them. The personalisation agenda has seen a change in individuals often undertaking self-assessments and then managing their own personal budgets to meet their needs. In the Care Act 2014 there is a shift to outcome-focused assessments being at the heart of self-directed support. Under the Talking Points: Personal Outcomes Approach (POA) developed by the Joint Improvements Team in Scotland, the outcomes of the service user and carer become the primary focus, not those of the organisation. So, we start with how the service user and carer want the story to end, rather than how the story started. Cook and Miller (2012) identify personal outcomes for service users and carers as including quality of life, change, and managing the caring role and process – ensuring that they feel listened to and respected.

Review and evaluate

A review can be seen as a formal process of reflection-on-action including all of the stakeholders. Reviews enable practitioners not only to ascertain whether the outcome has been successful, but also to reflect on how accurately the practitioners' views matched those of the service users, carers and agencies involved.

The review may mark the end of a particular piece of practice or the start of a further assessment of unmet needs. Regular reviews are particularly important when working with people with degenerative conditions such as Huntington's disease, where needs may change subtly over time. As Tom found when his wife first started showing symptoms of Huntington's disease:

> things creep up on you so gradually, things like for instance bottle tops being left undone, a slightly curious walk, the gait changes, the temper gets very slightly sharper, anybody who's experienced PMT would know exactly where we're coming from . . . But it starts to multiply you see, and you think, is this right?

> (Mantell, 2006, p181)

For the practitioner, reviews are also ongoing audit points along with supervision, peer discussion and observation of their reflective process. Such external checks counter the potential neutral (Baldwin, 2004) or insular nature of an individual's reflections, promoting continuous learning and development.

Reflection-on-action (see Chapter 1) is about evaluating how you could have better achieved the objectives of the service users and carers as well as your own. It may be about correcting mistakes or about ways to improve and refine your practice. It is about learning from practice, which can be divided into two forms of learning.

The first is single-loop learning (Argyris and Schön, 1996) and is where you tell the story again evaluating what you could have done differently to improve the process and outcome. It necessitates that you engaged with the service user and carer to ascertain the outcomes they wanted and that these outcomes were clearly recorded to guide and assess progress (Cook and Miller, 2012).

The second is double-loop learning and is where you go further, to question the governing variables, for example, challenging policy, as opposed to implementing them more effectively. As a specialist local authority worker for people with acquired brain injury, I brought to my manager's attention the fact that the eligibility criteria for disabled people did not include cognitive deficits and was therefore an inappropriate assessment tool for a wide range of people. More generally, improvements in developing services can be achieved by collating the information recorded with individuals (Cook and Miller, 2012). However, for double-loop learning (see Chapters 8 and 9) to be achieved, organisations need to encourage such practices (Baldwin, 2004).

As noted earlier, single-loop learning is more associated with a student or newly qualified practitioners, as they understandably tend to adhere rigidly to rules. As you engage in post-qualifying training and develop your expertise, you will also tend to incorporate double-loop learning and integrate single- and double-loop learning into your reflections before and in practice. Expert practitioners also tend towards viewing rules more for guidance than obedience. This discretionary approach reduces insensitive organisational bureaucracy but necessitates critical reflection to prevent 'street level bureaucracy', i.e. idiosyncratic routines or prejudice aimed at reconciling the conflicting demands of organisations, service users and the practitioner's own value base (Lipsky, 1980).

Activity 5.9

Professional discretion

In your practice setting, how much discretion do you have?
  How does this compare with that of your colleagues in other settings?
  How does it compare with that of other professionals with whom you work?
  What are the strategies that you adopt to avoid 'street-level bureaucracy'?

Comment

The managerial emphasis on quantifiable, evidence-based practice led in the past to a climate of concern with output, throughput and cost which severely restricted professional leeway (Johnsson and Svensson, 2004). Now evidence-based practice, such as the Personal Outcomes Approach (POA), is starting to provide alternatives to social workers, restoring the values and principles of professional practice, which were described as having been diminished through care management and bureaucracy (Miller, 2010, p120).

Understanding and desirable solutions

The model above provides a basic schematic of reflective practice. We tell the story to understand it better and inform our interventions. However, social work is a complex process. We have to be aware that there are multiple perspectives on a situation. Each party in the process has their own understanding of the situation and from that understanding flow their objectives and preferred solutions. For example, Karen cared for her husband Ralph but they had different views about how that care should be provided:

I might have been able to manage at home if he would be willing to have a nurse, or carers come in to help me. But he will not let them in the house.

(Mantell, 2006, p164)

Activity 5.10

Who's right?

Whose rights should prevail in circumstances like those of Karen and Ralph?

Comment

In my experience, the views of the service user tend to prevail in the short term, but if their carer reaches a point of being unable to continue, the service user may find that they are admitted to a care home, in a crisis situation, with limited choices. Central to this undesired outcome is the service user's level of mental capacity. Huntington's disease, for example, can cause rigidity of thinking, limiting the person's ability to consider alternatives. Advance planning may enable consensus to be achieved, but in some with conditions such as dementia or acquired brain injury, the person may lack insight into their needs. The provisions of the Mental Capacity Act 2005 have the potential to promote the views of service users through advanced decisions to refuse treatment, but also to shift authority to the views of the carer when the service user's level of capacity is in doubt, through lasting powers of attorney, for example.

Social workers, therefore, need to develop a multi-sited understanding of a situation to recognise that meaning is constructed by multiple agents in varying contexts or places (Marcus, 1998, p52). Social workers' ability to draw on a range of social sciences potentially increases their sensitivity to different approaches compared with those from more defined traditions.

In working with families there is often an implicit assumption that consensus is achievable, but this may not be possible. In such circumstances, whose meanings and, consequently, objectives are we aiming to meet? A relative of a service user who was a solicitor once said to me: 'Who is your client?' I replied that they both were. She was identifying a potential conflict of interest. One of the criticisms of social work has been the focus on one family member's needs to the detriment of another, for example, in Victoria Climbié's case.

Reflection is fundamentally about making the implicit explicit in order to critically scrutinise practice. Practitioners need to recognise and value different people's objectives but be explicit about whose objectives are being prioritised and, where appropriate, identify support or advocates for the other family members. This is not a straightforward process, as whose needs are paramount may change over time. One solution would be for social workers to move away from the terminology of carer and service user to identify a 'primary client', who remains the focus of their intervention. As the shift to individualised budgets proceeds, service users may demand that level of focus on their needs.

Time after time

Your first assessments may tend towards the mechanistic as you strive to become familiar with and master its components. Eventually, undertaking and reflecting on an assessment will become fluid, so much so that there is a risk of taking it for granted. Where this happens, it is easy to find yourself going through the motions, hearing what you expect to hear (confirmation bias) and responding to situations you have seen, rather than are seeing. This is more likely where you are faced repeatedly with similar situations. As Taylor (2005, p239) remarked: 'It is easy to do something when it is novel. It is another thing to maintain something when it has lost some of its initial appeal'. The reflective answer is to set an internal alarm bell to ring when situations seem the same because while situations may be similar, the individuals going through them are unique. At such points, it is essential to ensure you are actively rather than passively listening and that you remain receptive and curious about what you are hearing. My doctoral thesis was entitled 'Huntington's disease: The carers' story', because their stories were not being heard.

Taoists have a notion of 'the beginner mind', encountering all situations as if for the first time. Taking such a curious beginner's mind will not only help you to stay receptive to service users and their carers but will also help you to appreciate the world around you and reduce your own stress.

Chapter summary

This chapter has highlighted the reflective process that co-exists with social work practice. It has drawn on the example of people with Huntington's disease and their families to illustrate that the objectives of intervention are not always straightforward. Multi-sited meanings create multi-sited objectives. We should, however, embrace the polyphony this creates and not be too quick to determine the story we are constructing or dismiss the stories we are told. Having an open mind does not mean that you have to have an empty one and we must draw on our knowledge to appraise new infor-mation. However, as Issac Asimov remarked: 'Your assumptions are your windows on the world. Scrub them off every once in a while, or the light won't come in'. This requires an ability to live with uncertainty and curiosity to critically explore different narratives. Reflective practice enables social workers to develop the capacity for the creative (Trevithick, 2012) and for discretionary practice to meet people's diverse demands. However, you need to be sensitive to the person's lived experience, perspective and culture, your use of language and reflective on your own agenda(s). It is essential to be explicit about whose objectives you are prioritising and the assumptions you may be making:

> With care in the community of course, there's much more it being expected and assumed you're carers. And it's not always right.

> (Susan, who cared for her husband, in Mantell, 2006, p177)

Further reading

Excellent introductory text for developing your analytical skills.

Cottrell, S (2017) *Critical thinking skills: Effective analysis, argument and reflection.* Basingstoke: Palgrave.
   Slightly more advanced text on reflective practice in social work.

Gould, N and Baldwin, M (eds) (2004) *Social work, critical reflection and the learning organization.* Aldershot: Ashgate.
   Excellent introductory text to reflective practice in social work.

Gould, N and Taylor, I (eds) (1996) *Reflective learning for social work.* Aldershot: Ashgate.
   An accessible introduction to the Personal Outcomes Approach (POA).

Miller, E (2012) *Individual outcomes: Getting back to what matters.* Edinburgh: Dunedin Academic Publications.
   Read the original model, expanded upon within this chapter.

Parker, J and Bradley, G (2020) *Social work practice: Assessment, planning, intervention and review* (6th edn). Exeter: Learning Matters.

6

The role of reflection in breaking the cycle of unsafe practice

Sarah Houghton, Catherine Tucher and Denise Harvey

Achieving a social work degree

This chapter will help you to meet the current Social Work England Professional Standards (2019), develop capabilities from the Professional Capabilities Framework (2018) and introduce you to the Social Work Benchmark Statement (2019). The following are of particular relevance to this chapter:

Social Work England Professional Standards (2019)

3.5 Hold different explanations in mind and use evidence to inform my decisions.
3.6 Draw on the knowledge and skills of workers from my own and other professions and work in collaboration, particularly in integrated teams, holding onto and promoting my social work identity.

(Continued)

3.7 Recognise where there may be bias in decision-making and address issues that arise from ethical dilemmas, conflicting information or differing professional decisions.

3.10 Establish and maintain skills in information and communication technology and adapt my practice to new ways of working, as appropriate.

3.14 Assess the influence of cultural and social factors over people and the effect of loss, change and uncertainty in the development of resilience.

3.15 Recognise and respond to behaviour that may indicate resistance to change, ambivalent or selective cooperation with services, and recognise when there is a need for immediate action.

4.6 Reflect on my learning activities and evidence what impact continuing professional development has on the quality of my practice.

4.8 Reflect on my own values and challenge the impact they have on my practice.

6.2 Reflect on my working environment and where necessary challenge practices, systems and processes to uphold Social Work England's professional standards.

Professional Capabilities Framework (2018)

1. Professionalism
2. Values and ethics
3. Critical reflection and analysis
4. Skills and interventions

See Appendix 1 for the Professional Capabilities Framework Fan and a description of the nine domains.

Social Work Subject Benchmark Statement (2019)

5.2 viii the nature of analysis and professional judgement, and the processes of risk assessment and decision-making, including the theory of risk-informed decisions and the balance of choice and control, rights and protection in decision-making.

5.3 ix the ethical management of professional dilemmas and conflicts in balancing the perspectives of individuals who need care and support and professional decision-making at points of risk, care and protection.

5.11 ii apply ethical principles and practices critically in planning problem-solving activities.

5.13 iii balance specific factors relevant to social work practice (such as risk, rights, cultural differences and language needs and preferences, responsibilities to protect vulnerable individuals and legal obligations).

See Appendix 2 for a detailed description of these standards.

Introduction

The central purpose of this chapter is to explore the importance of reflecting on our experiences in order to minimise unsafe practice. By making sense of what we see, hear and feel, we can avoid acting in ways that can, albeit unintentionally, increase the risk to ourselves and to those we work with. This chapter will focus on the different aspects of practice that may make it unsafe: the practitioner as unsafe, the organisation as unsafe and the service user as unsafe.

Activity 6.1

Before you start reading this chapter reflect on what unsafe practice means to you. Write a definition of no more than three sentences which we will ask you to review at the end of the chapter to see if your views have changed.

What is unsafe practice?

Unsafe practice, sometimes referred to as 'professionally dangerous practice', can take a variety of forms but is in essence a way of practicing that puts either the service user or practitioner at risk of physical, social or emotional harm. We have chosen to use the word *unsafe* as the word *dangerous* often conjures up images of a mistake of great magnitude, and although unsafe practice encompasses this level of the spectrum, it is predominantly about the smaller actions which if left unchallenged can lead to serious consequences. Littlechild (2013) suggests unsafe practice may occur through the social worker's lack of skill to deal with hostility and/or aggression from the client or their family or could arise from a professional failing to recognise and deal with abuse, avoidance, disguised compliance or cultural relativism. An inability to reflect on one's assumptions, attitudes and knowledge base can, therefore, lead to pre-judgements and poor decision-making. Self-awareness through reflection is, thus, key to competent practice. Omitting to act, for example, not believing a service user or assuming that another professional will take action, can be just as unsafe as making a wrong decision. Organisational and management structures should support critical thinking, but if they are inadequate and not robust, they can create barriers to reflective practice. Bureaucratic services, high caseloads, lack of management support and supervision often being heavily task oriented, alongside a culture of organisations not valuing staff, create unsafe organisations. Professionals need to work in an environment that feels 'safe' to be able to process and make sense of their feelings and observations. It has been well documented that for this to occur, social workers need to have the opportunity to engage with reflective supervision, be supported in dealing with practice issues and have supervisors and managers that challenge decisions and judgements in a helpful way (Munro, 2008; Laming, 2009). No practitioner wants to be perceived as 'weak' or 'incompetent' because they have disclosed that an event has distressed them or that they are feeling 'stuck' and do not know how to take a case forward. Therefore, if social workers are to embed reflection as part of practice, they need to be able to show their vulnerabilities without fear of repercussion or judgement.

In today's modern society, the public place their trust in those professionals charged with providing welfare and support. When things go wrong with this provision, there is often a public enquiry/serious case review into the circumstances surrounding the incident. This gives rise to a culture of blame which in turn engenders defensive practice, which is often task-and process-driven rather than professionally curious, questioning, and inclusive. This has been highlighted in the previous chapter. Social workers' fear of ending up on the front page of a tabloid newspaper acts as a barrier to placing themselves in uncomfortable situations and confronting the challenging and difficult behaviour of service users and their families. It is a paradox, therefore, that although the aim of an enquiry/review is to improve practice, it conversely often creates a culture of more unsafe practice and impaired decision-making as social workers seek to protect their reputation in a risk averse way.

Over the last 20 years, there have been many examples of poor/substandard practice in both the statutory and voluntary sectors that have highlighted unsafe practices within the social care sector where the professionals involved have lost a sense of perspective in complex and challenging situations. Since the first child enquiry into the death of Maria Colwell in 1974, children have continued to die due to systemic and individual failings. The Laming report (2003) into the tragic death of Victoria Climbié in 2000 stressed the importance not only of agencies working together but also of professionals needing to ask difficult and different questions. The findings also highlighted that social workers often lacked the skills to manage the emotional and cognitive challenges that they faced daily. It could be argued this is due to years of underfunding, inadequate supervision and the erosion of relationship-based practice which has led to staff burnout and high staff turnover. The themes threading through subsequent high profile serious case reviews, such as Keanu Williams (2013), Child T (2011), Daniel Pelka (2013) and Peter Connelly (2009), have all referred to the invisibility of the child, agencies not working together, high caseloads and the lack of professional curiosity (see Chapters 1 and 5) and reflection. These same themes continue to reoccur over 40 years later as in the more recent serious care reviews of Baby D (2021), Child A (2021) and Emma (2022) which are all available to read with many others on the NSPCC (2022) repository.

In adult social work, the high-profile reviews into the tragic cases of Stephen Hoskin (2007) as explored in Chapter 5, and Gemma Hayter (Warwick Safeguarding Adults Board, 2010), highlighted the vulnerability of those marginalised in society and the often-unidentified risks of being abused by others whom they considered their 'mates'. In 2000, Mencap estimated that nine out of ten people with a learning disability are verbally harassed or exposed to violence because of their disability (Beadle-Brown et al., 2014). The fact that there has been no further research into the prevalence of abuse within this vulnerable group and no further data speaks volumes. There have been many recent cases of institutionalised abuse such as at Winterbourne View (CQC, 2011), a residential establishment for adults with Learning Disabilities where unsafe and unprofessional practice was identified at all levels, resulting in significant harm to the residents.

The Independent Jersey Care Inquiry report in 2017 underlined the complacency around assumptions that children in residential care are safe and acknowledged that the system had failed some children in a serious way. Frances Oldham QC in summing up stated that 'For far too many children who were removed from home situations deemed harmful or unsatisfactory, the States of Jersey proved to be an ineffectual and neglectful substitute parent'. The most alarming factor is that the report identified that there was often no legal basis for removing children and that decisions were based on 'prejudicial judgements' based on outdated traditions and a resistance to change in order to continue to protect the interests of those in power. Very few governance structures were in place, turnover of staff was high and leaders inadequate and poorly trained. Staff became complicit in the abuse, and as the report suggested, those who had genuine concerns felt disempowered to raise them in an effective way. There was no place for reflection and challenge in this culture of fear, which resulted in devastating consequences, often life long, for the children in state care.

Failings and unsafe practice have not, however, been confined to social care as the National Health Service came under fire with the highly critical Francis Inquiry Report (Francis, 2013) into the standard of care at Mid-Staffordshire Hospital Trust between 2005 and 2009. The Inquiry, which made 290 recommendations exemplified how these processes have tended to become long, drawn out, expensive and intensely bureaucratic, which in turn compounds the trauma for those affected. Despite this, lengthy process lessons have not always been learned, and in March 2022, the Independent Review of Maternity Services at the Shrewsbury and Telford Hospital NHS Trust (Ockenden, 2022) which covered the period 2000–2019 was published. It again highlighted poor practice and leadership and more importantly the lack of a voice afforded to the women and families involved, resulting in tragic outcomes and 'untold pain and distress'. The approach to care was based on the medical model; it being interventionist and clinically led rather than based on the social model of inclusivity and being person centred. One of social works contributions to the interprofessional team is raising awareness of a different approach based on the service user being at the centre of decision-making to ensure that care is not only safe but targeted. See Chapter 10 for further discussion of the social worker role in the interdisciplinary team.

The police were also criticised for their handling of large-scale child sexual exploitation cases in Rotherham between 1997 and 2013 (Jay, 2013) and elsewhere in the country, and a recent inspection by the HM Inspectorate of Constabulary and Fire & Rescue Services (2018) identified that the Metropolitan Police Service still has 'significant weaknesses' in the way it deals with cases involving children. At times, cases were found to be compromised due to poor investigations, volume of work and an absence of 'robust supervision'.

Activity 6.2

So why do you think that the issues within the serious case reviews are still being raised as a concern? Note down your thoughts to see how they compare with ours.

(Continued)

Comment

Although many of the key messages from serious case reviews and enquiries remain the same, there has been a change in thinking in the situations in which social workers find themselves. With the heightened awareness of child sexual exploitation, forced marriage, female genital mutilation, modern slavery and online abuse, social workers increasingly find themselves dealing with unfamiliar situations and feeling unskilled to manage them effectively. The PREVENT agenda (HM Government, 2011) designed to support people at risk of joining extremist groups and carrying out terrorist activities has added to the pressure on Social Services departments as they have become increasingly involved in identifying PREVENT cases because of their duty to counter radicalisation. The emphasis on early help networks has grown often leaving social workers as 'crisis managers' picking up cases when they have already 'gone wrong', negating the relationship-building phase which is so vital in effective practice. This is in spite of the fact that we know from research that 'effective relationships are central to successful outcomes' (Ingram and Smith, 2018). The shifting social care landscape of outsourcing social work tasks and services due to increasing demands and failing services to social enterprise, cooperatives, private companies and independent Children's Trusts has further added to this already complex environment.

The changing demographics in the United Kingdom: an increase in the older population, those living with long-term conditions, an increase in refugees and people with English as a second language and a rise homelessness have also impacted on the quality-of-service provision. There is more pressure to work jointly with colleagues in health care under the Joint Strategic Needs Assessment and an increased demand for assessments under the Mental Capacity Act (2005) for both mental capacity and protecting those who come under the Deprivation of Liberty Safeguards which is due to be replaced by Liberty Protection Safeguards. (Ministry of Justice, 2008). Roles often become blurred and there is a propensity to assume that other members of the multi-disciplinary team are carrying out functions and tasks, creating the capacity for things to go wrong. This was illustrated in the case of Gloria Foster (Surrey Safeguarding Adult Board, 2013), where different members of the team assumed others had re-arranged home care following the closure of the current provider, which resulted in her neglect and subsequent death.

These changes are against the backdrop of austerity and continuing cuts to front-line services and a greater need for transparency. As the demand for services increases, caseloads rise, putting more pressure than ever before on front-line staff. Attrition rates are high, particularly in the children's workforce (Department of Education, 2015), and many posts are vacant or filled by agency workers resulting in a high turnover of staff due to the time-limited nature of locum assignments (Stevenson, 2015). The 2021 figures released by the Children's Social Work Workforce (Gov.uk, 2022) highlight that in child and family social work; sickness rates, the number of social workers leaving the profession and the number of agency workers, have all risen. This was echoed in adult social care as figures published by Skills for Care in 2021 told a similar story. The prevalence of service users having multiple social workers not only increases the

(Continued)

(Continued)

potential for duplication and for vital information to be missed but also limits the opportunity to build effective relationships. There is a mounting pressure to record every interaction with a client at the cost of interacting with them. This paradox is mirrored in the sharing of information: developments in cyber technology allow us to be more interconnected than ever with other professionals, but rights legislation such as the Data Protection Act (2018) and Freedom of Information Act (2000) and fear of getting it wrong often prevents us from doing so. Serious case reviews have identified that had agencies shared information it would have enabled recurring themes, patterns and presenting risk factors to be recognised and alarm bells raised earlier, potentially averting tragedies from occurring. Despite these findings many agencies still work in silos and do not communicate effectively.

To address the effect of over-bureaucratisation on social work practice, the Government set up an independent review of child protection in England and Wales (Department for Education, 2009). This task force was set up in the wake of the Climbié case (Laming, 2003) and led to Professor Munro being asked to review child protection procedures in England and Wales. Her report noted the system had become over-proceduralised, with a target mentality and that the focus was on performance indicators rather than outcomes. She cautioned that when an organisation does not pay sufficient attention to communication skills, procedure may be followed in a way that is technically correct but so incompetent that the desired results are not achieved. Felton (2005) echoed this in her research warning that evaluating social work outcomes using quantitative methods can be reductionist and, thus, not aligned with the complexities of people's lives and the values of empowerment. In our experience as front-line social workers, processes and ensuring targets are met for Ofsted inspections often supersedes the importance of building relationships and achieving the right outcomes for the service user. For example, undertaking a home visit to a child on a child protection plan every 10 days is procedurally correct, but is pointless if the social worker does not actively reflect on if the child's needs and planned objectives are being met.

Munro (2011b) also highlighted that enquiries into high-profile child abuse cases primarily focused on aspects of professional error without addressing the causes. Indeed, the dominant response to the deaths of both children and adults in safeguarding cases has been a rational bureaucratic one of developing law, procedures and performance management targets to avoid future mistakes. By focusing on processes, attention to the psychological and emotional aspects of doing social work has been squeezed out and a feature of many of the reports is the numerous recorded instances where the failure of individual social workers to conduct quite simple tasks has contributed to the death of the child. There have been very few attempts at explaining these failures to act, in terms of questioning the notion of unsafe practice and why it occurs. Over the last few decades, social work education has placed an emphasis on rights, empowerment and anti-oppressive practice without attending to what are the often very real challenges of working with often aggressive and hostile involuntary service users in the statutory sector who do not want a social worker.

Concurrent to the enquiries has been the passing of legislation and the implementation of more regulations and guidance. The Care Act (2014) consolidated previous legislation relating to adult social care and statutory safeguarding adults'

(Continued)

guidance, but it also placed many more responsibilities on local authorities who were already experiencing cuts in funding. The Children and Social Work Act (2017) despite its initial opposition is broadly seen as positive legislation as it seeks to clarify the role of local authorities as corporate parents and creates a new safeguarding structure whose aim is to foster better interagency working and transparency. Local safeguarding partnerships, within local authorities, now have a leading role in coordinating effective local work to safeguard and promote the welfare of children. However, be aware that some of the procedures and laws that are introduced to improve practice may hinder it by shifting the emphasis from the service user to processes.

Unsafe practice in the light of COVID

At the time of writing, it is difficult to ascertain the true impact of the COVID-19 pandemic on practice and social workers capacity to keep those who are vulnerable safe from harm. Romanou and Bleton (2020), The NSPCC and Local Government Association (2020) all wrote about the perceived risk to both social workers and service users and proposed strategies that could be employed to minimise risk. What is clear is that the issues arising from the pandemic added a further layer of complexity to what was already challenging work, indicating that the role of reflection and robust supervision are even more vital. Social workers were challenged to work more flexibly and creatively, using platforms and methods that they were not familiar with, while managing increased caseloads due to people being so isolated. Guidance emphasized the need for interventions to be proportionate, planning more effective due to limited face to face time and the use of RAG (red, amber, green) rating tools to understand risk. As we emerge from the pandemic, it is valuable to reflect on what positives arose from the diverse ways of working and how these can be integrated into future practice.

Activity 6.3

Read a review from one of the high-profile cases that have been highlighted above and reflect on the behaviours that caused the failings and place them under the different headings. Note the themes that emerge:

- practitioners as unsafe.
- organisations as unsafe.
- service users as unsafe.

Comment

Review your thoughts at the end of the chapter and reflect on whether your views have changed.

The role of reflection in minimising unsafe practice

In the introductory chapter, we looked at how we might improve our professional practice by integrating Schön's (1983) concepts of *reflection-on-action* and *reflection-in-action* and Thompson and Thompson's (2008) *reflection-for-action*. How then do these concepts relate to unsafe practice in social work? Reflective practice is a dynamic concept, and the undertaking of 'safe and effective' social work means that the social worker needs to be continuously engaged in a process of reflective activity that includes all these concepts. In social work, reflection-for-action involves gathering and appraising what information is available both at the start of a case and throughout all of the involvement with the service user. Reflection-in-action means always keeping the situation under constant review while in the moment and revising or modifying the strategy as a result of these reflections. Reflection-on-action allows us to learn from the experience so that we can benefit from any insights and use these to inform our future practice.

Case study

Findings of a serious case review

The need for this continuous reflection can be illustrated if we look at the high-profile case of Child T under Dagenham & Barking in 2010. For a period of more than six years between 1998 and 2010, the two children of the family had been subject to child protection plans under three local authorities. Child T had a statement of special needs at the time of his death, was home-educated, and both children had missed substantial periods of schooling and developmental health checks. Since 2000, concerns had been raised about the mother's mental health and there had been no recent contact with specialist medical services or the multi-disciplinary child development team despite Child T having a disability. Mother's repeated formal complaints about social workers from all involved agencies deflected scrutiny of her care. All agencies made concessions following complaints which were not in the children's interests; for instance: re-allocating the case and not sharing information with the multi-agency network. Child T's mother killed him, aged 12, by forcing him to drink bleach. The 2011 Serious Case Review found professionals avoided challenging the mother due to her intimidating, aggressive and hostile behaviour towards them, resulting in poor child-centred risk assessments and interventions. Furthermore, they highlighted that ethnicity, religion and immigration status all had a 'significant influence' on the case history and how the family were viewed and managed.

Comment

Many different social workers managed the case but had there been a robust chronology to facilitate *reflection-for-action*, these behaviours should have raised a concern about the mother's avoidance of professionals and questioning about what this may mean for the children. If the social workers had *reflected-in-action*, they may have been able to access their feelings of being unsafe and intimidated and may have, therefore, considered the situation from the children's perspective and how they might have felt. If the social worker feels unsafe, then it is a good indicator that a powerless child or

(Continued)

adult at risk is likely to feel that way too. *Reflection-on-action* by the social worker may have resulted in the recognition of patterns of behaviour that were emerging and how the mother's accusations were a way of diverting attention away from her own behaviour. We all want to be liked and are anxious to be seen as practicing in an anti-discriminatory manner; however, these factors could also have led to professionals losing focus on the children and to underestimating the level of risk to them. Managers failed to recognise the impact of the mother's behaviour on the practitioners, resulting in inadequate guidance and support to the social workers dealing with the mother. The mother used hostile behaviour to keep control of discussions about her children and distance social workers and teachers, and she repeatedly accused social workers of being racist or culturally insensitive to her Indian background.

Case study

An example of reflection-on-action is given in the following extract taken from a recently qualified social worker's reflection on one of her new cases where the child had just been made subject to a formal safeguarding/child protection plan.

Before my first visit I read the Child Protection Plan and skimmed the Initial Case Conference Report. I felt prepared as I could see the central risks to the child (age 14) were explicit in the care plan, namely, David was not attending school and he was morbidly obese, due to parental neglect of his education and health.

Upon approaching the property, I noted the front garden had an old mattress, a pile of broken garden furniture, and rubbish strewn about. I had never encountered such a scene personally, or at the homes of service users during my student placements. The state of the garden I had to walk through to access the front door, as well as the dilapidated house in front of me, made me feel uneasy. I knocked many times before David's mother finally answered, and in a curt, gruff voice said, 'you must be here to see my son who does not need a social worker, you really don't need to be here, don't stay long'.

She walked away from me as I stepped into the property, but then as she continued to verbally criticise me and the Child Protection Conference, she turned and approached me while further raising her voice. She was taller and larger than me, and as she approached, my stomach tightened and heart started beating in my head. I felt intimidated, and out of my depth and unsure how to reply. I found myself quickly uttering that I must have come at a bad time and would return another day. I swiftly walked out of the property and felt a huge relief when I got to my car parked around the corner.

(Continued)

(Continued)

I felt very shaken in my confidence and ability as a social worker. I do not think I can achieve anything for David, but I know I need to overcome my fears and return to the family home to see him.

Activity 6.4

If you were the social worker in this case, reflect on the following:

• What are the barriers to implementing the care plan?
• How might these be overcome?
• What would your reflection-for-action look like?
• What might your reflection-in-action look like?
• What reflection-on-action would you consider to be central in being able to go forward with this case?

Comment

Think about your answers. This social worker is learning to reflect on her practice, particularly being a newly qualified social worker in a front-line child protection team. In terms of assessing David's well-being, how does her response to the initial home visit impact on him? What does the mother's presentation tell you about her parenting capacity and what it might mean for David? You might consider how it could have been dangerous for her to persist considering the mother's hostile presentation, or how she could have responded to her differently and what this could have meant for facilitating a working relationship with the mother and David. If she felt intimidated in this environment, you may reflect on how David might feel given the power imbalance and not having the option to walk away as the social worker did. Do you think the mother would have 'picked up' on the social worker's fear; would that have made the situation more unsafe? What is the impact of feeling scared on her ability to reflect-in-action?

In addition to reflecting on oneself, the process of reflection must also include an appraisal of whatever relevant research evidence and guidance in relation to best practice is currently available. Tapping into the experiences and knowledge of colleagues and supervisors can also offer different perspectives to reflect on. No two cases are the same but the more tools you have in your practitioner 'tool-box', the more likely it is that you will find an appropriate approach. To be an effective reflective practitioner you need to be an informed one.

Organisations as unsafe

From our original definition, *organisational dangerousness* covers the processes by which organisations, albeit unwittingly, act in such a way as to collude with, maintain or increase unsafe practice. Often, this form of unsafe practice goes unrecognised because it is embedded in the culture of the organisation. Senior managers have often not practised on the front line for many years and can have unrealistic expectations of social workers' capacity. The impact on service users of the constant turnover of staff and being shifted from social worker to social worker and team to team is rarely considered in assessments. Organisations are frequently hierarchical and led from the top down, often making it difficult for social workers to challenge decisions. Service improvement is typically measured internally and externally using quantitative methodologies when it is a qualitative service. Research has highlighted the limitations of quantitative measurement, including the tendency to miss areas where evidence or data are not available, and to exclude less quantifiable aspects of quality (Raleigh and Foot, 2010; Faulkner and Faulkner, 2018).

Miller (2012) in her work challenges the whole notion of outcomes per se, arguing that personal outcomes which are defined by an individual are often compromised and in conflict with the organisation's desired outcomes, which are often driven by the organisation's value base and external performance measures. This can create an environment in which service users and organisations are working in opposition and not together to achieve agreed goals. In adult care, this often results in already stretched budgets being spent on the wrong services and the notion of person-centred care being eroded. Although OFSTED inspections of children's services tend to be very target-driven and predominantly quantitative, the CQC (Care Quality Commission) standards are more qualitative which allows organisations to deliver care in different ways depending on the needs of the service users e.g. effective practice can take many forms.

Activity 6.5

Next time you have supervision, reflect on the CQC inspection questions listed below against your caseload. Consider your answers and reflect on what would you do to change how you managed the case?

- Are services safe?
- Are services effective?
- Are services caring?
- Are they responsive to people's needs?
- Are services well led?

Comment

When performance targets become the focus of interventions, then supervision often mirrors this and becomes task-orientated and paternalistic rather than reflective and holistic. Even prior to the COVID-19 pandemic, many organisations had reverted to 'hot desking' to save money and facilitate more flexibleworking from home. This has been packaged as a more 'efficient' way of working, but the purpose appears to be to save money rather than the focus being on the service being more effective. Although this may facilitate a better work life balance for some social workers, it has inadvertently reduced reflective spaces and prevented spontaneous reflective conversations within

(Continued)

(Continued)

teams. It has also reduced the opportunities for newly qualified social workers to learn from observing more experienced staff and could lead to isolation and increased stress levels. These losses are important as Ruch (2002) considers that reflective practice in social work permits a holistic understanding of the knowledge generation process and goes on to stress the importance of attending to both rational and emotional responses to practice encounters. The purpose of emotions in reflection is addressed in Chapter 3.

Activity 6.6

Care plans, safety plans and written agreements are often used by organisations to ensure that service users are kept safe. In light of what you have read so far, do you think that they are effective? Note down the reasoning behind your thoughts.

Comment

While they are a valuable tool in person-centred care, Ruch (2002) highlights that care plans, safety plans and written agreements have their limitations. She reflects on a case in children's services which involved a family with a history of sexually abusive relationships, and the department's 'rational' response to concerns for the children which was, to repeatedly devise ever more complex written agreements. She, as we did, failed to understand the basis for the reasoning that a piece of paper would safeguard the children concerned in what was becoming an increasingly 'irrational' situation. As practitioners we need to focus on the actual risk to the service user of the presenting behaviours rather than a plan that in essence protects the organisation.

Organisations as systems

The Social Care Institute for Excellence (SCIE, 2012) noted that any social worker's performance is a result of both their own skill and knowledge and the organisational context in which they are working. Consequently, poor practice is often a combination of 'flawed design and a clumsy user'. Taken from the aviation model, it purports that most practitioners are competent, motivated, and hardworking so the aim should be to design a system in such a way as to make it harder for people to do something wrong and easier for them to do it right. Sadly, this is not the experience of many social workers as they find themselves feeling undermined as practitioners by their employer due to the convergence of pressures, such as cumbersome processes, 'clunky' computer/recording systems and high caseloads, resulting in time constraints on social worker to service user, face-to-face direct work sessions, particularly in statutory settings (Whittaker and

Havard, 2016). Individual and group/peer case reflection practices may not be initiated or sustained by the organisation, thus undermining structured opportunities for creative thinking, colleague challenge and exploration of purposeful direct practice methods/ tools. Social workers who have overcome this by initiating and embedding regular peer supervision and practice reflection sessions within their work environment not only develop their own practice abilities, they also positively influence the organisational culture by instilling these practices as the norm within their organisation.

Activity 6.7

Reflect on the organisation in which you work:

- Does the culture and systems in your placement make it harder for you to do your job well? If so, is it a safe place to practice?
- Is there a physical space in which you can reflect on cases with your peers?
- Is your supervision regular and reflective or task-orientated?

Comment

If you found that the systems and culture obstruct rather than assist your work, then are there any channels for suggesting changes? If there are no formal channels for meaningful reflection, can you create informal opportunities? Our experience is that when approached, experienced practitioners are often very willing to listen, challenge and support you in your reflective journey.

Supervision plays a crucial role in ensuring that we practice safely, and it should be regular and cover both accountability and reflection to enable you to develop as a practitioner (see Chapter 9).

Continuous professional development

Serious case reviews and public enquiries have highlighted that the lack of training and up to date knowledge of staff have contributed to their inability to manage the case safely. Continuous professional development (CPD) is a professional duty of social workers and is part of the registration process. Un-informed practitioners can be both dangerous to themselves and others. Despite this, social workers are frequently blocked from attending training due to the converging pressures of staff shortages and limited budgets. Being 'too busy chopping wood to sharpen the axe' creates inefficient and ill-equipped practitioners, which is counter-productive and can be dangerous.

Practitioners as unsafe

Despite what we saw in the case of Child T, when the social worker's desire to uphold professional anti-discriminatory practice was capitalised on, we need to ensure that concerns about such behaviour do not become an excuse for continuing with the status quo rather than challenging discriminatory practice. We need to constantly challenge how we practice, for example, through the recent decolonising social work agenda. As caring professionals, we need to be alert as to how our own values and sensitivities can produce flaws in our practice and decision-making.

The rule of optimism

Social work is a helping profession intended to facilitate change within individuals and families. Munro (1996) believes that this requires optimism by practitioners about the capacity of individuals to change. The gap between professional expectations and reality, i.e., an overly positivistic view, can however be undetected or overlooked by an inexperienced or complacent practitioner. Overly positivistic thinking by a practitioner can become a barrier to swiftly recognising 'disguised compliance', challenging the individual or family when their engagement is not meaningful or recognising that a person will not be able to keep themself safe. This is more likely to occur in the absence of frequent, robust and reflective case supervision with an experienced practitioner/ manager. In a review of child Serious Case Reviews in England, Kettle and Jackson (2017) identified that insufficient professional curiosity combined with an overly optimistic view of parental behaviour had led to interventions which were insufficiently authoritative and left children at risk of abuse. This affirms the importance of robust supervision that is sufficiently reflective and not performance indicator driven.

Strengths-based approaches

Strengths-based practice approaches in children's safeguarding, such as: *reclaiming social work, signs of safety* (Turnell and Edwards, 1999) and *family safeguarding models* are increasingly being utilised internationally and across British local authorities as the preferred practice framework, as they involve working in partnership with families. While these approaches may superficially appear to be over-positivistic and void of professional curiosity, they do differentiate between and assist practitioners to find a firm footing between the two polarities of 'the professional is always right' (paternalism) and unconditional acceptance of what the service user or their carer says (professional dangerousness). The practitioner must squarely face the harsh realities of the alleged or actual maltreatment without dehumanising or demonising the people involved'. Turnell (1998) suggests this requires a receptiveness and open-mindedness about the people involved that allows for possibilities and change without minimising the level of harm or risk.

The systemic unit models, sometimes referred to as 'reclaiming social work' or the 'Hackney model' (Forrester et al., 2013) brought together a small team of practitioners who had an overall oversight of all cases allocated within the team. Using a systemic approach, based on family therapy within the family, was central to the model with clinicians forming part of the small team. There have been mixed reviews on its impact at reducing risk but the learning from this model has resulted in local authority children services departments implementing more family focused safeguarding models which include specialist support for parents with substance misuse issues, domestic abuse survivors and parents with poor mental health. This requires social workers to be able to work and communicate effectively with many different professionals. This is in line with the recommendations of the Independent Review of Children's Social Care to develop inter-professional teams which can draw on a range of expertise (Macalister, 2022).

Failure to do this could potentially put children at risk. This is echoed in working with adults especially when conducting assessments under the Care Act (2014). The guidance issued by SCIE (2015) requires local authorities to focus on a person's strengths and capabilities to ensure that care is person centred, and maximises, opportunities to meeting the outcomes they want to achieve. These models will, however, only be successful if the organsational structures and support for staff are robust.

Plans not aspirations

All social work, whether working with adults or children, requires planned practice interventions that are SMART (specific, measurable, achievable, responsible and timely—see Chapter 1). Social work that sets unrealistic targets and does not adhere to timescales and allows drift is unsafe and puts the service user and children at risk.

Information and power

The impact of managing the power imbalance between social worker and service user has already been alluded to in Chapter 5, but it is worth mentioning that if this is not recognised both parties can be put at risk. This is particularly important when delivering potentially upsetting information to service users in terms of their own and/or their children's safety. For example, a children's social worker that decides that a child is not safe within their family home will need to deliver the news to parents in a way that reassures them, but also informs them of the concerns. Similarly, an elderly person who needs to move from the home they have lived in all their life into a care home would need to be dealt with compassionately while explaining the reasons for the decisions taken (Care vs control).

Know your limitations

Practitioners need determination to go into the unknown and push outside their comfort zone, but they need to reflect-in-practice to ensure that they are safe and not becoming the 'problem'. As explored in Chapter 5, it is important that the Dunning-Kruger (1999) effect does not occur whereby confidence outpaces competence and mistakes are made. If you are struggling with a case or unsure what the next steps should be it is always prudent to explore in supervision and seek support rather than put yourself and others at risk.

Professional boundaries

Being an open-minded, caring, non-judgemental and empowering practitioner neces-sitates that both you and the service users you are working with understand your professional role. Clear boundaries are not only a professional requirement and provide a framework for the relationship in which you have a Duty of Care; professional boundaries are also a protection to you, your organisation and clients, particularly as you can be dealing with issues that are often intensely personal and difficult. Further-more, dealing day after day with difficult issues, trauma and crises, often with indi-viduals who lack awareness of and/or are unable to regulate their own emotions, can be draining, stressful and cause compassion fatigue. Cooper (2012) highlights the need for practitioners to be self-aware of their own emotional reactions to service users, including transference onto the service user of their own emotions and sharing personal infor-mation in an attempt to show empathy, and how this can impact on their profession-alism. The development of effective ways to ameliorate stress or distress in order to avoid being overcome with burn-out and/or secondary post-traumatic stress is also integral to safe practice.

Are you over-sharing?

Due to the prevalence of social media, attempts by service users to locate and/or learn about the personal lives of social workers is common, therefore ensuring secure social media with the highest of privacy settings, including the use of a pseudonym instead of a proper name, for example, on Facebook, is pertinent to ensuring social worker safety and the maintenance of professional boundaries. Our individual motivation for entering social work varies, but a common theme is the desire to help or to do good. We get, or hope to get, something out of being a social worker. It is essential, however, to recognise your own needs and subjectivity so that you do not risk making professional decisions based on your needs instead of your clients' (Cooper, 2012).

Service users as unsafe

Service users may intentionally behave towards social workers in a manner that is aggressive in an attempt to distract or intimidate, or they may display volatility due to becoming emotionally overwhelmed, substance abuse or mental ill-health. Some dis-abilities, for example, an acquired brain injury could also cause problems in emotional regulation and impulse control, increasing the risk of frustration and aggression. In order that behaviour is not mis-interpreted, it is essential that practitioners ensure that they have the understanding and expertise to work with people in a sensitive and appropriate way to prevent the risk of ill-informed interventions in which the service user may be subject to confirmation bias based on stereotypical perspectives, which can cause avoidable harm.

Practitioner fear

In safeguarding, unsafe practice occurs when practitioners do not identify significant harm and/or leave a service user at risk of significant harm as a consequence of their attitudes, assumptions or behaviour. Safeguarding, particularly child protection social work, is inherently intrusive into private family life, as the practitioner must adhere to and implement specific legislation and laws to ensure children are safeguarded (for example, regular statutory home visits for children subject to child protection plans). Caregivers, and sometimes children themselves, can be resistant to the processes that result from professionals' worries about parenting, particularly as safeguarding processes are compulsory and may feel unjustified to families, often resulting in covert and overt hostility towards social workers. Social workers may encounter subtle attempts to distract, divert attention, intimidate or undermine their confidence. These attempts may be masked in the form of questions or making remarks about social workers' private lives; canvassing whether they are parents themselves, or threatening to formally complain.

Experienced social workers are adept at adapting their techniques to different circumstances and using de-escalation techniques with service users who display extreme hostility and intimidation. For students or newly qualified practitioners this, however, can be daunting, and they can find themselves feeling fearful during encounters with passive aggressive or overtly uncooperative and/or angry family members and can also feel in acute physical danger when facing hostility or verbal/and or physical aggression. According to Ferguson (2005), avoiding unwanted hostility or conflict can, however, result in practitioners unintentionally and intentionally colluding with caregivers, thereby further endangering the child or adult whom the social worker has been entrusted to safeguard. It is, therefore, important to develop strategies to manage these situations.

Reflection-for-action on key documents, noting any alerts about the service user or relatives, and considering how emotive your visit may be, can help guide you on whether you should see them alone or with a co-worker and what steps you need to take to keep yourself safe. Referring to your organisation's lone working policy can also help you with this decision. Reflecting-in-action may enable you to prevent a situation escalating if you encounter an already hostile situation while with a service user. Using role play either with your supervisor or within the university setting can help you explore in a practical way how you can respond to these challenges when they arise.

What counts as threatening behaviour?

We have all encountered threatening behaviour at some time or other, some more than others. According to Koprowska (2005), hostile and aggressive acts include the following: shouting; swearing; using abusive language; taking up an aggressive stance, such as jabbing a finger in the face, making verbal threats in person or in writing, spitting, invasion of personal space, unwanted touching, throwing objects, brandishing a weapon, hitting, other physical or sexual attacks, preventing someone from leaving, damaging property.

It is however vital to remember, that encounters between social workers and service users are not always characterised by hostility. Many service users in all fields engage with services on a voluntary basis and get on well with their social workers. Nonetheless, high numbers of staff across the whole social care workforce have experienced some form of abuse, aggression or harassment from service users or a service users relative (Schraer, 2014) In a survey conducted by Unison in 2022, 40 per cent of social work staff in the United Kingdom reported having faced abuse from service users, their families or members of the public during the first few weeks of the year (Turner, 2022). In addition, 44 per cent of survey participants reported a rise in such behaviour since the onset of COVID, while just 2 per cent felt it had decreased.

Activity 6.8

Think about the cases you are involved with and ask yourself would you accept any of the behaviour that has been directed at you in your personal life?

If not ask yourself why you are accepting this behaviour in a professional context.

Comment

If we experience bad behaviour often enough, we tend to accept it as normal. Reflect in supervision as to what you think are acceptable behaviours and which should be challenged. The NHS have a zero-tolerance policy. Most people, but not all, go through stages of escalation before they become violent, and challenging their behaviour at an early stage can prevent it escalating. However, challenging someone can trigger/cause arousal levels to escalate rapidly so consider putting in place precautionary steps to ensure you are safe, such as having a co-worker present, choosing an environment where help is easily at hand environment, and having a plan in place if you need to exit quickly.

Case study

Children's social worker Julie was working with Karen (age 20). Karen has a mild learning difficulty and a young child, Tom, and they both live with her mother Jo, who manages Karen's benefits. There had been concerns that Jo had neglected Karen as a child and now concerns have arisen that Karen may be neglecting her baby. Karen had split up from Tom's father but told Julie that her mother took her to meet some strange men and that one of them was her new boyfriend, although she could not remember his name. Later that day Julie saw on Karen's social media account that she was newly engaged to this man. Julie raised a safeguarding concern with Adult Social Services. Jo phoned Julie angrily stating if she did not leave her family alone, she would find out where she lived and harm her. She accused Julie of targeting her family because they were Travellers and would therefore complain to Julie's manager, to get Julie taken off the case. Two months later the police concluded their investigation of Jo which found she had stolen most of Karen's monthly benefits and had been sexually exploiting her, resulting in Jo's arrest and charges

(Continued)

against her. During a supervision session with her manager, Julie reflected on the tactics Jo used and what her curiosity and intuition uncovered about the family dynamics and exploitation of Karen.

Activity 6.9

Consider what the possible risks and outcomes might have been for Karen and her child Tom had Julie backed off after receiving numerous hostile communications from Jo, and not listened and acted upon her curiosity and intuition.

Comment

Being professionally curious and inquisitive is a key assessment skill that assists practitioners to form a working hypothesis. Had Julie backed off when threatened by Jo the consequence would have been Jo's continued sexual and financial exploitation of Karen and risks to Tom. Reflect in supervision about a time when you may not have taken into account your intuition and how that impacted on your assessment or casework.

Activity 6.10

Remember your definition of unsafe practice from the beginning of this chapter? If you were re-writing it now, what would you change?

As a result of reading this chapter, write down three ways in which you are going to adapt your practice to ensure that you are a safe practitioner.

Chapter summary

In conclusion, we want to draw together some of the main practical suggestions that will assist you in minimising unsafe practice.

- When reflecting-for-action, before every visit you should find out as much as you can by reviewing the case notes, discussions with colleagues and relevant research.
- When reflecting-in-action, whilst interacting with service users, be aware of your emotional responses to any aggressive behaviour and how it impacts on your behaviour. Set out the non-negotiable areas at an early stage in the relationship.

- Always set aside some time for reflecting-on-action, reviewing features of the case after the visit, to allow you to learn future strategies and revise your assessment.
- Finally, think 'outside the box' so you can identify ways the culture and systems of the organisation can support and not inhibit your practice.

Further reading

Banks, S (2020) *Ethics, critical and radical debates in social work* (5th edn). Bristol: Policy Press.

Bernard, C and Thomas, S (2016) Risk and safety: A strengths-based perspective in working with Black families when there are safeguarding concerns. In Williams C and Graham M (eds) *'Social work in a diverse society' transformative practice with Black and ethnic minority individuals and communities*. Bristol: Policy Press.

Bhatti-Sinclair, K and Smethurst, C (eds) (2017) *Diversity, difference and professional dilemmas: Developing skills in challenging times*. Open University Press/McGraw Hill.

Faulkner, S and Faulkner, C A (2018). *Research methods for social workers: A practice-based approach*. Oxford University Press.

Fook, J (2016) *Social work: A critical approach to practice*. London: SAGE (4th edn, November 2022).

Gould, N and Baldwin, M (2016) E Book – *Social work, critical reflection and the learning organization*. London: Routledge.

Kennedy, S (2020) *Seeing the child in child protection work*. London: Red Globe Press.

Koprowska, J (2020) *Communication and interpersonal skills in social work* (5th edn). Exeter: Learning Matters. (5th edn coming in 2019.)

Munro, E (2020) *Effective child protection* (3rd edn). London: SAGE.

Trotter, C (2014) *Working with involuntary clients: A guide to practice* (3rd edn). London: Routledge.

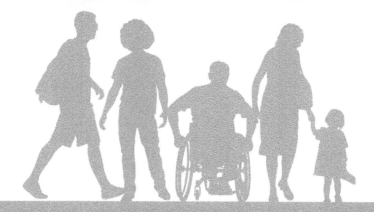

7

Gender in practice

Linda Bell and Chris Smethurst

Achieving a social work degree

This chapter will help you to meet the current Social Work England Professional Standards (2019), develop capabilities from the Professional Capabilities Framework (2018) and introduce you to the Social Work Benchmark Statement (2019). The following are of particular relevance to this chapter:

Social Work England Professional Standards (2019)

1.1 Value each person as an individual, recognising their strengths and abilities.
1.2 Respect and promote the human rights, views, wishes and feelings of the people I work with, balancing rights and risks and enabling access to advice, advocacy, support and services.
1.3 Work in partnership with people to promote their well-being and achieve the best outcomes, recognising them as experts in their own lives.

(Continued)

(Continued)

1.5 Recognise differences across diverse communities and challenge the impact of disadvantage and discrimination on people and their families and communities.
1.6 Promote social justice, helping to confront and resolve issues of inequality and inclusion.
2.2 Respect and maintain people's dignity and privacy.
2.5 Actively listen to understand people, using a range of appropriate communication methods to build relationships.
2.6 Treat information about people with sensitivity and handle confidential information in line with the law.
3.2 Use information from a range of appropriate sources, including supervision, to inform assessments, to analyse risk and to make a professional decision.
3.5 Hold different explanations in mind and use evidence to inform my decisions.
3.6 Draw on the knowledge and skills of workers from my own and other professions and work in collaboration, particularly in integrated teams, holding on to and promoting my social work identity.
3.7 Recognise where there may be bias in decision-making and address issues that arise from ethical dilemmas, conflicting information or differing professional decisions.
4.1 Incorporate feedback from a range of sources, including from people with lived experience of my social work practice.
4.3 Keep my practice up to date and record how I use research, theories and frameworks to inform my practice and my professional judgement.
4.4 Demonstrate good subject knowledge on key aspects of social work practice and develop knowledge of current issues in society and social policies impacting social work.
4.8 Reflect on my own values and challenge the impact they have on my practice.
5.1 As a social worker I will not: Abuse, neglect, discriminate, exploit or harm anyone, or condone this by others.
6.1 Report allegations of harm and challenge and report exploitation and any dangerous, abusive or discriminatory behaviour or practice.

Professional Capabilities Framework (2018)

3. Diversity and equality
5. Knowledge
6. Critical reflection and analysis
7. Skills and interventions
8. Contexts and organisations

   See Appendix 1 for the Professional Capabilities Framework Fan and a description of the nine domains.
   The chapter will also introduce you to the following standards as set out in the Social Work Subject Benchmark Statement (2016):

5.2   iii the relevance of sociological and applied psychological perspectives to understanding societal and structural influences on human behaviour at the

(Continued)

> individual, group and community levels, and the relevance of sociological theo-
> risation to a deeper understanding of adaptation and change.
>
> 5.2 v social science theories explaining and exploring group and organisational
> behaviour.
>
> 5.4 iv explanations of the links between the factors contributing to social differences
> and identities (for example, social class, gender, ethnic differences, age, sexuality
> and religious belief) and the structural consequences of inequality and differential
> need faced by service users.
>
> 5.5 v the nature and function of social work in a diverse and increasingly global
> society (with particular reference to prejudice, interpersonal relations, discrimi-
> nation, empowerment and anti-discriminatory practices).
>
> *See Appendix 2 for a detailed description of these standards.*

Introduction

This chapter will ask you to reflect upon the impact of gender on your practice as a qualified or student social worker. Specifically, it will help you to explore how your identity may influence your behaviour and attitudes in practice. The chapter will also ask you to reflect on the extent to which your practice is influenced by others' gendered expectations of what roles and behaviours are appropriate for you.

What do we mean when we talk about 'gender'?

In everyday discussion, the word 'gender' may be used interchangeably with 'sex'. However, for some people 'sex' seems to imply distinctions based upon biological difference whereas 'gender' may be understood more in terms of the individual's personal identity (see Jenkins, 2014; Chandler, 2017). Gender identity could incorporate physical characteristics but may also be influenced by practices and expectations that are culturally or socially determined. Whilst historically, gender may have been seen as inextricably linked to biological differences, nowadays this view can be open to question. One of the interesting features of current debates concerning gender is the focus on whether the terms 'man' and 'woman', 'masculine' and 'feminine' can be considered to be false binaries, and that they reduce a complex range of phenomena to either/or questions. Are these merely stereotypes, perhaps they represent polar opposites or are they on a continuum?

Sociologists continue to disagree about the significance of the body to 'social' aspects of gender (*embodiment*) (sociology of gender, https://www.oxfordreference.com). Is it possible to disengage the body from social identification with a particular gender? Does 'gender' itself exist as a concept? A more recently discussed aspect of gender identity is whether someone identifies with the gender to which they were assigned at birth (cis-gender) or one that they have acquired since then (for example, identifying as trans or non-binary).

Feminists have for a long time been challenging people to look beyond stereotypes in order to consider and reflect on the *power implications* of different kinds of pre-conceptions about sex and gender (see Himmelweit, 2008): how do these occur, internationally and within different social and cultural settings (Hawkesworth and Disch, 2016)? For feminist authors writing about sex and gender in earlier decades, primacy was often given to sex/gender aspects of identity, at the expense of other forms of identification (e.g. by taking a 'feminist standpoint'). However, Harding (2004), a proposer of feminist standpoint theory, also relied on ideas about oppression derived from class struggle. More recently, it was recognised that 'gender' inevitably intersects with other identities such as age, sexuality, race/ethnicity as well as social class. This is especially significant for social workers and those with whom they work (Christie, 2006; Cree, 2018; Cocker and Hafford-Letchfield (eds), 2022).

These are themes that will be explored further in this chapter; however, to return to the question of societal pressures and expectations to conform ('genderism') the next exercise will ask you to reflect upon your own experiences in the workplace.

Activity 7.1

Do you think your gender (however it can be defined) has an impact on the roles and behaviours expected of you at work?

If the answer to this question is yes, what are these expectations and to what extent do you feel comfortable in conforming to or rejecting them?

Comment

It is possible that you have not experienced many such pressures or expectations around gender at work. However, when we have asked students to think about these questions, they often identify some quite subtle mechanisms at play in the workplace. These can range from questions of 'who gets listened to in meetings' to the types of work that get allocated to particular individuals. Of course, it will probably not surprise you that students often report that 'gendered' expectations do not exist in isolation; they frequently conflate with those same 'identity' questions of sexuality, class, age, culture and ethnicity. Therefore, when considering gendered aspects of power, it is worth considering how this may be affected by other sources of discrimination and advantage (Reynolds, 2013). These, albeit contested, theories concerning *intersectionality* provide a useful entry point to these debates (Cooper, 2016; Collins and Bilge, 2020; Hafford-Letchfield and Cocker, 2022).

Making sense of gender

As a social work student, you will have encountered discussions of gender in relation to helping to confront and resolve issues of inequality and inclusion. You may have been asked to reflect on the impact of gender in your relationships with users of services, and with your colleagues and supervisors; this is important when promoting social justice and challenging the impact of disadvantage and discrimination on people and their families and communities. However, when reflecting on the impact of gender in social work practice, students are confronted with a range of potentially conflicting perspectives. Nevertheless, Hicks (2001, 2015) notes that, within social work, gender is often assumed to be a rather static quality, a 'given' which in turn can lead to a narrow conceptualisation of social problems and social work interventions. Therefore, there is a challenge in identifying how gender may have an impact on the way specific issues may be experienced very differently by individuals. This may seem obvious; however, for practitioners, there is a risk of relying upon normative generalisations and assumptions to make sense of complex phenomena.

Human beings can feel very uncomfortable and confused by complexity (Gilovich, 1991). As a species, we have evolved to look for patterns to help us make sense of our world (Shermer, 2008). This creates a risk of interpreting what we see through the lens of our preferred theories or prejudices. Psychologists refer to this as *anchoring bias*: we anchor our interpretation to what we already know. Similarly, *confirmation bias* leads us, sometimes unwittingly, to look for evidence that confirms our preconceived ideas (Handley et al., 2015; Cournoyer, 2017). Social psychologists and other social scientists highlight a human tendency to 'privilege custom and tradition over progress and social change' (Jost, 2015, p607). Similarly, Sennett (2004) argues that a frequent societal response to economic and social insecurity is to look for an attractive, if illusory, degree of certainty in an uncertain world. This psychological and social conservatism may be helpful in understanding the current, somewhat heated, debates around conceptualisations of gender that challenge the notion of a male-female binary (Webb and Childs, 2012).

Within recent years, the recognition of 'gender fluidity' has been embraced as a liberation from the biological determinism of our genetic inheritance (Fawcett Society, 2016).

People have always lived and felt non-binary – there's just a label for it now. And behind that label is a community, people who respect you and lift you up. We're not a trend. We're humans and this is integral to our sense of self. Acknowledging our humanity and identity doesn't harm you.

('Clo' quoted in Marsh, 2016)

Conversely, social conservatives caution against a new 'politically correct' orthodoxy. Perhaps predictably, this is framed as a particular threat to children; 'The intention is to break down children's sense of what sex they are and also wipe from their minds any notion of gender norms' (Phillips, 2016).

The current arguments concerning gender fluidity may appear to be new. However, they have their origins in the unresolved questions about the extent to which gender can be detached from biology. Writing 20 years ago, MacInnes (1998, p9) provided a helpful starting point in attempting to untangle some of the then-emerging debates:

We increasingly acknowledge the equal rights of women and men, but cling to the conviction that the different sexes of our bodies contain the key to other, more fundamental distinctions.

Arguably, MacInnes's observation is equally true today as when it was written. Biology still underpins many of the assumptions and myths about gender (Furness, 2012). For some commentators, there is an apparent desire to understand the social world through the prism of neuroscience: in short, to ask to what extent can social relations be understood by identifying fundamental gender differences in the structure and functioning of the brain. It may be the case that these differences exist and have an influence on both cognition and behaviour (McCarthy et al., 2012). However, Fine (2010) argues that conclusions have been drawn about gender differences, which are simply not supported by science. Similarly, Kimura (2000) cautions against biological determinism; noting that the differences between individuals of the same 'sex' may be greater than the differences *between* sexes.

In summary, gender is a key element of our personalised identity: it is fundamental to how we see ourselves and how we would like others to see us. This raises the question of the extent to which our gendered identities exist separately from our social interactions. Butler (2004, p1) explores how gender is 'performed'; she uses the term 'improvised', not in isolation, but in relation to others:

> ... one does not 'do' one's gender alone. One is always 'doing' with or for another, even if the other is only imaginary.

Activity 7.2

What would you consider to be the key influences on your gender identity?

Would you agree with Butler (2004) that your gender identity is 'performed' in relation to others?

Comment

Perhaps the best conclusion we can make is that the construction of gender identity, for each individual, is subject to the operation and interaction of a complex array of variables. Some of these variables are biological, some may be specific to individual life experiences, and some may link to social or cultural norms. Added to this, the 'performance' of gender can be contextual; for example, is one's gender performance different at work than at home? Does it vary in different work or domestic situations? (Miller, 2017). Furthermore, the study of 'intersectionality' illustrates the interaction of gender, race, class, sexuality, age and religion to provide a more nuanced understanding of individual identity, particularly in relation to advantage, discrimination, power and oppression (Collins and Bilge, 2016, 2020).

Gender roles in social work practice

Hood et al. (1998) illustrate the extent to which women were perceived to bring to post-war British social work special qualities that were also seen as being essentially 'feminine': the ability to engage with others and to set both children and adults at their ease (Curtis Report, 1946, para. 446). Empathy, sensitivity and the ability to read and manage others' emotions were skills and qualities typically associated with women. Hochschild (1983, 2015) has argued that women's greater facility with emotion is a valued and essential characteristic of occupations where women predominate. In fact, because women are paid to understand others' feelings and to nurture and provide emotional support, this work should be recognised as being 'emotional labour'. Gorman and Postle (2003) suggest that emotional labour is integral to good social work practice but, because it can be seen as something women do naturally, it is often unrecognised or undervalued by social work agencies (Barlow and Hall, 2007). Instead, greater value is often afforded to processes and qualities that can be perceived as essentially 'masculine': managerial skills, the ability to remain emotionally detached, or technical skills with IT or administrative systems (Berdahl et al., 2018).

Within this context, it is not surprising that, in order to succeed in leadership roles, some argue that women might be expected to adopt behaviours that are associated with masculinity (Kerfoot, 2001). Women who display these characteristics may even risk being perceived negatively by both male and female colleagues (Heilman and Okimoto, 2007). However, others have argued that since a 'care' orientation is central to social work values, feminist leadership and working within an 'ethic of care' relates effectively to a transformational leadership style (Simola et al., 2010; Cooper and Romeo, 2022). Simpson (2004) suggests that, compared to women who may have superior experience or qualifications, men benefit from an assumption of enhanced competence and expertise. However, this may not always have been an advantage, as men may find themselves expected to deal with professional situations that their knowledge and experience have not equipped them for. Schaub (2022) argues that how we support men to undertake social work can both enable gender equality and help people of all genders to undertake caring roles (Reynolds, 2013). Certain organisations such as the European Institute for Gender Equality now have a monitoring role in identifying sexism at work and promoting gender equality.

Approximately 85 per cent of UK children and families social workers are female (Department for Education, 2018) and only 13.6 per cent of students on social work courses are male (Crabtree and Parker, 2014). Consequently, a number of authors have speculated whether social work is an unusual, or non-traditional, occupation for a man (Williams, 1995; Christie, 2001, 2006). Nevertheless, there is a great deal of empirical evidence that, despite their minority status, men enjoy gender privilege concerning their career prospects: men may quickly gain promotion to higher-status management positions and are statistically over-represented in senior positions (McPhail, 2004; Lazzari et al., 2009; Schaub, 2022). However, as highlighted by McLean (2003), the majority of men in social work are not employed in senior or managerial positions. Therefore, men in lower-status roles may have to navigate contradictory expectations of what are appropriate workplace behaviours for males or may feel isolated in primarily female work environments (Crabtree and Parker, 2014).

Research by Shen-Miller et al. (2011) suggests that, within non-traditional occupations, men do internalise expectations of how they *ought* to behave as men. These behaviours are often reflected in 'traditionally masculine' responses to situations that were emotive (for example, when men confront danger or remain calm in challenging situations). The researchers concluded that this limited the scope of the men's work and reinforced stereotypical constructions of masculinity in the workplace. These themes are explored in the following case study.

Case study

Dan is a student social worker in a local authority children and families team. He enjoys what he calls the 'buzz' that he gets from his work, but often feels stressed and out of his depth. However, he feels quite pleased that other members of the team respect him and that he is seen as capable and reliable. At his placement mid-way meeting, his practice educator commended Dan for his progress and said that he was functioning at a level far higher than she would expect. Dan thinks that he has learned a lot from watching how his female colleagues defuse certain situations; but, he also thinks that they appreciate his support in a crisis, particularly when he accompanies them on 'difficult' visits. Dan hopes that he can act as a role model to young male service users to show them that men can be caring and sensitive, but still be men.

Activity 7.3

Looking at the case study, can you identify any issues for Dan?

Comment

The characteristics of stereotypical forms of masculinity might help us to understand some of Dan's experiences. For example, we could question how easy it would be for him to admit when he was feeling stressed or out of his depth. This could be particularly problematic, as Dan seems to value the status he receives from being seen as capable and reliable. This may, of course, pose some issues for him, and perhaps for service users and colleagues too. Other issues could be evident if Dan's gender is seen to be beneficial on 'difficult visits'. Perhaps he might reflect on what his role is expected to be in these situations. Would taking a feminist perspective, which also recognises masculine privilege (as suggested by Schaub, 2022) be helpful here?

Research summary

Crabtree and Parker (2014) explored the experiences of male student social workers. They concluded that:

- male students experienced: *gendered contradictions and paradoxes of the liminal journey that constitutes social work education* (p37).
- within social work education and practice, male students experience men and masculinity as being constructed as inadequate and/or abusive.

(Continued)

- consequently, male social workers feel the need to be perceived as being different from other men; yet, paradoxically, are expected to demonstrate stereotypically masculine behaviours: stoicism, stress resilience and the ability to cope with aggression and violence.

Gender and the emotional challenges of social work

We have already explored the concept of emotional labour (Hochschild, 1983, 2015). In Chapter 3, Gill Butler develops the theme of emotion in social work and argues that emotional intelligence is an integral part of effective social work practice. Social work's person-centred value base aligns with notions of caring, nurturing and emotional support. However, social workers are required to engage with particularly distressing and emotionally challenging situations. Research has revealed the incidence of anxiety, fear and emotional distress in social work practice, yet recognition and support within agencies are variable (Smith, 2005; Ferguson, 2008, 2011). The failure to acknowledge the emotional aspects of the work is convincingly addressed by Ferguson (2005, 2011) and summarised in Chapter 6 in its focus on professional dangerousness.

Activity 7.4

Think of an experience at work or on placement that you found to be emotionally challenging.

- What did you feel at the time?
- Did you get any support at work? Who from?

Comment

Smith (2005) demonstrates that the support of colleagues, including the line manager, is key in helping social workers deal with the anxiety and distress that they may encounter through their job. Failure to acknowledge and address the emotional impact of work can result in an emotional 'burnout' (Hochschild, 1983) or lead to dangerous practices (Ferguson, 2005, 2011). Within recent years, there has been a rapid expansion of interest and research concerning resilience and social workers. However, it is perhaps surprising that consideration of gender has been largely absent from the analyses of social worker resilience. Although it does not specifically address gender, the following research summary explores the connection between emotional resilience and the lived experience and personal identity of social work students. Consequently, it touches upon many of the themes that we have discussed in this chapter. In particular, the study revealed that the social work students interviewed equated the expression of emotion with a lack of professionalism.

Research summary

Focusing on resilience and personal identity, Rajan-Rankin (2014) conducted semi-structured interviews with 10 undergraduate social work students. The research highlighted the following themes:

- Students experienced discomfort, to a greater or lesser degree, in dealing with emotion during their course. Emotional containment was seen as important and the study highlighted the tensions between the expression of emotion and perceived notions of professionalism.
- Social support was essential for coping with stress. Formal supervision and informal networks were seen as important.
- Identity and difference were explored with some students feeling that it was not safe to be themselves. The study did not focus on gender but on race, religion and sexuality.

Case study

Julie is a social work student on placement. She has been working with a 15-year-old young person called Adam, who has a history of offending behaviour. Teachers and other social workers view Adam as being uncommunicative and aggressive. Julie acknowledges that his behaviour has often left her feeling anxious, frustrated and irritated. However, she tries not to show this in her work with Adam, not least because she feels that he may be trying to provoke her. She is determined not to give him the satisfaction of knowing that he is irritating her. In supervision, Julie has recognised that some of her irritation stems from feeling that she is 'not getting through to him'. Because this makes Julie doubt her own competence, she feels angry towards Adam. Julie feels that her reactions are unprofessional but resolves not to let him upset her. She secretly acknowledges that she feels intimidated by many of the young male service users she works with but works hard to ensure that she does not demonstrate any vulnerability.

Julie learned that Adam had been in a fight outside school, where he was attacked by a group of young people. The teacher whom Julie spoke to suggested that Adam had been 'winding people up, like he usually does', but he would not say anything about what happened. Julie visited Adam and asked him to describe what occurred. Adam started to speak, then began to cry. Julie was very surprised; because he had always seemed so combative, Julie had not expected him to cry. Adam quickly got embarrassed; he said he was 'OK' and did not want to talk about it. Julie changed the subject, then immediately regretted doing so.

Activity 7.5

Try to put yourself in Julie's position. What would you do next?

(Continued)

Comment

The case study illustrates a familiar question for social workers: how to respond to someone who is distressed. In this situation, Adam appears to have become embarrassed about crying in front of Julie. You might consider whether Julie was right not to explore the cause of Adam's distress. If you do not think she was right, what could she have done differently? You might also reflect on whether it would have been easier, or more difficult, for both participants: if they were both females; if the social worker was male; or if the service user was female and the social worker male. Think carefully about your responses; why would gender matter in this situation? Similarly, you may wish to explore whether some of Julie's apprehension may have stemmed from stereotypical assumptions about masculinity and, in particular, male service users. Within social work, masculinity and male service users have often been perceived as threatening, redundant, or problematic (Christie, 2001, 2006; Scourfield, 2006; Crabtree and Parker, 2014). But some recent research has directly confronted these stereotypes (Philip et al., 2018). Finally, you might speculate about what the information revealed in the case study might imply for the longer-term emotional resilience of both Julie and Adam.

Reflecting on gender in social work training

Within social work, feminist perspectives have been particularly effective in ensuring that qualified social workers are aware of the discrimination and disadvantage that both women and otherwise non-gender-conforming people encounter. Similarly, throughout their careers, it is likely that social workers will encounter the consequences of abuse, violence and criminal activity; the overwhelming majority of this behaviour is perpetrated by men. Therefore, it is unsurprising that a considerable body of literature has explored the links between a range of social problems and the nature of 'masculinity'. In essence, this literature highlights the problems that men cause and asks whether there is something specifically problematic with male biology, psychology and socialisation. These debates are not confined to academia: a recent best-selling popular psychology book is *The Problem With Women Is... Men* (Orlando, 2008).

Reference to Orlando's book is not included here to trivialise important issues, but to illustrate a further consideration: the extent to which discussion of gender can be impeded by polarisation and defensiveness. Arguably, the issue of gender in social work training has tended to focus on women's experiences, specifically of discrimination and disadvantage. Men largely feature as sources of problems; either through their individual behaviour or through the structural advantages they experience in a male-dominated society. It is perhaps worth stressing that the influence of gender is not, inevitably, female-centric. Similarly, there are risks in assuming that structural advantages are equally distributed, that men and women are homogeneous groups, and that individual men and women are representative of, and responsible for, their gender group. Within an educational setting, these risks are illustrated by Gough (2001), who noted that many male students felt the need to 'defend' their gender or 'bite their tongue' during gender-related discussions. Similarly, Crabtree and Parker (2014) and Schaub (2022) have noted that male students occupied a vulnerable position that oscillated between privilege and marginalisation.

Feelings of 'guilt' are arguably consistent, but an under-analysed feature of social work training; specifically, whether feeling guilty is both appropriate or useful for practice. Lloyd and Degenhardt (2000) advocate directly challenging male students to take responsibility for the behaviour of their gender. However, this raises the question of whether, for example, a male social worker is somehow implicated in the violence and abuse perpetrated by male social work clients. Similarly, is it problematic to note, for example, that the majority of aggressive acts are committed by men and conclude that men, all men, are aggressive? Arguably, there is a risk of confusing correlation with causation: as Hicks (2015, p473) points out, the majority of abuse may be committed by people of one gender, but does this show that gender *causes* abuse?

The range of perspectives concerning gender is confusing and emotive for anyone who may be looking for some certainty when attempting to apply theory to their own experiences. Arguably, our understanding of the process of reflection should help us with this confusion. The work of Schön (1983) suggests that we should be wary of attempting to apply, uncritically, a particular theory; or, rejecting it if it does not appear to correspond to our own experience. He asks us to engage in a 'reflective conversation' where we blend our theoretical knowledge with our own personal experience to gain a greater understanding of a specific situation. Schön (1991) allows for, and positively embraces, the notion that real-life practice situations can be messy, involve uncertainty, and may challenge our preconceptions and beliefs.

Activity 7.6

Reflect on your experience of how gender was addressed in your social work training:

- Try to recall one specific session or topic. How did you feel during and after the session?
- In what ways did it inform your understanding of practice?
- Were there any aspects of this session that were unsuccessful? Why do you think it was unsuccessful?

Case study

Lynn is in her late 40s; she has embarked on social work training, having spent the last 15 years raising a family. She is now in her second year at university and has been pleasantly surprised by how well she has done academically. Reflecting on her own experiences of school, she realises that she was not encouraged to fulfil her potential. Although her brother was encouraged to go to university, Lynn's parents believed that girls should not be

(Continued)

encouraged to pursue academic or professional careers. Lynn married young but is now divorced; reflecting back she realises that her ex-husband always seemed to be threatened by her intelligence and was absolutely set against her going to college. Through talking to other women on the course, Lynn has noted that hers was not a unique experience.

Lynn has found that the teaching of gender issues in her course has helped her make sense of some of her experiences. Lynn was particularly interested to learn about the feminist perspectives on caring. She noted that, when her mother became ill, the family and other professionals seemed to expect Lynn to care for her; the same expectation did not seem to apply to Lynn's brother. Lynn remembers the stress and the guilt that she experienced trying to reconcile all the conflicting demands that she experienced.

This chapter has provided a brief summary of a number of perspectives on gender. We hope that you will have gained an appreciation of the complexity of the issues but feel more confident in applying some of the perspectives discussed to your own social work practice. In Chapter 3 on emotional intelligence, Gill Butler argues that through reflection-in-action the emotionally intelligent practitioner understands what others expect from them, and how to behave or react 'appropriately' in a given situation. This goes to the heart of what we have discussed in this chapter. However, we find it interesting to understand how the gender of practitioners may, perhaps unconsciously, influence their practice. In particular, to what extent do we internalise others' expectations of us and practise in a manner that reflects these expectations? We hope that this chapter will have enabled you to think more critically about these questions: specifically, what are the benefits of conforming to how we feel we ought to behave, and what are the costs if we do not?

Chapter summary

- The influence of gender is a key feature of social work practice, yet the range of theory can be confusing for students looking to apply a particular perspective to their own experiences.
- Schön (2017) provides a useful framework for acknowledging and understanding that reflective practice requires a flexible and critical approach to the application of theory to the 'messy' real world of practice.
- Students could be reluctant to openly engage with and discuss some of the issues concerning gender. This may be because the issues could be seen as being contentious and students are anxious about 'saying the wrong thing'.
- Exploring some of the theory and research concerning gender, and reflecting on your own experiences, views and behaviour will help you understand how your gender identity has an impact on your experience of practice.
- It is beneficial to consider the emotional impact of social work and reflect upon how your gender may affect your responses to particular situations and the support you may receive from others.

Further reading

Austin, A (2018) Transgender and gender diverse children: Considerations for affirmative social work practice. *Child and Adolescent Social Work Journal*, 35(1): 73–84.
 An accessible and interesting summary of some of the themes highlighted in this chapter.

Kane, EW (2013) *Rethinking gender and sexuality in childhood.* London: Bloomsbury Academic.
 A considered and informative study of a neglected area of practice.

Holmes, M (2007) What is gender? Sociological approaches. SAGE.
Pilcher, J and Whelehan, I (2017) *Key concepts in gender studies* (2nd edn). SAGE.
 Two useful texts overview from a sociological perspective.

Rao, A, Sandler, J, Kelleher, D and Miller, C (2015) *Gender at work: Theory and practice for 21st century organizations.* New York, NY: Routledge.
 A useful text that covers many of the critical themes explored in this chapter.

8

Reflective practice on placement

Terry Scragg

(Continued)

Professional Capabilities Framework (2018)

5. Knowledge
6. Critical reflection and analysis

See Appendix 1 for *the Professional Capabilities Framework Fan and a description of the nine domains.*

Social Work Subject Benchmark Statement (2016)

3.1 v   the nature of social work practice. The process of reflection and evaluation, including familiarity with a range of approaches for evaluating welfare outcomes and significance for the development of practice and the practitioner;
3.2 v   skills in personal and professional development. Take responsibility for your own further and continuing acquisition of knowledge and skills.

See Appendix 2 for a detailed description of these standards.

Introduction

The purpose of this chapter is to explore the use of reflective practice whilst you are on placement as part of your social work degree programme. Discussion of the origins of reflective practice, its evolution and its relevance to social work is found in other chapters in this book. This chapter describes a range of practical activities that can increase your engagement with reflective practice which will enhance your learning during your placement (see also Chapter 2 for an introduction to ways of getting started in reflecting on your practice).

As your course progresses your knowledge and understanding of the use of reflective practice will increase and you should become more confident in recognising how you can apply the skills of reflection to different practice situations. When you begin your first placement you may find that your reflection is mainly at a descriptive level, but as you advance through your placements you are increasingly able to use reflection to analyse your practice culminating in your final placement where you are able to reflect in a critical or transformational way. Once you are qualified as a social worker, you will find reflective practice continues to play an important part in your continuing professional development, and you will be assessed in practice to gain a post-qualifying award as part of the assessed and supported year in employment (ASYE) and the employer's standards for social workers (for further information, see Websites at the end of this chapter). The opportunity to develop your skills in reflection whilst a student on placement can help you to value the importance of this activity throughout your professional career (Roulston et al., 2014).

Although this chapter is primarily concerned with the student's understanding and development of reflective practice, it should also be of interest to practice educators. The practice educator's focus on supporting the students to develop their skills in reflection is mirrored in their own need to 'reflect on their own practice, monitoring and analysing the outcomes of their reflection so that new learning can be identified and shared with the student and others' (Ixer, 2003).

Reflection within the placement setting

Throughout your placements, you will use a variety of approaches to develop your reflective practice. The important element in the process is that it takes place within a relationship where your practice educator can facilitate your learning through regularly reviewing your work with service users, challenging you to describe your practice, giving you feedback, and identifying your future learning needs. The main context for this to happen is the supervision session where you meet with your practice educator. To create the right conditions for reflection your practice educator needs to be familiar with your practice, understand the main social work theories relevant to your particular agency setting, and the processes involved in reflective practice. For supervision to be effective, it relies critically on the quality of the relationship between practice educator and student, and is undertaken on a regular basis where there is sufficient time in an appropriate setting and in conditions of privacy and without interruptions. The practice educator also needs to be able to ask the right questions that will help you analyse your practice in a way that leads to greater insight and understanding of your actions, and those of others. You should not expect your practice educator to have all the answers to practice issues, but rather to be able to facilitate an increased awareness of the range and possible approaches that you can test out in the future.

Activity 8.1

What is your experience of supervision?

- do you feel supported and is there mutual respect between you and your practice educator?
- are you happy with the frequency of supervision sessions?
- are you happy with the way the sessions are organised?
- are you able to contribute to the agenda?
- are you making a substantial contribution or always leaving it to your practice educator to take the initiative?
- do you receive a copy of the supervision record following each session?
- are there changes that would make the sessions more effective for you?

(Continued)

(Continued)

Comment

Your response to these questions will indicate whether you are satisfied with the supervision arrangements and that you feel confident that supervision takes place within a supportive and trusting relationship, where your practice educator offers non-judgemental feedback on your practice and that you feel 'safe' to disclose your anxieties or concerns about practice situations within supervision (Ixer, 2003). Where you have concerns you should discuss these with your practice educator and work together to identify how the supervision arrangement can be changed to meet your needs, and also ensure that they meet the requirements placed on the practice educator as part of their contractual agreement with the university.

Research summary

A study by Roulston et al. (2014) found that students valued supervision in a safe and supportive environment where they had a positive working relationship with their practice educator which was conducive to learning. Approachable and supportive practice educators, who also demonstrated their experience and commitment to the role, were valued by students and were influential in helping the student to develop professionally. Students also valued constructive feedback on their practice dilemmas, and discussion of their feelings and values, with time to reflect on their practice. The findings of this research suggest that the quality of the supervisory relationship is a key influence on the students' learning and level of satisfaction with the placement.

Being prepared for supervision

You can increase the potential for satisfactory supervision sessions if you ensure that you are prepared in advance:

- Make notes before the session of any issues or activities that you have been involved in since the last session (in addition to your reflective journal extracts) that you want to discuss. Share this with your practice educator prior to the session so they are prepared to discuss the issues you want to raise. You could email it along with any journal extracts you are providing for your practice educator.
- Ask your practice educator to support you in dealing with difficult situations through the use of rehearsals or role-play so that you are more confident when you experience the real situation.

- Supervision is a two-way process of interaction. Make an active contribution and demonstrate your commitment to developing your practice.
- Make your own supervision notes so that you have a personal record of the discussion, decisions taken and any actions suggested by your practice educator.

How reflective practice can help you during your placement

Your practice educator should ensure that there is clarity about the purpose of reflection and that it is an activity concerned with professional learning and development, that only personal issues are addressed in so far as they affect your professional practice, and that you are comfortable discussing your performance (Fook and Askeland, 2007) within carefully established boundaries (Hunt, 2001). The establishment of ground rules and boundaries early in the placement is essential as is a supervision agreement that outlines the practicalities that can form the basis for clear expectations on your part and those of your practice educator (Maclean and Lloyd, 2013).

An important prerequisite for your understanding and confidence in the use of the reflective practice is that at an early stage, both you and your practice educator explore what each of you identifies as the main elements of reflective practice and how and when it is used during the placement, recognising that it is one element among a range of potential learning opportunities. It is likely that during the first placement your understanding of reflective practice may still be developing, and therefore it is important to avoid the risk that you could be placed at a disadvantage because your level of understanding does not accord with those held by your practice educator (who in turn may have a limited understanding). Clarity between you both on the purpose and forms of reflective practice can help avoid the potentially discriminatory element in the assessment of your practice which could further increase the imbalance in power between you and your practice educator (Ixer, 1999).

Activity 8.2

Both you and your practice educator should do the following:

- Describe what you understand by the term *reflective practice*.
- Compare your definitions.
- Agree on a common understanding of reflective practice.
- Agree on how and when you will make use of reflective practice.

Comment

The purpose of this activity is to ensure that there is a broad understanding of what the term reflective practice means to you and your practice educator. This can help avoid some of the risks identified by Ixer (1999), if applied without prior exploration and agreement between the two parties, which could result in placing the student at a disadvantage and undermining their self-development.

Developing your reflective journal

Reflection can take a number of forms, with the most common approach being the journal (sometimes described as a diary or log) which you complete regularly throughout your placement and where selective entries are used as the basis for discussion with your practice educator. Describing your reactions to practice experiences is helpful in enabling you to clarify your thoughts and emotions, externalise your ideas and help you work out future strategies. If you use it to describe particular experiences that are significant to you, for example, a critical incident or completing a process recording of an interview with a service user, it can also help you to measure your progress over the duration of a placement (Cottrell, 2015). It then has the potential to be a useful reminder of how your understanding of practice situations can change over time.

There is no right or wrong way to write up a reflective journal. Your approach will be one that is right for you, but it is helpful to go beyond pure description and incorporate your reactions, thoughts and feelings, and what you have learned and what you hoped to achieve (Parker, 2010). The following general guidelines will enable you to capture the essential elements of particular experiences and help in getting you started:

- Set aside sometime each week for writing up your journal but remember that it is advisable to write down particular experiences while they are still fresh in your memory. The longer you leave recording your thoughts after an experience, the harder it becomes to recall exactly what happened and how you felt about it.
- Write your journal entries in the first person (I felt . . ., I thought . . .).
- Give yourself sufficient time to mull over your thoughts and ideas.
- Don't worry about style or presentation as this is your personal journal.
- Describe what happened, but also ask yourself critical questions about the how, why, and what of a situation.
- What does your account tell you about your thoughts and feelings about the experience you have described?

Case study

Jack is in his first placement and has been asked by his practice educator to use an early supervision session to discuss how he can use his experiences to develop his understanding of reflective practice. Prior to this session, they had compared their understanding of reflection and its application to practice. The practice educator, Sarah, suggests that he starts a reflective journal where each week he records his thoughts about events in the placement, particularly focusing on critical incidents or other occurrences that have been particularly problematic or challenging and have significance for him, in a narrative form. She suggests that he records his reactions without attempting to overly edit his responses. The very act of writing his diary enables Jack to transform his thoughts into a narrative process that he can then use in supervision sessions. Sarah asks him to email his diary entry to her prior to their fortnightly supervision sessions, ensuring that no service user, carer or

(Continued)

professional can be identified in his journal entries. Sarah reads Jack's journal entry before they meet and identifies questions that she wants to raise with him. When they meet, Sarah invites Jack to select from his journal events he has described and she uses the sessions to explore what the events meant for Jack in terms of his thoughts and feelings and what he has learned from the process. What she is doing is asking Jack to 'reflect on his reflections' in order that he develops greater insight into his own practice. As Jack is new to using reflection his narrative is largely descriptive. Sarah understands his stage of development and progressively encourages Jack to take an increasingly analytical approach in his reflection, focusing on critical incidents, particularly those where he felt uncomfortable or where things didn't go as he had hoped for, and in this way helps him to develop the skills that will lead him to increasingly identify a better understanding of his thoughts and feelings and the way this helps him to make connections with his personal assumptions about his practice. Sarah uses Schön's (1983) stages of reflection to provide a structure for the discussion. Through this process, she challenges Jack to reflect on his experiences and helps him to appreciate the intuitive, emotional and analytic dimensions of social work practice (Munro, 2011).

Asking reflective questions

As you become more familiar with writing up entries in your reflective journal you could introduce the following set of questions as a starting point when you are thinking back over a practice experience that you will subsequently discuss with your practice educator:

- What was the event?
- Was it planned or unplanned?
- What exactly did I do (describe it precisely)?
- Why did I choose that particular approach?
- What social work theories seemed to be relevant to the situation?
- Did I work in an anti-oppressive way?
- How successful was I?
- Could I have dealt with the situation better?
- How could I do things differently next time?
- Has the reflection on my practice changed the way I intend to do things in the future?

Although we all at times reflect some degree and draw conclusions from our experiences, here we are using the structure of a questioning process that can be applied routinely as part of your reflection on your practice, whether you record an experience in your journal or not. It can become part of an ongoing structured dialogue with your practice educator that goes beyond random reflections and is part of an ongoing process that helps you build knowledge and understanding about practice. Reflecting on an experience in this structured way is about learning from the process with the aim of gaining insights that help you influence your future practice. A final thought: ask yourself when you are reflecting on personal experiences whether you tend to adopt particular patterns of thoughts and feelings and whether this limits your potential to understand practice situations.

Activity 8.3

In order to develop your skill in writing reflectively, think back to a situation that challenged you in some way and feels free to write spontaneously whatever thoughts and feelings come into your head when you think about the situation. Through this process, you are giving yourself permission to engage with your emotions and not censor your thoughts and feelings as you become aware of them when you recall an experience.

Comment

Freeing up your writing in this way can enable you to be honest about your practice, something you might not want to do when you discuss a situation with your practice educator, for fear of being judged as not sufficiently 'professional'. If your relationship with your practice educator is founded on mutual respect and openness between you then you should increasingly feel you can reveal more about your thoughts and feelings which can significantly increase your awareness of your values, attitudes and responses to practice situations.

Your reflective journal as evidence in assessment

To satisfactorily complete your placements, you will need to submit a portfolio that demonstrates your achievements against the domains of the Professional Capabilities Framework. Entries in your reflective journal can provide valuable evidence of your progress throughout your placements, and you should identify journal entries that demonstrate how your skills in reflecting on your practice have developed during the duration of the placement.

Different approaches to reflective practice

Although the reflective journal is described as an ideal tool to help you develop your reflective skills, other forms can include critical conversations with your practice educator, process recordings, and activities such as rehearsals and role play where you can test out different approaches to working with service users in a safe setting. You can also use the comments from your practice educator when they have observed your practice, and also participation in team or multi-disciplinary meetings, where you explore your understanding of organisational systems, processes and cultures and how these influence agency practices. Trying different approaches can help you learn what works best for you and in what types of situations (Quinn, 2000). Where there seems to be some agreement among researchers, is that critical incidents increase the potential for effective reflective thinking (Griffin, 2003; Lam et al., 2007). These researchers suggest that practice situations which generate anxiety, or appear perplexing to a student, have greater value in terms of practice learning.

Activity 8.4

Discuss with your practice educator the different forms that reflection can take and identify jointly what would be most helpful for your development.

Comment

It is useful to avoid concentrating too narrowly on particular forms of reflection and consider the potential range of opportunities during your placement that could form the basis for reflection which would provide you with a richer and more fulfilling experience. The reflective journal is an excellent starting point as it offers you the potential to use narrative as a method to tell your story about your reaction to events, particularly the emotions and feelings experienced from contact with service users and others. Use the journal alongside other forms of reflection or as an adjunct to other approaches.

Research summary

Research by Wilson and Kelly (2010) explored the challenges and opportunities that students identified themselves with when on placement. Although there was a high level of satisfaction by students with both their academic programme and practice learning opportunities, the research nevertheless highlighted some key areas for improving the student learning experience. The researchers found that many students reported a high level of stress during their practice placements, often related to unexpected learning challenges and demands by practice educators and tutors. Students were also concerned about dealing with conflict situations and challenging behaviour. Where practice educators supported students to develop their skills through role play and rehearsal, this was strongly valued by students.

Ensure reflection is challenging

Together with your practice educator you should avoid the trap of reflection becoming a mechanical routine and use unthinkingly with a checklist approach taken to each experience or event discussed. This can result in engaging with critical thinking or the emotional impact of social work without the self-questioning, experiment and rehearsal for future action, creating the 'risk of navel gazing' (Boud and Walker, 1998). It is also important to avoid reflective practice focusing exclusively on your individual practice and failing to consider the wider issues, including the practices, processes and routines that you observe in your placement agency. Finally, also consider the wider social and economic policies which may play a contributory role in the problems experienced by service users and carers (Quinn, 2000).

Using an experiential learning approach

We have seen how the use of reflective questions can help you structure your thinking when you are writing up journal entries. To take things a stage further you can increase the effectiveness of reflection if you adopt ideas from experiential learning where you move beyond a mere description of an experience and use the well-tested technique of the experiential learning cycle. There are a number of different models of experiential learning that are all essentially similar, asking you to describe an activity, evaluate and analyse your practice and identify possible future action, the most known being Kolb (2015) and Johns (2017). For the purposes of this chapter, I have drawn on Gibbs's (1988) Reflective Cycle which students find helpful in exploring their experiences (see Chapter 1). The value of using the experiential learning cycle is that it recognises that it is insufficient to have an experience and assumes you will learn from it. Once you become familiar with using the learning cycle you can use it regularly to reflect on interventions working through the cycle to help you identify if there is a particular stage(s) where you experience problems. Take an example of a first meeting with a service user where you have been asked by your practice educator to undertake an initial assessment prior to further intervention. Use the stages in the learning cycle as you reflect back on that meeting:

Stage **1: Description** – what was the experience (what am I reflecting on)?
Stage **2: Feelings** – what were your personal thoughts and feelings during the experience?
Stage **3: Evaluation** – what went well and not so well about the experience? What made it difficult?
Stage **4: Analysis** – what sense did I make of the situation? What was really going on?
Stage **5: Conclusion** – what should or could I have done differently and what can I conclude about my way of working? Who or what might help?
Stage **6: Action plan** – what am I going to do differently in this type of situation next time? What steps do I need to take on the basis of what I have learnt? What support do I need to help me achieve change?

These questions can be built on with a greater depth of questioning as you become more skilled at reflecting on your practice and the work you undertake with service users becomes more complex and demanding. By adopting this approach your practice educator is helping you to understand that there is considerable potential for personal development and improvement in practice by using a questioning approach as an example. By consciously adopting a critical approach using the learning cycle it takes you beyond pure description to actively engaging with each stage of the cycle.

Case study

You are a student in an adult services team working with older people in the community. A referral has been received regarding Mr Brown stating that he is in his late 70s and has suffered a cerebral haemorrhage (stroke) and has been admitted to the hospital. Following medical treatment and a period of rehabilitation, he is now considered ready for discharge. You are asked by your practice educator to visit Mr Brown and undertake a needs assessment of his readiness for discharge so that community support services can be planned. You meet Mr Brown in the hospital ward and explain that you are a student social worker and that you have come to complete an assessment so that the service can assess his need for support following discharge. You find it difficult to communicate with him as the stroke has affected his speech and he becomes tearful at times during the interview. You learn that Mr Brown has some mobility problems due to his right side being affected by the stroke. As you struggle through the needs assessment form it is clear that Mr Brown's main concern is anxiety about how he will cope when he leaves the hospital as he lives alone and has no family support. Although he wants to return to his own home he will clearly need support to help him with everyday domestic tasks. You speak to the ward sister to try to obtain more information about Mr Brown's ability to manage on his own after the stroke but feel the ward sister is primarily concerned with a date when Mr Brown can be discharged as there are pressures on beds. You mention that Mr Brown wants to return home if he can be supported although the ward sister suggests that Mr Brown would be better suited to a residential home. You stated that you were not in a position to make any commitments about his discharge and wish to consult your supervisor. You return to the office to discuss Mr Brown with your practice educator.

Comment

This case study provides an opportunity to explore a range of themes, including the consequences of a stroke for an older person, the impact of a stroke on speech and mobility, changes in emotions or depression that are often a consequence of this condition, and anxiety about coping in the future. There is also your reaction to working with an older person, where you may experience communication problems, and where there are pressures from health professionals related to resource issues between hospitals and community services.

For example:

- What were your initial thoughts about being allocated the case?
- What information would have helped you better prepare for the interview?
- Did your thinking change as you gain more information?
- What were your thoughts and feelings as the interview progressed?
- What theories could offer ideas?
- Was there anything you would do differently if you were allocated a similar case in the future?
- What does this case tell you about the challenges different services experience when resources are limited and there is pressure on professionals to suggest solutions that are not necessarily in the best interests of service users?

(Continued)

(Continued)

By using this process you will be able to develop an understanding of the issues that you face when working with service users and from this experience increasingly construct a body of informal knowledge from your practice (Parker and Bradley, 2017). It is important that you not only make links between theory and practice following an intervention but also that you regularly start to identify particular theoretical perspectives that can help you anticipate some factors that are likely to be present in a particular case.

Impact of working with loss and grief

A further dimension of your practice is recognising that working with service users who are experiencing change and loss (as in the previous case study), and the possible grief responses this can engender, may raise strong personal feelings about the loss you may have experienced, or reawaken existing pain or arouse fears about one's own mortality. At a personal level we will all experience loss and bereavement at some time in our lives and how this is experienced is unique to each individual. Models of grief following a personal loss can help you understand more fully understand the experience of a service user who is affected by the death of a loved one or a life-changing health condition. Here, the works of Kubler-Ross and Kessler (2014), Murray-Parkes (1982) and Worden (2018) are helpful in understanding an individual's likely reaction. It is important to remember that these authors caution that an individual's reaction may not be experienced as a linear process but dependent on a wide range of factors related to whether grief follows the death of a loved one, or from other losses such as health or trauma, and that progress through the stages of grief can be one where there can be both progressions and regressions.

Activity 8.5

After reviewing the grief models consider how can you incorporate this knowledge into your work with service users.
Do these models help you make sense of any personal experiences you may have had or work with service users?

Comment

When working with a service user knowledge of the stages of grief and the possible range of reactions can be helpful as this can reassure the person that the thoughts and feelings they are experiencing are not abnormal, and offer the social worker a framework to help guide the bereaved person in their grief work. It is also important to recognise that 'being with them' as described by Dent (2005, p23), means listening intently to their story, acknowledging their feelings and supporting them in the transition to a different life without the deceased. Machin (2009) reminds us, that to be an effective practitioner means achieving a balance between two key elements in practice – professional objectivity and human subjectivity. Reflection on such interventions through a supportive supervisory process can enable you to process the personal impact of working with loss and grief and explore your own coping styles and achieve the balance between the two elements of good practice. For a discussion of social work with service users experiencing loss and bereavement, particularly older people, see Scragg (2012).

The contribution of social work theories

It can sometimes be difficult to identify specific theories and practice models that neatly fit when engaged with service users. The immediacy of involvement in direct practice can mean that consideration of social work theories periodically takes a backseat. We have seen in the previous case study that to fully engage in a purposeful way with a situation it is important to be well briefed and confident that your knowledge and understanding, however incomplete, provide you with some indication of what you are likely to face when you meet a service user for the first time. When you are allocated a new service user, do you think about which theories might offer some pointers to how you approach the meeting with them? From what you know of the situation, which theories seem to offer some understanding of the service user's predicament, what they might be experiencing, and which practice methods could offer a way of working effectively in the situation?

Activity 8.6

To help you think about how to apply theoretical perspectives to practice situations, Maclean and Harrison (2015) offer some key statements that can help in this process:

- What are the key aspects of the service user's identity?
- What are the key presenting issues?
- What are the key aspects of the agency context and practice?
- What are the key points of the work to be undertaken?

Imagine that you are working with a young man with a learning disability who is moving from his parental home to live independently for the first time in supported accommodation. What theoretical perspectives and practice approaches does this case suggest might offer a better understanding of the issues both he and his family face and how direct work with him could better meet his needs?

(Continued)

(Continued)

Comment

There are several areas which you could focus on in this activity. He is a male, has a learning disability and wants to be independent. His parents may be anxious about whether he will be able to manage independently, and whether he has the skills and confidence to live independently. What support will he need to manage successfully? Practice issues would include a needs assessment, the consideration of risk factors, care planning, identifying support for independent living skills, and working with the housing provider. Personalisation would be the main practice focus in this situation, ensuring the service user is at the centre of the process (SCIE, 2010). Some of the above areas suggest an interaction of theory and practice that can provide ideas about how you could approach a similar situation. Ideally, you want to move to a position where you recognise how theory underpins practice and practice informs theory (Thompson and Thompson, 2008), rather than relying on theories to provide ready-made solutions. As you gain experience and explore more complex practice issues you should begin to recognise where theories can offer new insights or help you make sense of experiences which at first were puzzling. So theory helps us not only understand a situation but also to select the most appropriate method of intervention, as Howe (2009, p2) observed: 'If you can make sense of what is going on, then you are halfway towards knowing what to do'. Applying social work theories can mean your practice is sensitive, intelligent and organised. Knowing the evidence base for using a particular practice method helps to develop your rationale for considering a particular approach.

Integrating theory and practice

In her review of child protection Munro (2011) describes how social workers draw on both theory and practice experience in their work and together these enable them to make assumptions based on sound judgements that can help in decision-making. Skills developed through academic studies enable them to make sense of practice situations, whereas intuition derived from repeated practice experience can lead to beliefs or 'gut feelings' about situations that provide some security when operating in a world of uncertainty.

Similarly, as you gain more experience working with service users you will come to recognise how emotions influence each encounter and what you are experiencing emotionally when you connect with the service user and their experience. Ruch (2002) suggests that there is a range of potential sources of information available to the social worker when responding to a new situation – theories, professional and personal experience, the experience of service users and knowledge passed on by colleagues – that can all help you enter a situation with some understanding of possible outcomes. But these are only assumptions, and even if they have proved reliable in the past, they may not account for incidents in the service user's life that you have no control over, or personal issues in your own life that affect your interactions and responses to encounters with service users.

Although each situation is unique, by building up practice experience (intuitive understanding) and analytic knowledge (application of theoretical models), and exploring through reflection you will develop knowledge and skills over the duration of your placements, which will enable you to practice confidently at a professional level.

Practical application of the integration model

One practical approach that you can use to develop your confidence in applying theory to practice is to identify a particular theory or practice model from your university course or techniques used in your placement that has a sound theoretical foundation, that you can 'test' to see how far it can inform your work with service users while on placement. I have chosen an example from my own experience working with students placed in substance misuse services, of motivational interviewing (MI). MI has its origins in Rogers (1951) client-centred therapy and was developed by Miller and Rollnick (2013) as a way of helping individuals who were struggling with addiction and want, or need to change, but are ambivalent about the degree of change they need to make. They describe a four-stage process of *engaging* and building a trusting relationship, *focusing* to establish an agreed direction towards change, *evocative* questions that help the individual identify why they want to change, and *planning* the how and when of change. MI is now used in a wide variety of social and health services where professionals support individuals who wish to change their behaviour (Hohman, 2012).

Activity 8.7

Discuss the relevant theory with your placement supervisor and identify the different elements of MI and how these can be applied in practice. Support this by reading either a chapter from Goodman (2013) or an article (Vowell, 2022) which describes MI and notes the key points. Here an opportunity to shadow a professional using MI in a practice situation is invaluable. This can enable you to understand how the different elements of MI are used in a real-life interview. Ensure the professional understands the purpose of the shadowing exercise that you are clear about what you hope to identify during shadowing and that you have the opportunity to discuss your experience with the professional following the session.

Activity 8.8

Following a shadowing experience asks yourself the following questions:

* What was the purpose of the interview with the service user?
* What did I learn from the situation?

(Continued)

(Continued)

- Was I able to identify elements of MI during the shadowing experience?
- What questions did it raise for me about the technique?
- Would I feel confident to begin using some of the techniques in an interview with a service user?

Comment

Shadowing is an invaluable opportunity to observe how professionals incorporate elements of MI in work with service users and provide ideas on how you could use some of the techniques when starting to work with service users and give you the confidence to develop your own style of working.

Once you have gained some experience working with service users, then with appropriate guidance from your placement supervisor and practice educator test out the techniques of MI with service users where this is deemed suitable.

Case study

Karina is a student placed in a substance misuse service and has been asked to work with a young man, Dave, who has self-referred to the service as he is concerned about his increasing cannabis use as his job is at risk and it is impacting his family relationships. Following guidance from her practice supervisor her first contact with Dave will be primarily to engage with him, build rapport and establish a trusting and respectful relationship as an initial stage and create a preliminary agenda that they both agree to work on as a shared approach to change. This early stage in supporting Dave in his desire for change provides an opportunity for Karina to reflect on the initial processes of MI, before moving on to identifying Dave's ideas and commitment to reduce his cannabis use and how this can be planned if he is serious about change.

Comment

Once you start working with service users it will provide you with the opportunity to explore the degree of 'fit' and begin theory and practice. When you have completed work with a service user discuss this with your placement supervisor and practice educator as this will help you stand back from the experience and reflect on your experience and what you have learnt from the process. You could also take this further by reading articles that critically evaluate particular intervention strategies in a more objective and critical context that can help inform future practice (Copley, 2018).

Although I have chosen a particular example of MI for the purposes of illustrating the integration model the process can be applied to any area of practice where you wish to explore particular theoretical and practice models, recognising that slavishly adopting these techniques or being over-prescriptive in their application will inevitably be tested in practice where service users present their own unique life stories and experience. Exploring practice models using critical analysis and reflection means you learn to evaluate the effectiveness of different theories which can build your confidence in relating these to practice situations. In this way you become more critical about different theoretical approaches, identifying what works in what situations and why, leading to better-informed practice that is the hallmark of the professional social worker.

Chapter summary

This chapter has introduced you to reflective learning in the context of your practice placement. It has identified the importance of supervision and your relationship with your practice educator, and the value of working together to identify your understanding of reflective practice and how you can use this in your placement to support your learning. We have seen how you can use a range of practice opportunities to explore reflectively, particularly the use of the reflective journal. Case studies have provided examples of how you can develop skills in the use of a reflective journal and using a structured approach to analyse your practice and learn from experiences and events during your placement. A case study of work with an older person provides an opportunity to explore challenging issues that offer ideas for future practice in different contexts, including work with service users experiencing grief following the loss of a loved one. Finally, the chapter reminds you of the importance of social work theories that should be an integral part of your practice, and testing these in a real-life encounter with service users can provide a unique learning opportunity that can inform future practice, by trying out particularly approaches and techniques. Combined with a growing understanding of different situations this can enable you to develop both analytic and intuitive skills that can offer a degree of certainty when faced with future challenges, but where it is still important to appreciate how the uniqueness of each encounter suggests that a healthy scepticism is important in any practice situation.

Further reading

This book is written with the student social worker in mind and describes the key social work theories and how they relate to practice through the use of activities and case studies.

Deacon, L and MacDonald, SJ (2017) *Social work theory and practice.* London: SAGE.
   Written by experienced practice educators', this guide explains the major theories used in social work practice. Particularly helpful in relating theory to practice when on placement.

Maclean, S and Harrison, R (2015) *Theory and practice: A straightforward guide for social work students* (3rd edn). Rugeley: Kirwin Maclean Associates Ltd.

A comprehensive exploration of the essential components of good practice learning, such as the integration of theory, reflection, assessment and the use of supervision.

Parker, J (2010) *Effective practice learning in social work* (2nd edn). London: SAGE.

Websites

The Assessed and Supported Year in Employment (ASYE): www.skillsforcare.org.uk.
Standards for employers of social workers in England: www.local.gov.uk/workforce.

Part III

Maintaining reflective practice

9

Working with your team manager

Terry Scragg

Achieving a social work degree

This chapter will help you to meet the current Social Work England Professional Standards (2019), develop capabilities from the Professional Capabilities Framework (2018) and introduce you to the Social Work Benchmark Statement (2019). The following are of particular relevance to this chapter:

Social Work England Professional Standards (2019)

4.2 Use supervision and feedback to critically reflect on, and identify my learning needs, including how I use research and evidence to inform my practice.

4.3 Keep my practice up to date and record how I use research, theories and frameworks to inform my practice and my professional judgement.

(Continued)

(Continued)

4.4 Demonstrate good subject knowledge on key aspects of social work practice and develop knowledge of current issues in society and social policies impacting social work.

4.5 Contribute to an open and creative learning culture in the workplace to discuss, reflect on and share best practices.

4.6 Reflect on my learning activities and evidence of what impact continuing professional development has on the quality of my practice.

4.7 Record my learning and reflection on a regular basis and in accordance with Social Work England's guidance on continuing professional development.

4.8 Reflect on my own values and challenge the impact they have on my practice.

Professional Capabilities Framework (2018)

6. Critical reflection and analysis
7. Context and organisations

   See Appendix 1 for the Professional Capabilities Framework Fan and a description of the nine domains.

Social Work Subject Benchmark Statement (2019)

5.3 xii continuous professional development as a reflective, informed and skilled practitioner, including constructive use of supervision.

5.6 xi the contribution of different approaches to management and leadership within different settings, and the impact of professional practice on the quality of care management and leadership in public and human services.

5.17 ii advance their own learning and understanding with a degree of independence and use supervision as a tool to aid professional development.

   See Appendix 2 for a detailed description of these standards.

Introduction

This chapter will introduce you to the world of management, particularly the work of the team manager who is the person you will come into regular contact with both as a student on placement and when newly appointed to your first social work post. Working with your team manager will be one of your most significant workplace relationships and it is important that you understand the changing world of social work management, the pressures and demands placed on front-line managers and how you can work effectively with your manager. For the purposes of this chapter, I have assumed that your manager is also supervising your practice and that you meet regularly to discuss your work with service users as part of your social work degree programme, post-graduate award or ASYE.

The first part of the chapter will examine the role of a front-line manager, who has key responsibilities in terms of leading a team, managing resources and allocating work, and maintaining standards and supporting staff who are directly involved in providing or arranging services. The second part is concerned with how you can make the best use of the knowledge and skills of your manager and what you need to do to ensure that you are getting the best from the relationship. Here we are talking about 'managing your relationship with your manager', in other words, understanding what you need to do to ensure that you are meeting your manager's needs and at the same time receive the support you need to enable you to practice effectively, develop your skills and advance your career. The third part focuses on the important work of supporting staff and those activities that enable staff to perform well, including supervision, consultation and review. All these activities have a valuable developmental function, particularly helping the newly qualified social worker to develop a critical awareness of the potential of reflective learning.

Part one: the work of the front-line manager

Front-line managers have to make the most effective use of their staff and other resources they manage. They need a clear understanding of the task and how it can be achieved, an understanding of the skills and abilities of team members, and the agency's wider resources. They also need knowledge of how the staff team can mobilise resources in the community, either through a partnership with other provider organisations or by direct intervention. To achieve this, they have to establish a form of work allocation and workload management that is achievable with the resources available to them to ensure that staff can manage their personal workloads without creating stress and burnout (SCIE, 2012).

Front-line managers also influence decisions due to the *positional* power invested in their role (Smith, 2010). If they are also recognised as having expertise in particular areas of social work practice they can influence decisions through *expert* power. Although power can be used *coercively* in organisations, front-line managers can use their power and influence ethically to bring about necessary changes and improvements in services.

They also have a key role in supporting, monitoring and developing social care practice. They are the 'bridge' between senior management, practitioners and service users, interpreting organisational policies and procedures, legislative requirements and practice standards to their teams. They also play an important role in communicating and explaining senior management decisions and in turn provide information where policies and procedures are not working, representing the opinions of front-line staff to senior management (Scragg, 2009).

In their research on front-line managers, Henderson and Seden (2003) argue that employers want managers to manage dilemmas, constraints and challenges which face teams at the front line of services, where they operate in situations of conflicting requirements. From an analysis of managers' job descriptions, Henderson and Seden identified the requirements of employers falling into three main functions, which were in turn identified by front-line managers who participated in their research. These are:

- strategic – they are required to develop strategies, systems and procedures to meet the overall objectives of the service.
- operational – they have to ensure that the service is effectively managed and that they adhere to departmental objectives and resolve operational problems.
- professional – they have to take responsibility for managing staff, induction, supervision, training, development and appraisal. They need to ensure that all staff are empowered to undertake the tasks allocated to them, to consult them and involve them in decision-making. They also need to provide effective support and take corrective or disciplinary action where necessary.

What these three functions tell us is that front-line managers face a number of dilemmas on a regular basis. They have to focus on the operational and professional components of their role – day-to-day support and supervision of staff, allocating work, developing and enabling team members, and ensuring that they meet practice standards while at the same time responding to the demands of senior managers as part of the strategic planning process based on their local knowledge of the community their team serves. This also means that front-line managers may have to implement decisions delegated to them by senior managers, which they may find personally difficult.

Case study

Sarah is a newly appointed team manager in a social work team, having been promoted from a practitioner role in the same team. Although she had a clear understanding of the work of the team manager based on her relationship with the previous postholder, she is surprised at the range and variety of demands she now has to meet in the new role. She feels comfortable working with her team colleagues and supporting their practice and maintaining relationships with a range of external organisations that work in partnership with her service, but she finds she is also expected to respond urgently to the demands of senior managers for information and to participate in strategic planning meetings, as well as manage a range of staff and financial resources within the limits set by her line manager. She now has to balance the demands of supporting and managing practice with those of strategic and resource management, including implementing decisions that she finds difficult to sell to her staff team.

Activity 9.1

When you are on placement, speak to your team manager and ask them about the demands of their role and the range of tasks they are expected to manage. Tell them you have been reading about how the management of social work has changed, for example with the emphasis on managing much tighter eligibility for services and highly constrained financial resources, and ask them how these changes have impacted their work as a manager. This will give you an insight into their work and help you understand the multiple pressures on them and why they have to balance the demands for services with the resources available to them.

(Continued)

Comment

I hope that you now have a more informed insight into the work of a front-line manager and understand some of the many pressures they experience stemming from their wide-ranging agenda. How your manager balances these pressures, in response to the wider demands of the organisation, and at the same time ensures that they are able to create time and space to support individual practitioners and the wider team will in the end be the test of their overall effectiveness. This places particular demands on front-line managers who are required to integrate the skills of strategic management with the knowledge and judgement of an expert practitioner.

Part two: Managing your relationship with your manager

Front-line managers have a crucial role in supporting you and providing opportunities for you to engage in work-based learning through a range of practice opportunities. If you are to develop your practice from these opportunities it is important that your relationship with your manager meets your needs. Your relationship is one where you have the choice to be passive and succumb to being managed, or to develop an active approach to managing your manager. Managers do not just manage other people, they are managed themselves through the actions of their staff. Developing your skills in managing your relationship with your manager means that both of you can benefit and in turn the service becomes more effective.

Relating to your manager's world

Try to understand your manager's role, the demands on them, and how you can help them achieve their aims. Recognise that your manager is dependent on you, just as much as you are dependent on them. The following are some of the things you can do to increase your understanding of your manager:

- Be aware of the pressures and demands on your manager.
- Understand some of the constraints they work under that limit their ability to make decisions about resources that meet your recommendations.
- Understand why they may not always be available for consultation as a result of the demands on them to respond to a wide range of agendas.
- Focus on possible solutions rather than appearing to challenge their authority, so that there is a win–win outcome with the desired end obtained without you or your manager losing face.

An important part of successfully managing your relationship with your manager is your own confidence in communicating effectively and adopting an assertive approach. If you are able to communicate assertively it is more likely you will meet your own needs, but also gain the respect of your manager. In turn, your manager is likely to feel more confident about your practice if they see you as a practitioner who takes your development seriously and strives to develop a relationship that is effective at both managerial and practice levels.

Case study

Paul had a positive experience of supervision while he was a student, where his practice supervisor challenged him to take increasing responsibility for his own development as he neared the end of his degree course. Now professionally qualified, he is meeting with Sarah, his team manager, to establish arrangements for supervision and the support he wants her to provide for him. He is conscious of the demands on her time but wants to ensure that he will be able to use the supervision sessions to support his practice, to critically reflect on his interventions with service users, and also have the opportunity to discuss his wider pro-fessional development. In preparation for this first meeting, he has spent some time identifying his own learning needs and what he would ideally like the supervision sessions to provide. In this way, he is adopting a proactive approach to his own development, which will be welcomed by Sarah, who wants her team members to actively manage their own development with her support.

How you manage your relationship with your team manager will be crucial to your future development. If you can establish a relationship where you both adopt an approach that recognises the value of reflective learning and questions current practice which has become habitual or is claimed to be 'best practice', the more strategies you will develop over time that enable you to respond to the demands made on you and the service.

Actions that are likely to increase your potential for success include:

- being clear about your role and taking responsibility for your own learning.
- developing yourself to meet the demands of your practice.
- identifying your strengths and weaknesses and what you need to do to improve your practice.
- being open to changing your behaviour as a result of feedback from your manager and other colleagues.
- recognising when you need help or support and ask for it.
- giving honest and constructive feedback.
- checking when you are not clear about your manager's statements or behaviour.
- stating your own position openly, clearly expressing your thoughts and feelings.

Taking responsibility for developing yourself and your relationship with your manager can help you to become an active participant in the organisation which should help you to become a more satisfied and effective member of the team, and a better and more respected advocate for the people you serve (Hafford-Letchfield, 2009).

Part three: Creating a learning environment to support practice

We have seen that a particular role and function of the front-line manager is to promote and sustain practice standards through knowledge of statutory requirements, social work standards and organisational procedures, combined with support for individual practitioners and teams through supervisory and other learning activities (Kearney, 2004). The starting point for ensuring practice standards is achieved is through the manager's knowledge about how practice should be undertaken, how services are best delivered and being able and willing to share this knowledge with staff.

Rosen (2000) argues that managers can best achieve this through 'modelling practice', with staff doing what managers do, rather than what they say should be done. One way this can be achieved is through managers acting as a professional consultant to the team, consulting about what could be done (methods of intervention) or what should be done (meeting statutory or procedural requirements).

In order to create and sustain a culture in which continuous learning and development take place, it is important that a manager promotes their own learning and engages in reflection on their own practice and in turn is more receptive to the development of reflection in colleagues (Thompson, 2015). The manager is in a key position to influence the development of high standards of practice. To achieve this, a manager needs to understand how practice should be carried out and be up to date with knowledge-based practice developments.

The importance of the workplace as a setting for learning with the demands and challenges of practice – solving problems, improving quality or coping with change, and growing out of the interaction with colleagues – is central to the notion of reflective learning, with Eraut (2001) identifying the appointment and development of front-line managers as one of the most important mechanisms for promoting learning in an organisation. The appointment of front-line managers and their professional behaviour influences how staff practice; as will the standards managers set for themselves. Darvill (1997), writing about work-based learning, sees this as influenced to a great extent by the manager's own style of working and how much they are seen to value this aspect of their role. He sees the front-line manager possessing influence in promoting a vision of the team and supporting a learning culture, and adopting a strategic approach to the development of individuals and the team.

Ways in which managers can encourage continuous learning

Front-line managers have an important role in relation to continuous learning and should see themselves as learners. They are the most visible member of the staff team, with a complex set of roles and relationships, and therefore set an important example to other members of their team. They can facilitate staff learning through a range of activities (based on Darvill, 1997):

- declaring the importance they place on their own learning.
- actively using team meetings, supervision and case reviews as a way of asking probing questions about the practice, and encouraging receptivity to new ideas.

- striking a balance between encouraging staff to take risks in testing solutions but remaining accountable for minimising risk to service users.
- encouraging staff to trust the freedom of the learning process in being open about their concerns where they feel their practice falls below their own professional standards.
- recognising that some learning may reinforce bad habits or questionable practice. Positive learning demands a willingness to question habits, experiment and use the time to reflect and develop new ways of seeing.

The front-line manager as a facilitator of workplace learning can create a climate where learning can take place. The creation of a climate for learning is seen by Thompson and Thompson (2008) as shaping the organisational culture in ways that are supportive of learning and reflection, although they recognise that you may be faced with a situation where your manager is someone who has little interest in supporting staff and sees this as a chore. Thompson and Thompson argue that if you encounter this situation you need to consider what you can do to identify those who will support you rather than accepting you have to do without learning support. If this is not possible, they suggest that you should consider whether you need to start looking for employment in a more supportive environment, as damage can be done to your morale in the short term and career in the long term in such an environment. What these comments point to is the crucial importance of organisational structures and support systems to enable the development of social work expertise.

Research summary

The Chartered Institute for Personnel and Development (CIPD) training and development survey (2004) found that the three most important activities in helping employees learn effectively were the building of a culture in the organisation supportive of learning, ensuring that managers have the skills and are committed to supporting learning and development, and ensuring that employees are given time to participate in learning opportunities in the workplace. The commitment to learning at the most senior levels in organisations was seen as crucial in order to create a learning culture, alongside an environment where individuals felt able to make mistakes and learn from them, and where they were encouraged to question, take risks and try new things. The survey also found that employees believed that they learned most effectively from workplace learning opportunities, with coaching and mentoring considered highly effective ways of helping individuals to learn. This latter aspect resonates with Gould and Baldwin's (2004) study of social work and learning organisations, with the need for practitioners to be given time to learn at work. They describe the difficulties practitioners found in persuading their organisations to grant space for reflective activities, and without these opportunities there was little chance of developing strategies for effective practice.

Comment

We can see in the above paragraph and research summary that the culture of an organisation is a significant factor in its effectiveness. Where practices need improvement, it can sometimes be difficult to introduce change due to the strength of established beliefs (Scragg, 2010). Organisational cultures that have evolved over time

(Continued)

about how a service is managed and delivered can be so much part of everyday practice that they go unquestioned. These beliefs and assumptions about a service can be unspoken and taken for granted – 'the way we do things around here'. Where organisations fail to make needed improvements, the power of a culture can be a major factor in resistance to change. Attempting to change a service often means challenging existing beliefs and assumptions about a service (Scragg, 2011). This can require a fundamental rethink about what constitutes good practice in order to promote a new cultural paradigm (Johnson and Scholes, 2008).

Opportunities for using reflective practice

Reflective learning takes place through an understanding of professional knowledge developed in practice and the systematic analysis of that experience (Gould, 1996). Using this approach, reflective practice involves drawing selectively and appropriately on our professional knowledge base, integrating theory with practice, rather than relying on theory to provide ready-made answers. In this way, we learn from experience by reflecting on it and being open to new ideas.

Front-line managers and their staff have a range of opportunities available to them where reflection-on-practice can take place. The following examples are provided to give you some ideas about the possibilities open to you and your manager.

Supervision

Supervision provides a unique opportunity for supporting staff and providing a context for the development of reflective practice and should be seen as an elementary requirement in social work services and is the cornerstone of good social work practice (Laming, 2009). Supervision encompasses a potentially wide range of functions (see Carpenter et al., 2015) the following issues are recognised as fundamental to high-quality supervision:

- Agreeing on a guaranteed time in an uninterrupted setting where the worker is able to reflect on their interventions, including current activities and future plans that improve outcomes for service users. This should also include caseload management and guidance.
- Recognising the demands work at the frontline places on the individual and supporting the social and emotional needs of workers.
- Using supervision as a setting for reflective learning and identifying continuing professional development opportunities for the worker.
- Acting as a mediator providing communication between the frontline and senior management, including the organisation's priorities and workers' concerns that senior managers need to hear.

A key feature of supervision highlighted by Carpenter et al. (2015) is the quality of the relationship between supervisor and worker. Where this is seen as a positive relationship by workers it is seen to impact the turnover of and retention of staff through greater job satisfaction (Gibbs, 2001).

Supervision and reflection

It is through the process of reflection in supervision sessions that professional learning can take place, both in analysing the explanations and the evidence on which assessments and interventions were based and in identifying where there are developmental needs in relation to practice. This requires the supervisor and supervisee to separate out what went well and what hindered practice interventions so that they can first articulate for themselves and then communicate to service users what has underpinned their assessments and their choice of interventions and thereby use supervision to provide accountability to people using the service as well as governance of the service (Cunningham, 2004).

Critically appraising practice in this way should not be seen as a personal attack on the supervisee's practice but as a valuable external perspective that can offer new insights and angles on a problem. This process will be more effective where the organisational culture is non-defensive and values learning, and where practitioners feel comfortable when the supervisor challenges their judgements and assumptions (Munro, 2011b).

Practitioners benefit from the process of knowledge that can be learnt from high-quality supervision. This is where managers focus on the developmental aspects of supervision, although this can often be neglected under the pressure of work, with time and opportunity to share and reflect on practice – for example, time for debate and development of critical thinking skills – submerged by the focus on micro-details of individual cases (Sawdon and Sawdon, 1995). The pressure on front-line managers to monitor the performance of staff and focus on the need to meet quantifiable outcomes risks undermining the practitioners' ability to think creatively, which challenges the rational-technical approach that has stifled social work practice (Munro, 2011b). This view is reinforced by a survey of workers that found a significant number of respondents dissatisfied with their supervision arrangements, particularly lack of focus on personal development and emotional issues (BASW/CoSW, 2011).

A more reflective approach where there is time to mull over experience and learn from it avoids what Thompson (2015) describes as a routinised response to practice where practitioners come to rely on routines that are applied in complex situations, often inappropriately, stemming from (among other things) the use of untested assumptions, a reliance on stereotypes and missed opportunities for learning and professional development. It is the front-line manager's responsibility to ensure that a team or organisational culture does not encourage a routinised approach in spite of organisational pressures towards conformity. In her research, Ruch (2005) has challenged bureaucratic responses to the complexity, risk and uncertainty in social work, and has argued for a more creative and thoughtful approach to practice, recognising diverse sources of knowledge that are embedded in practice as well as theoretical perspectives.

A further dimension of supervision that you may find helpful is when you are faced with a challenging intervention or a 'fast developing' situation that cannot wait for a formal supervision session. Knowing that you can access your manager in real time and seek guidance whether face to face or by email or by phone, proves a reassurance when you are faced with novel practice situations (Lambley and Marrable, 2013).

Activity 9.2

Reflect on a recent experience of supervision. How far did this cover the functions described above?
   If the session did not meet your needs, can you identify what aspect(s) of supervision were unsuccessful?

- Was it to do with location?
- Was it to do with structure?
- Was it to do with the content?
- Was it to do with the process?
- Was it related to your supervisor's contribution?
- Was it related to your own contribution?
- What could your supervisor change to ensure that the next session is more successful?
- What could you do to ensure that your next session is more successful?

Comment

This activity should have helped you judge the effectiveness of your supervision sessions and whether they are meeting your needs. If they are not, it could be concerned with a lack of clarity about the expectation that both you and your supervisor have about supervision, what are important functions and its purpose. A contract that sets out the purpose, processes, practical arrangements and expectations of supervision can help create a more effective supervisory relationship in the future. Here a supervision template that constitutes an agreement between participants is an important basis for you and your supervisor to be clear about what you each expect from supervision sessions. For an example of supervision agreement and recording templates, see hcpc (2021) at www.hcpc.uk.org.

Consultation

A second area that provides an opportunity for reflection is consultation. This is a problem-solving process where you can use your manager as a consultant. The difference between consultation and supervision is that it can be a one-off event for which you (as consultee) set the agenda, while your manager's role (as a consultant) is to facilitate your working through a specific issue that concerns you. You are drawing on the experience and expertise of another person who can offer you the help you need. You can, of course, use other people from your team, or in the wider service if you feel they have the particular expertise to help you.

Using Schein's (1998) approach to consultation, it is a process where your manager, acting in the role of consultant, works collaboratively with you in a manner that enables you to develop your own assessment of the issue and use your skills to act. This process is as follows:

- Stage one: active listening on the part of the manager as they encourage you to describe the issue that concerns you and try to understand the issues from your perspective.
- Stage two: diagnostic intervention, which focuses on helping you to think about what is going on in the situation through reflection on previous actions or interventions.
- Stage three: action alternatives, when the focus shifts to what you want to consider in terms of action and you begin to describe an action that will follow the consultation.

Ideally, your manager will ask you questions that stimulate you to form your own ideas as to why events have occurred and what might be done. This also takes the pressure off the manager of having to be the expert and provide solutions, and in turn helps you to come to a judgement about the issue and to learn about the process of problem-solving. In this way, consultation provides a valuable opportunity to reflect on a practice situation and through a problem-solving process build your confidence to act in the future and also to experience using the expertise of your manager in a non-managerial relationship.

Case study

Paul has been asked to take responsibility for working with a service user where a succession of workers has tried a range of interventions, without success. He is concerned that his intervention will lead to similar frustrations and has asked his manager Sarah if she will help him to work through some of the issues and discuss various approaches to work with the service user. She agrees to meet with him and discuss his concerns. Her approach is not to suggest how he approaches the service user, but to explore the issues, probe and test his assumptions and support him to make his own decisions about the options he could consider when he meets the service user for the first time. In this way, she hopes to help Paul become more confident in his practice and also to model an approach to problem-solving where her team members do not become dependent on her for answers to problems but develop confidence in their own problem-solving abilities.

To work effectively in a consultative relationship, it is important that you take responsibility for how you want to work with your manager (or another member of the team) in a consultative role, including:

- openly sharing your concerns about the issue and why you need help in thinking through your approach;
- accepting constructive feedback from your manager;
- participating in problem-solving and not expecting to be told what to do;

- reflecting on the issues and exploring the options open to you;
- taking responsibility for implementing the action you have decided on.

Finally, it is important to recognise that consultation is a process that is usually reserved for more experienced members of staff who can be relied on to exercise a high degree of professional autonomy in their practice. It is therefore something you may come to value as you gain experience in your first social work post, where you are able to demonstrate over time that you have the confidence of your manager and can use consultation effectively to support your approach to practice situations (Bamford, 1982).

Reviewing and evaluating interventions

A further opportunity to review practice and in turn reflect on the effectiveness of interventions can be undertaken by evaluating practice. Although supervisory sessions and consultation provide opportunities for reflection, other contexts are also important to develop these skills. Review and evaluation are parts of the five stages of systematic practice: assessment, intervention, review, termination and evaluation (Thompson, 2015).

Reviewing practice enables practitioners and their managers to explore current approaches and whether adjustments need to be made in the plan, or radically different tactics need to be used. A service user's situation can change over time and assessment may need to change too as an initial assessment may have been based on partial information. It is important, then, that practice is reviewed periodically so that adjustments can be made to the intervention plan. A consequence of not reviewing practice regularly is that time, effort and energy can be wasted because the intervention is misdirected. The review gives you an opportunity to amend or confirm your plan of intervention.

Once an intervention is completed there is the opportunity to evaluate what worked and what was less successful, and what can be learned from the process. This process should take you back to the initial assessment and your original objectives and how far you were able to meet these, and what was not achieved, given the time, resources and priorities (Thompson, 2015).

Evaluation of interventions is also important, not only in terms of specific interventions but also in relation to the organisation, which needs to review the effectiveness of the services it provides where resources are limited. A key part of the evaluation is the need for practitioners to understand that it can enhance the effectiveness, accountability and transparency of practice. From a wider perspective, it is increasingly expected by those who fund services and those who use them, so that together evaluating interventions and outcomes enables practitioners to be more effective and efficient (Alston and Bowles, 2003).

Evaluation is also an important element in practitioners developing a research-mindedness approach to their practice and countering the risks when so much practice *inevitably happens on the hoof without the opportunity for critical evaluation* (Gould and Baldwin, 2004, p46). Evaluating your practice periodically has the potential to help you develop more effective interventions by adopting a research approach to your practice with the potential to improve it and ensure that you remain conscious of the need for continual improvement. Review and evaluation have a further potentially important role in providing the social work profession with the evidence to demonstrate its effectiveness and respond to attacks that stem from politically driven agendas which undermine the confidence and morale of practitioners.

Research summary

The Management of Practice Expertise Project undertaken by the former National Institute for Social Work (2000) had as one of its aims to identify which kind of approaches to management enabled staff to develop and sustain their practice expertise. This was conducted through a survey of supervision arrangements and policies in social services departments, a study of a group of practice sites and conferences, and workshops that brought together managers and practitioners to explore relationships between management, supervision and practice development. In a discussion paper published as part of the research, it found that front-line managers were vital to the practice and service delivery of an organisation and that they were the keystones between senior management and front-line staff, their teams and other teams, and between the agency and other services and individuals. The key role of the front-line manager was concerned with holding together the different worlds and avoiding the damaging fragmentation if these different worlds did not maintain relationships with each other. Further important roles were the deployment of resources and ensuring that standards in practices were set and maintained, that staff were supported when engaging in the complex and demanding practice, and that they were continually developed in knowledge-based practice. This is particularly achieved where the managers model practice and their work is visible, for example, in residential settings and where they act as consultants to team members, playing the role of crucial opinion leaders (Rosen, 2000).

Conclusion

Developing an effective working relationship with your manager is a crucial part of your development as a social worker. How you build this relationship will be important in defining how far you move beyond a comfortable openness in your dialogue to a position where you can explore more of your biases and interpretations and articulate your reasons for particular approaches to intervention that can lead to real change in your practice. Much of the success of this relationship will also depend on your manager and how far they have developed their own skills in reflecting on their practice and how far they are able to move beyond defensive routines that have become such a powerful part of the prevailing ethos in many organisations and thus be willing to explore the complex world of social work practice.

Chapter summary

The role of front-line managers has changed significantly, from the traditional focus on supporting practice to one that more closely resembles that of the general manager, with responsibilities for the efficient management of resources, the effective performance of staff and the achievement of the strategic goals of the organisation, using their positional power to influence change. Front-line managers are increasingly balancing the demands of the organisation with the need to ensure the maintenance and support of practice as a result of the managerialist ethos in social care organisations. You can significantly influence your relationship with your line manager through the adoption of a proactive and positive approach to managing this important relationship. Working with your manager to develop a mutually satisfactory working relationship can benefit you both, and in turn service users and the wider organisation, as your practice improves and develops. Front-line managers have a wide range of methods available to them to support your development, through supervision, consultation and evaluation of your practice. Each has the potential to use reflection as a means of widening your under-standing of practice. Knowing how to take advantage of the different techniques available can help you decide how your manager can best support you. Working with your manager to explore the complexities of practice means a degree of openness and willingness to challenge assumptions that can be uncomfortable but has the potential to open your practice to deeper examination.

Further reading

Explores a wide range of key issues in the management of social work organisations, including leadership, performance and organisational learning.

Hafford-Letchfield, T (2009) *Management and organisation in social work* (2nd edn). London: SAGE.
> Professional leadership is increasingly important at all levels in social work organisations, not only for those in formal leadership roles, but all practitioners who can make an important contribution to services through their leadership activities.

Scourfield, P (2018) *Putting professional leadership into practice in social work*. London: SAGE.

10

Reflective practice for inter-professional co-produced social work collaboration

Anita Atwal

Achieving a social work degree

This chapter will help you to meet the current Social Work England Professional Standards (2019), develop capabilities from the Professional Capabilities Framework (2018) and introduce you to the Social Work Benchmark Statement (2019). The following are of particular relevance to this chapter:

Social Work England Professional Standards (2019)

4.5 Contribute to an open and creative learning culture in the workplace to discuss, reflect on and share best practice.
4.6 Reflect on my learning activities and evidence what impact continuing professional development has on the quality of my practice.
4.7 Record my learning and reflection on a regular basis and in accordance with Social Work England's guidance on continuing professional development
4.8 Reflect on my own values and challenge the impact they have on my practice.

(Continued)

Professional Capabilities Framework (2018)

1. Professionalism
2. Values and ethics
3. Diversity and equality
4. Rights, justice and economic wellbeing
6. Critical reflection and analysis
7. Skills and interventions
8. Contexts and organisations
9. Professional leadership

   See Appendix 1 for the Professional Capabilities Framework Fan and a description of the nine domains.

Social Work Subject Benchmark (2019)

5.3 vii   the professional and ethical management of potential conflicts generated by codes of practice held by different professional groups;
5.5 vii   the factors and processes that facilitate effective interdisciplinary, interprofessional and interagency collaboration and partnership across a plurality of settings and disciplines;
5.6 viii the importance and complexities of the way agencies work together to provide care, the relationships between agency policies, legal requirements and professional boundaries in shaping the nature of services provided in integrated and interdisciplinary contexts;
5.16 iii respect and manage differences such as organisational and professional boundaries and differences of identity and/or language.

   See Appendix 2 for a detailed description of these standards.

Introduction

Health and social care professionals must function in complex and changing service systems. Social workers need to continuously update their knowledge and skills to manage complex societal, political as well as health and environmental challenges. Teams are viewed as an important part of managing service users who face life-changing impairments and/or challenges with participation in society. According to the Canadian Interprofessional Health Collaborative, interprofessional collaboration is a 'partnership between a team of health providers and a client in a participatory collaborative and coordinated approach to shared decision-making around health and social issues' (Canadian Interprofessional Health Collaborative, 2010, p6). Interprofessional education is used within the training of social workers and other health-care professionals to develop social work students as future interprofessional team members and leaders.

Social workers operate within diverse teams made up of many different health and social care professionals. These teams can be based in many service areas including primary health and social care. Teamwork is important as it is considered a mechanism to achieve positive outcomes and improve service user safety. The team can have a direct impact on service user outcomes, as shown in some of the serious case reviews that are discussed in this chapter. Teams in health and social care are unique in that their members do not choose to work together; rather the team members are brought together, either because of their clinical skills, their location or they are employed within the same organisation. The primary focus is to solve problems. The skills needed to work within diverse and complex teams that manage challenging health and social conditions should not be underestimated. A definition of a team used by the NHS Leadership Academy (Lynas, 2014, p3) is 'a group of people who are working through collective endeavour toward a common goal'.

Working within teams requires social workers to work across, and work with, different professional groups. Whilst collaboration is an important component of best practice, it is often difficult to put into practice. The interprofessional literature and even practice have excluded the most important people from the team – service users and carers.

Service users have had to fight long and hard in order to become a part of the decision-making process and to be an equal player within health and social care teams. Co-production is an essential part of professional practice. It is defined as a 'value-driven approach that blurs barriers between the state, services, and citizens; involves relationships of reciprocity and mutuality; and applies an assets-based model of service users' (Boyle, 2010, p3). Co-producing value in health and social care starts from the fact that service users and professionals exist within a larger system that can promote or impede progress towards optimal care. Batalden et al. (2016) have proposed a theoretical framework for co-production. A key part of the framework is to incorporate service users' priorities and values in order that service users can partake in decisions whenever possible. This requires respectful and open interaction and effective communication. Self-management is an important component of co-production. Likewise, service user groups have been vocal in acknowledging the importance of citizen control and power, but to be successful this requires changes to organisational cultures, leadership and management strategies. Whilst social workers are committed to the principles of co-production, there is evidence of social workers not including families, carers and service users within the decision-making process as identified in some of the case studies in this chapter.

This chapter will consider how reflection can enable social workers to work more effectively within interprofessional teams. Throughout it, you will be asked to complete self-reflective activities that can be used whilst on placement. Teams that reflect on issues together can work through events that could be viewed as a 'near miss' and/or have been subject to safeguarding concerns. Teams may also want to spend time reflecting on what went right – how the teams worked together to achieve the best possible outcome for the service user.

Activity 10.1

Based on your reading of the previous nine chapters or on your own experience of practice, consider:

- What methods do I use currently to reflect on issues that may arise whilst working within teams?
- Are they useful in evaluating my practice?
- Do I share them openly with others in a formal or informal setting?
- How successful are they for me?

Reflection in teams

Reflective practice is considered an essential attribute of health and social care professionals who want to adopt a collaborative approach that improves the quality of care. Reflection is a key ingredient in effective education and practice and involves higher-order thinking processes (tackling problems which appear to have no clear or obvious conclusion). Reflective time on practice placements is thought to enhance the integration of theory and practice and enrich the student's learning experiences whilst on placement (Duffy, 2009). Reflection may be triggered by an awareness of a gap between theory and practice, a difference between what 'should be' and 'what is' (Sullivan and Decker, 2005). Our actions and the quality of our care are improved by reflection-on-action.

Reflection is a process and, just like learning, it is a process that also has outcomes. Reflection has positive outcomes of shared meanings, greater coordination, and clearer communications. When teams reflect together, they gain insights and coordinate their actions to accomplish change.

(Moore, 2012)

Clark (2009) suggests that what is needed for transformative interprofessional learning is secondary or second-order reflection. This requires stepping back from oneself and a professional perspective to be able to consider one's own self (p216). It is through this 'stepping back' process that an individual can become aware of the social and shared dimensions of interprofessional education – learning with, from and about others. This process is closely aligned with thinking about one's own thinking or metacognition.

Reflective journaling is considered an effective method to provide the conditions for effective reflection (see Chapter 4). Using journals whilst on placement can be useful in encouraging students to apply theory to their practice and make meaning out of the experience. It is possible to gain more insight into and awareness of the self as one learns about others. Self-assessment tools, conflict management skills and leadership ability may all be useful in developing values, skills and abilities for interprofessional and collaborative teamwork.

Activity 10.2

Here are some questions to ask yourself about collaboration and teamwork.

- *What does collaborative working involve?*
- *Spend a few minutes listing the knowledge and skills required.*
- *What type of teams have you seen and/or worked in?*

Comment

You may have included:

- making time to get to know other professionals and their roles and how they may be evolving in new contexts;
- thinking about language and terms used and their relevance and meaning to other professionals or workers;
- exploring your own prejudices about other professional groups and their models of practice;
- reflecting on values and not making assumptions about shared beliefs or views;
- being clear about resources and their impact on collaboration;
- being confident about your professional practice and ability in the collaborative working role;
- being credible – delivering as promised to action plans and keeping others involved informed of progress;
- gaining consensus on leadership and accountability in a specific practice situation.

The type of teams could have been one of the following as defined by Katzenback and Smith (1993):

Working groups: team members hold some shared information and undertake some team activities, but there is no joint responsibility or clear definition of team roles.
Pseudo teams: members are labelled as a 'team' but, in reality, have little shared responsibility or coordination of their teamwork.
Potential teams: team members are beginning to work in a collaborative manner but have few of the factors needed for effective teamwork, e.g. joint goal setting.
Real teams: members share common goals and share some accountability.

Team reflection

It is important to reinforce that diverse teams have a better outcome for service users, with teams that have both gender and diversity reported to be more innovative (Gomez and Bernet, 2019). Some professions such as Allied Health (HCPC, 2021) are not diverse and therefore in some instances teams are homogenous. This in turn may result in teams being unable to bridge cultural and social nuances. Social workers may want to reflect more carefully on diversity within the teams they belong to and issues that arise from professional practice. To do this we need to think carefully about the structure that works best for the team and when and how team reflection should occur.

Free flowing conversation

Some teams may prefer an approach where the style is 'open conversation' by that we mean there is no agenda and/or order.

In a team meeting, you may start by thinking about Mrs Smith's recent re-admission after she was assessed by a social worker and a paramedic after a call from the fire brigade.

This is a good example of cross-agency and integrated working that lends itself to team reflection. The social worker and the paramedic worked in partnership to assess activities of daily living such as getting in/out of a chair. In this instant, the social worker and the paramedic jointly made the decision to recommend a review at a local hospital.

The team could use a technique known as Pluses and Deltas. The Paramedic and the social worker could reflect alongside other team members on what went well (Pluses). In this instance, both understood each other's role and were able to discuss their assessments. They were able to make a joint decision with Mrs Smith. In relation to the Deltas (what could be done better) both the social worker and the Paramedic perceived they would have valued an assessment by an Occupational Therapist. The Occupational Therapist could have assessed not only Mrs Smith's ability to carry out our everyday tasks but also suggested any assistive devices and carried out a safety assessment.

The team can also carry out a stop/start/keep reflection. In this instance, the social worker and the paramedic may reflect on their practice in relation to anything they feel they should stop doing. Is there anything they should start doing? For example, they may suggest that they have access to a community occupational therapist. In relation to what they should keep they may decide that the model of joint working enhances patient care and therefore should be kept.

Why interprofessional skills are needed

In the NHS Plan (NHS England, 2020) there is a growing awareness of the need for greater coordination between professionals, services and agencies. The Care Act (2014) made it a statutory obligation that Local Authorities co-operate with public services as well as with private health and social care providers, the aim is being to promote the integration of care between and within health, social care and other agencies. In reality, complex multidisciplinary care is often fragmented (Coulter et al., 2013). To promote integration, health professionals require the skills to work within complex teams. This is a key challenge for social workers, as it is dependent upon social workers having a strong professional identity and professional confidence to articulate core skills and values. Social workers need to have an excellent understanding and awareness of the roles and skills of professionals to ensure that their service users have access to the right support at the right time. Social workers have the ability to bring to the team a unique perspective but can only do this if they have an excellent team playing skills and an understanding of team dynamics.

The key to interprofessional practice is 'blending professional skill, values and knowledge across disciplines' (Sweifach, 2015). In order to ensure that services are truly integrated, social workers need to be able (and willing) to work across traditional health care and social care boundaries. A Canadian study used focus groups to explore barriers and facilitators to interprofessional collaboration from the perspective of social work (Miller and Ashcroft, 2016). The study found that culture, self-identity, role clarification, decision-making, communication and power dynamics were viewed as important factors in the work of social workers.

Manthorpe and Martineau (2014) conducted a review of serious cases of persons with dementia. Key findings from the review can be attributed to factors related to interprofessional working. The review drew attention to fragile communication between the care home and the local authority social services department, the local primary care team and specialist mental health or acute hospital services. In addition, there was a need for greater engagement by health care and social work professionals with care home staff, especially in supporting them when residents' needs increase, with management of pressure ulcers and distressing behaviour. Likewise, another case review identified that poor communication between a care home and Accident and Emergency resulted in a falls referral not being made for a 94-year-old lady with complex health conditions (Hardy et al., 2017).

Similar issues of a lack of coordination and communication were found in serious case reviews by the National Society for the Prevention of Cruelty to Children (see Table 10.1).

Table 10.1 Summary of cases from serious case reviews published by the National Society for the Prevention of Cruelty to Children (2018)

Case	Background	Issues
2016, Bristol Child Brooke	Sexual exploitation of looked-after children.	Multiagency system was not set up to respond quickly and flexibly to adolescents with complex needs.
2016, East Sussex Child M	Death of a 17-year-old girl in March 2013 from a drug overdose.	Lack of coordination in the early stages between Child M's school, substance misuse, mental health services and children's social care provision.
2016, Surrey Child AA	Serious, non-accidental head injuries to a 10-week-old baby, whilst in the care of parents.	There were differences of opinion between children's social care and community health services; this was compounded by a lack of clear and current assessment and coordinated planning.

Table 10.1 Summary of cases from serious case reviews published by the National Society for the Prevention of Cruelty to Children (2018) *(Continued)*

Case	Background	Issues
Mr I Wokingham	Mr I had suffered a brain injury and a lower leg amputation. He was prone to depression and developed an increasingly severe dependence on alcohol. He resented contact from the services and was aggressive to visitors including the regular care staff who had been managing his health and well-being.	Restructuring of services and confusion between two teams. One team had no access to recent mental health records.

Reflecting on values in teams

Codes of ethics and practice help to define the uniqueness of each profession. As well as distinguishing the key characteristics of a professional group, they provide the standards against which members' practice will be judged in disciplinary hearings. This dual purpose, protecting service users and upholding social work values, should reassure the public. However, this is not always the case.

As a social worker, you have a code of ethical conduct from the professional body of your country, for example, Social Work England. You also need to be mindful of legislation, such as the Human Rights Act 1998, case law, NHS, and employer values. Ethics is a complex and difficult area, as one professional may not view a situation in the same way as another. For example, one professional may place an emphasis on protection and another on empowerment. Ethical issues need to be discussed and debated within teams, and some health and social care providers may set up inter-professional ethics rounds to help with challenging decisions. In some cases, inter-professional ethical dilemmas may arise when considering the safeguarding of persons deemed not to have the capacity to make sound decisions. In such cases the root cause of harm that may occur to service users is often attributed to communication errors within teams.

Leadership is an important part of teamwork to ensure that team members' voices are heard. The leader of the multidisciplinary team is usually a member of the medical profession. A study investigating the role of general practitioners in primary care for older adults (Grol et al., 2018) found that team members from primary care and social services indicated that general practitioners had an indispensable role in teams but may need convincing to take a lead in organising multidisciplinary teams for older people. Indeed, it has been suggested that teams need an accepted leader if teams are to function well (Pileño et al., 2018). Can social workers lead and manage teams? One of the identified barriers is the failure of social work courses to teach leadership skills (Austin et al., 2011; Haynes, 2022). It has been recommended that social workers can facilitate collaboration in teams by enacting leadership abilities in practice and policy (Miller and

Ashcroft, 2016). Social workers need to remember that are already leaders and/or 'everyday leaders' are team players and are visionaries not just influences. The very nature of social work practice means that social workers lead in practice as they understand complex problems (Haynes, 2022). One study found that members of a community mental health team highly valued the input of social workers as part of a multidisciplinary team (Anendstern et al., 2021).

The role of a leader within teams (Waldfogel et al., 2016) has been identified as:

- managing issues of governance, e.g. setting clear objectives/purpose for the team/what is expected of members;
- ensuring that others in the organisation have an understanding of the role of the team and why the team is important. Hayes (2022) suggests that social workers advocate for open and honest communication that will foster collaboration.
- negotiating locally for the funding/resources needed for the team to be effective;
- escalating issues of concern that may impact the safety of the service user.
- Hayes (2022) Suggests that social work leaders will also look for strengths and weaknesses in team members and the goal of the social work leader is to ensure that the team works through challenges.

The type and amount of interaction in team meetings can be used as an indication of teamwork. A study by Atwal and Caldwell (2005) revealed some key differences in the way in which different professions interacted. Occupational therapists, physiotherapists, social workers and nurses rarely asked for opinions and for orientation. The consultant (the individual in charge of the medical team) tended to set high rates for asking for orientation, giving opinions and giving orientation.

Activity 10.3

Please read and reflect using the prompts outlined below on this case study about Sophia and her family.

You are the lead social worker supporting Sophia, aged 15, and her family. Sophia is a young person with physical and learning disabilities who lives at home in a supportive and close-knit family. Sophia has had good educational and children's service health care support throughout her life, but as she draws near to school-leaving age and moves towards adult services, she and her family have been expressing concerns about the future and the opportunities for continued health care support and potential employment opportunities. At a recent review meeting, Sophia and her family voiced these concerns and the lack of future plans in place for her transition to more adult-focused services. Major worries were gaps in terms of links with adult health services for monitoring and treatment of her physical disability, and access to learning disability agencies' support. Following this meeting, you contacted your professional colleagues in health about Sophia's future needs and provisions before a further meeting with Sophia and her family.

The following reflection prompts are adapted from Spike and Lunstroth (2016) and can be used to reflect on the case study.

(Continued)

- What are the ethically relevant features of the situation you encountered?
- What is at stake for all of those involved and for those who might be affected? Are there limits to the ethical responsibilities of those in the situation?
- If the chosen action were to be generally observed, would the consequences and possible side effects still be reasonably acceptable to all those affected?
- What are the implications of this situation for you, the team, the service user and their carer?

Comment

Possible questions may be:
  What are the ethically relevant features of the situation you encountered?

- Do we have enough knowledge to act with credibility?
- Would there be new resource issues to work through as Sophia has a number of health-care needs?

  What is at stake for all of those involved?

- What are the social or economic factors?
- What is the impact of Sophia's transition into adult services on the family?

  Would the consequences and possible side effects still be reasonably acceptable to all those affected?

- How much involvement has Sophia had in planning her transition to adult services so far?
- What role has her family played?
- To what extent are resources an issue in relation to empowerment and choice?

  What are the implications of this situation for you, the team and service user and their carer?

- Will more or a different form of support be required if Sophia leaves full-time education?
- Am I familiar with acute health-care service processes or do I have the appropriate multi-professional links to gain access to those services?
- What is the current situation like for others in transition using these local health care services?
- What other professionals are involved in the transition process and what role do they play?

Within the team meeting different opinions may arise which can lead to inter-professional conflict. In order to be person-centred, social workers may find themselves having a different opinion from that of other members of the team. As professionals are trained to utilise different approaches, philosophies and even values this is an important part of teamwork. It should be viewed as a strength as all opinions should be listened to, debated, and discussed within teams so the best decision can be made. However, conflict can be viewed in a negative way and can undermine professional confidence. Within the literature, conflict is often regarded as an indicator that teamwork is absent. It is defined as 'disagreement with the other about what should be done in a task or how a task should be done' (Barki and Hartwick, 2004, p236). The difference in opinions should not be viewed as an indication of weak teamwork, but rather an indication that different professions have different views and values. This is a key strength of a team. The role of the leader within the team is to allow each member of the team to have a voice and for the team to make a decision based on all team members' contributions. The identified barriers to conflict resolution in teams include a lack of time and workload; people in less powerful positions lacking the recognition or motivation to address conflict; and avoiding confrontation for fear of causing emotional discomfort (Brown et al., 2011). Cohesive groups are not necessarily a sign of teamwork. Janis (1972) identified a 'disease' that infects cohesive groups, which he termed *groupthink*. During groupthink, members do not voice alternative opinions. Consequently the group can make errors that could have been avoided. The causes of groupthink have been identified as cohesiveness, isolation, leadership and decisional stress.

Activity 10.4

The Thomas-Kilmann Conflict Mode Instrument (Thomas and Kilman, 2018) can be used to help you manage conflict within the practice. Have you ever used any of the following stages identified in the model?

Accommodating. You put the other person/group ahead of your own needs, even to your own detriment. Maintains relationships. Can breed resentment when over-used. Effective when the other person/group offers a better solution than your own.

Avoiding. The action of inaction. You are not pursuing your own needs, nor are you helping the other person/group to meet their own. Effective for trivial issues, or as an interim solution while emotions settle down. Postpones meaningful resolution.

Compromising. Each person/group gives up something to meet the other halfway. The middle ground. Effective for when both goals are equally important. May lead to dissatisfaction.

Competing. A very assertive approach, when your goals or needs come ahead of those around you. This may be viewed as an authoritarian approach. Effective for emergencies or when a quick decision is needed. May lead to hostility or resentment.

Comment

Within teams, I tend to use the compromising approach particularly in relation to discharge planning. In many instances you need to balance the needs of the organisation, health and social care resources, the needs and wishes of service users and carers, the functional and mobility assessment of therapists and nurses, as well as the health and social care condition.

Reflection on professional identity

Team meetings are settings in which assumptions are constantly challenged and where team members can share skills and knowledge. Social workers need to be able to voice their opinions within teams. This may mean speaking up against other professionals and/or representing the service user's view. Social workers need to have a good understanding of power dynamics within teams, as well as which professional traditionally holds the most power in decision-making situations (Miller and Ashcroft, 2016) and physician collaborative practices.

Activity 10.5

Describe the social worker's role in one sentence.

Comment

Now compare your answer to the International Federation of Social Workers' (2014) definition:

> *Social work is a practice-based profession and an academic discipline that promotes social change and development, social cohesion, and the empowerment and liberation of people. Principles of social justice, human rights, collective responsibility and respect for diversities are central to social work. Underpinned by theories of social work, social sciences, humanities and indigenous knowledge, social work engages people and structures to address life challenges and enhance wellbeing.*

(IFSW, 2014)

To work within teams, social workers need a strong professional identity and it is essential that they are able to clearly state their role within the health and social care team. Yet, if you ask several social workers to define their roles you are likely to get different descriptions. If, however, you learnt the International Federation of Social Worker (IFSW) definition and repeated it to a member of the multi-disciplinary teams, they would probably look at you blankly. This is because social work encompasses a wide range of roles. However, social work would benefit from a much briefer and more accessible definition.

Social workers need to have the professional confidence to be able to negotiate their role in an interdisciplinary team without consultation with other members of their profession (Oliver, 2013). Interestingly, Bell and Allain (2010) advocated a dynamic core social work identity that is adaptive to changing contexts. It is important to acknowledge the socialisation process that occurs which enables a student and/or social worker to understand and sign up to the culture and values of other professionals, that is, it allows students to know 'who they are'. Interprofessional education is a mechanism which allows students to gain a dual identity – not only of their own profession but also of other professional groups. However, during this time the students risk asymmetric dualistic classification (Bock and James, 1992 – see Chapter 3 for further discussion), in which different professional groups are divided between the 'in-group' (those with whom they share a common identity) and/or the 'out-group' (consider the group to be of competition and/or no shared values).

This continual battle to ensure professional survival has a significant influence on interprofessional relationships. Team members may not be able to know when and how to access other members of the multidisciplinary team which is complicated by the number of professionals within the health-care arena, each with different roles and values. The consequences of social workers not working with other professionals can have a serious negative effect on service users, families and society. Social workers are working within health and social care organisations that are facing considerable funding constraints alongside the limited availability of resources to meet changing health and social care needs. It is important to understand how the political landscape has shaped social work and the different professions. What is clear is that professions including social work change and adapt roles according to market forces (Larson, 1977). In some instances, the expanding role of professionals brings interprofessional jealousies and safeguards, hence the need to negotiate roles within the team. Professionals are accused of 'poaching desirable skills' and delegating less desirable ones with the intention of securing status and control.

A similar picture is emerging in the United Kingdom due to the considerable problems facing nursing recruitment. We are currently seeing the expansion of apprenticeships as well as new professionals such as physician assistants, and the expansion of paramedics role. Shaun Lintern, a reporter who helped expose the Mid-Staffordshire care crisis (see the Francis Inquiry, 2013), argued that we should be replacing health-care assistants rather than nurses with nursing associates – up-skilling rather than down-skilling the workforce (Lintern, 2018).

One way of social workers achieving a strong sense of professional identity is for social work educators to enable students to gain a better understanding of their personal selves and self-awareness through reflection (Bell and Allain, 2010). The public image of social work effects how other professionals perceive and potentially stereotype social workers. Stereotypes are shared beliefs about individuals based on knowledge of the social groups to which those individuals belong (Quadflieg and Macrae, 2011). Research that has explored social workers' perceptions of doctors suggests doctors were less likely than social workers to identify service user/family problems related to adjustment to illness and problems connected to hospital and community resources (Mizrahi and Abramson, 2000). A survey from the United States found that social workers do feel valued and are respected for their skills and knowledge and experience within interprofessional teams (Sweifach, 2015).

Activity 10.6

Bell and Allain (2011) explored stereotypes with social work students. Complete the same task in this activity.

Rate from highest to lowest the following professions/occupations according to the competences that follow:

(Continued)

health visitor – teacher, – police – Early Years worker – family social worker – school nurse – Child & Adolescent Mental Health staff – doctor.

academic ability – professional competence – interpersonal skills – leadership ability – ability to work independently – team player – ability to make decisions – practical skills – confidence.

Then compare your ratings to those in the table below.

Competence	Highest	Lowest	Your answer
Academic ability	Doctor	Police	
Professional competence	Doctor	Police	
Interpersonal skills	Early Years worker	Police	
Leadership ability	Police	Health visitor	
Ability to work independently	Doctor	Police	
Team player	Family social worker	Doctor	
Ability to make decisions	Doctor	Early Years worker	
Practical skills	Early Years worker	Child and Adolescent Mental Health staff	
Confidence	Doctor	Health visitor, family social worker	

Comment

How did your findings correlate with the findings from the study?
  Were you surprised?

Working collaboratively in health care requires social workers who can facilitate decision-making in the team. They also require social workers to understand the stages of team development. To do this we can refer to the Tuckman theory of group development (Tuckman and Jensen, 1977).

Forming. Teams may not know each other very well and trust may be limited. In addition, team members may have been brought together because of their expertise and not because they have been asked to work together.

Storming. The group form may be in conflict with power struggles and/or frustration in relation to the task that the group needs to solve. This phase can be destructive.

Norming. Accepted communication and group rules are established and adhered to. Team members may become complacent. There is a need to be aware of 'social loafers' (Karau and Williams, 1993). 'Social loafing' is when a team member exerts less effort to achieve a goal when they work in a group than when they work alone.

Performing. The team focus is on the goal and communication becomes open and fluid.

Technology may be used within teams to resolve some of the problems associated with face-to-face teamwork. Key problems are usually associated with communication issues such as the location of professionals and/or availability of professionals. It has been suggested that virtual teams are more effective than face-to-face teams as members do not wait for meetings to make decisions. In addition, team members are more willing to contribute since they do not have many of the psychological and practical obstacles that exist within traditional, face-to-face teams (Majchrzak et al., 2004).

Activity 10.7

Babiker et al. (2014) list a toolbox for working in teams. These skills will ensure you have the personal skills that will equip you to work within diverse teams. Read and reflect on them before entering professional practice and or placement.

- Always introduce yourself to the team
- Clarify your role
- Use objective (not subjective) language
- Learn and use people's names
- Be assertive when required
- Read back/close the communication loop
- State the obvious to avoid assumptions
- Ask questions, check and clarify
- Delegate tasks to specific people, not to the air
- If something doesn't make sense, find out the other person's perspective
- Always do a team briefing before starting a team activity and a debrief afterwards
- When in conflict, concentrate on *what* is right for the service user, not *who* is right/wrong

---

Chapter summary

There is an increasing need for social workers to be equipped with collaborative working skills and this chapter aims to provide you with the basics. Further reflection on the attributes required and your individual readiness for the role will both support and enhance your future professional development. Soukup et al. (2018) outlined the characteristics of a multidisciplinary team for cancer patients, which can be applied to any setting with any service user group. The characteristics of a successful team are teams that have a common purpose, measurable goals, effective leadership, effective communication, good cohesion and mutual respect.

Further reading

Addresses collaboration in the community, child, mental health and acute care. Contains good personal accounts and addresses power within teams, models of professionalism, identity, ethics and service users.

Barrett, G, Sellman, D and Thomas, J (2005) *Interprofessional working in health and social care.* Basingstoke: Palgrave Macmillan.
  A broad focus on multi-agency working, for example, youth work, police, teachers and the legal profession. Useful case studies and an emphasis on social justice anti-discriminatory practice and anti-oppressive principles.

Quinney, A and Hafford-Letchfield, T (2013) *Interprofessional social work: Effective collaborative approaches.* London: SAGE.

Conclusion

In this book, we have seen that reflection is an intellectual and emotional process that enables us to create meaning and learn from experience (Fook, 2008). The book has covered a range of topics from the perspective of reflective practice. It has introduced you to the concepts that have informed our understanding of reflective practice and the way knowledge is potentially used by professionals and what you need to consider if you are to become an effective practitioner. By understanding how you can become a more skilled reflective practitioner, we hope it will help you narrow the gap between the theory and practice of social work and generate practice-based knowledge that can guide your actions.

Social work deals with people who need practitioners to be responsive and reflective instead of simply carrying out everyday practice in a routine or ritualistic manner. Reflection on practice can help you guard against the risks of 'working on autopilot' in which you follow the same pattern of practice that governs and directs your action.

Reflecting is an essential element of our ongoing commitment to anti-discriminatory practice. It provides the opportunity to focus on your practice and confront your values, attitudes and feelings. This critical, informed, consideration enables you to understand and work towards resolving the contradictions that are inherent in much social work practice.

In Part 1 of this book, we have provided you with some of the key concepts that have informed the development of reflective practice and how it can be applied to practice situations through the use of the reflective cycle (Chapter 1). The chapter recognises that reflective practice can provoke anxiety when first encountered by students and that positive relationships and processes need to be in place for reflection to take place safely. Building on the previous chapter we provide you (Chapter 2) with a number of practical ways of getting started when reflecting on your practice. From identifying a safe space where you feel comfortable to reflect on your practice through to the use of a range of specific techniques, we offer you a wealth of ideas to choose from to get you started as a reflective practitioner. Finally in this section (Chapter 3), we explore the role of emotions and how the emotional content in social work has been neglected but is essential for helping practitioners understand some of the complexities inherent in practice. An understanding of emotional intelligence is identified as a particularly useful framework in helping you explore more fully your responses to complex practice issues.

In Part 2, we provide you with a range of case examples and exercises that can help you increase self-awareness and manage stress (Chapter 4). These techniques, adapted from cognitive behaviour therapy, are designed to help you to develop more positive thinking when examining your own thought patterns and develop more confidence at a personal and practice level. Drawing on research (Chapter 5), we examine work with carers that poses important questions about the role of service users and carers in the social work relationship and alerts you to some of the complex issues involved when you are working in these situations. This chapter draws extensively on case studies to help you reflect on the importance of carers' and users' perspectives and their participation in the social work process. We then consider (Chapter 6) an area that is important to all social workers, that of unsafe practice where service users or practitioners are at risk. Drawing on a number of key national reports, we examine high-profile failures in practice and the lessons for practitioners. The chapter suggests ways in which the use of reflection can help minimise unsafe practice when working with service users who are hostile and aggressive, concluding with strategies to ensure personal safety. We then consider the role of gender in social work (Chapter 7) from a range of perspectives, including how socialisation can shape expectations of gender roles and how these may impact on you in practice situations. The chapter explores what constitutes gender identity and how stereotyped assumptions about emotions are bound up with notions of gender. The chapter provides you with opportunities to explore gender issues in the context of both social work training and practice settings. Finally, in this section (Chapter 8), we examine applying reflective practice in your placement, within supervision with your practice educator, exploring your practice through the use of experiential learning approaches. The important contribution of social work theories is recognised and how you can explore theories relevant to your practice and their effectiveness in work with service users.

Finally, Part 3 focuses on management and how reflective practice can be promoted and maintained through a range of management and organisational processes. We first explore the world of team managers (Chapter 9) and their crucial role in ensuring that they balance the demands of practice with those of the wider organisation, with suggestions of ways that you can proactively manage your relationship with your manager, and some of the techniques that you can use to reflect on and about practice with your team manager. Finally, we acknowledge that social work increasingly takes place in an interprofessional context (Chapter 10), where working effectively requires specific skills and a strong professional identity. The chapter provides you with activities that will enable you to prepare yourself for work in multi-disciplinary teams and working collaboratively with colleagues across a range of agencies. We hope that these two chapters will provide you with a deeper understanding of the world of management and the interprofessional context which you will begin to experience as a student on placement and more fully engage with as your career develops.

Thinking about Johari's window (see Chapter 1), we hope this book has added to 'what you know you know'. Critical thinking can help you to explicitly gain knowledge and fill the gaps in 'what you know you don't know'. Reflective practice helps you to uncover 'what you know, but don't realise you know' – the gut instinct or 'the unearthing of implicit assumptions by professionals in their own work' (Austin et al., 2012, p181). Curiosity, being open to polyphony (many voices) and exploring new activities will help you to understand 'what you don't know that you don't know'. Reflective practice is consequently a challenging activity, in which you need to be open to exploring and changing the sense you make of the world (Fook, 2008) and through exploring your emotions, yourself. We wish you well on your journey of discovery.

You will be helped on the first stages of this reflective journey by your practice learning educator. We also hope that once you are qualified, you will retain a commitment to reflective practice as part of your continuing professional development, making time to engage in reflection and be willing to challenge current practice where it fails to provide satisfactory answers, recognising that there is no end point to learning for the effective social work practitioner.

Appendix 1

Professional capabilities framework (2018)

The 9 domains

1. PROFESSIONALISM – Identify and behave as a professional social worker, committed to professional development.
2. VALUES AND ETHICS – Apply social work ethical principles and value to guide professional practices.
3. DIVERSITY AND EQUALITY – Recognise diversity and apply anti-discriminatory and anti-oppressive principles in practice.
4. RIGHTS, JUSTICE AND ECONOMIC WELL-BEING – Advance human rights and promote social justice and economic well-being.
5. KNOWLEDGE – Develop and apply relevant knowledge from social work practice and research, social sciences, law, other professional and relevant fields, and from the experience of people who use services.

6.   CRITICAL REFLECTION AND ANALYSIS – Apply critical reflection and analysis to inform and provide a rationale for professional decision-making.

7.   SKILLS AND INTERVENTIONS – Use judgement, knowledge and authority to intervene with individuals, families and communities to promote independence, provide support, prevent harm and enable progress.

8.   CONTEXTS AND ORGANISATIONS – Engage with, inform and adapt to changing organisational contexts, and the social and policy environments that shape practice. Operate effectively within and contribute to the development of organisations and services, including multi-agency and inter-professional settings.

9.   PROFESSIONAL LEADERSHIP – Promote the profession and good social work practice. Take responsibility for the professional learning and development of others. Develop personal influence and be part of the collective leadership and impact of the profession.

Published with kind permission of BASW – www.basw.co.uk

Appendix 2

Subject benchmark for social work

5 Knowledge, understanding and skills

Subject knowledge and understanding

5.1 During their qualifying degree studies in social work, students acquire, critically evaluate, apply and integrate knowledge and understanding in the following five core areas of study.

5.2 Social work theory, which includes:

i   critical explanations from social work theory and other subjects which contribute to the knowledge base of social work

ii   an understanding of social work's rich and contested history from both a UK and comparative perspective

iii the relevance of sociological and applied psychological perspectives to understanding societal and structural influences on human behaviour at individual, group and community levels, and the relevance of sociological theorisation to a deeper understanding of adaptation and change

iv   the relevance of psychological, physical and physiological perspectives to understanding human, personal and social development, well-being and risk

v   social science theories explaining and exploring group and organisational behaviour

vi   the range of theories and research-informed evidence that informs understanding of the child, adult, family or community and of the range of assessment and interventions which can be used

vii the theory, models and methods of assessment, factors underpinning the selection and testing of relevant information, knowledge and critical appraisal of relevant social science and other research and evaluation methodologies, and the evidence base for social work

viii the nature of analysis and professional judgement and the processes of risk assessment and decision-making, including the theory of risk-informed decisions and the balance of choice and control, rights and protection in decision-making

ix   approaches, methods and theories of intervention in working with a diverse population within a wide range of settings, including factors guiding the choice and critical evaluation of these, and user-led perspectives.

5.3   Values and ethics, which include:

i   the nature, historical evolution, political context and application of professional social work values, informed by national and international definitions and ethical statements, and their relation to personal values, identities, influences and ideologies

ii   the ethical concepts of rights, responsibility, freedom, authority and power inherent in the practice of social workers as agents with statutory powers in different situations

iii   aspects of philosophical ethics relevant to the understanding and resolution of value dilemmas and conflicts in both interpersonal and professional context

iv   understanding of, and adherence to, the ethical foundations of empirical and conceptual research, as both consumers and producers of social science research

v   the relationship between human rights enshrined in law and the moral and ethical rights determined theoretically, philosophically and by contemporary society

vi   the complex relationships between justice, care and control in social welfare and the practical and ethical implications of these, including their expression in roles as statutory agents in diverse practice settings and in upholding the law in respect of challenging discrimination and inequalities

vii   the conceptual links between codes defining ethical practice and the regulation of professional conduct

viii   the professional and ethical management of potential conflicts generated by codes of practice held by different professional groups

ix   the ethical management of professional dilemmas and conflicts in balancing the perspectives of individuals who need care and support and professional decision-making at points of risk, care and protection

x   the constructive challenging of individuals and organisations where there may be conflicts with social work values, ethics and codes of practice

xi   the professional responsibility to be open and honest if things go wrong (the duty of candour about own practice) and to act on concerns about poor or unlawful practice by any person or organisation

xii   continuous professional development as a reflective, informed and skilled practitioner, including the constructive use of professional supervision.

5.4   Service users and carers, which include:

i   the factors which contribute to the health and well-being of individuals, families and communities, including promoting dignity, choice and independence for people who need care and support

ii   the underpinning perspectives that determine explanations of the characteristics and circumstances of people who need care and support, with critical evaluation drawing on research, practice experience and the experience and expertise of people who use services

iii   the social and psychological processes associated with, for example, poverty, migration, unemployment, trauma, poor health, disability, lack of education and other sources of disadvantage and how they affect well-being, how they interact and may lead to marginalisation, isolation and exclusion, and demand for social work services

iv   explanations of the links between the factors contributing to social differences and identities (for example, social class, gender, ethnic differences, age, sexuality and religious belief) and the structural consequences of inequality and differential need faced by service users

v   the nature and function of social work in a diverse and increasingly global society (with particular reference to prejudice, interpersonal relations, discrimination, empowerment and anti-discriminatory practices)

5.5   The nature of social work practice, in the United Kingdom and more widely, which includes:

i   the place of theoretical perspectives and evidence from European and international research in assessment and decision-making processes

ii   the integration of theoretical perspectives and evidence from European and international research into the design and implementation of effective social work intervention with a wide range of service users, carers and communities

iii   the knowledge and skills which underpin effective practice, with a range of service users and in a variety of settings

iv   the processes that facilitate and support service user and citizen rights, choice, co-production, self-governance, well-being and independence

v   the importance of interventions that promote social justice, human rights, social cohesion, collective responsibility and respect for diversity and that tackle inequalities

vi   its delivery in a range of community-based and organisational settings spanning the statutory, voluntary and private sectors, and the changing nature of these service contexts

vii   the factors and processes that facilitate effective interdisciplinary, interprofessional and interagency collaboration and partnership across a plurality of settings and disciplines

viii the importance of social work's contribution to intervention across service user groups, settings and levels in terms of the profession's focus on social justice, human rights, social cohesion, collective responsibility and respect for diversities

ix   the processes of reflection and reflexivity as well as approaches for evaluating service and welfare outcomes for vulnerable people, and their significance for the development of practice and the practitioner.

5.6   The leadership, organisation and delivery of social work services, which includes:

i   the location of contemporary social work within historical, comparative and global perspectives, including in the devolved nations of the United Kingdom and wider European and international contexts

ii   how the service delivery context is portrayed to service users, carers, families and communities

iii   the changing demography and cultures of communities, including European and international contexts, in which social workers practise

iv   the complex relationships between public, private, social and political philosophies, policies and priorities and the organisation and practice of social work, including the contested nature of these

v   the issues and trends in modern public and social policy and their relationship to contemporary practice, service delivery and leadership in social work

vi   the significance of legislative and legal frameworks and service delivery standards, including on core social work values and ethics in the delivery of services which support, enable and empower

vii   the current range and appropriateness of statutory, voluntary and private agencies providing services and the organisational systems inherent within these

viii   development of new ways of working and delivery, for example, the development of social enterprises, integrated multi-professional teams and independent social work provision

ix   the significance of professional and organisational relationships with other related services, including housing, health, education, police, employment, fire, income maintenance and criminal justice

x   the importance and complexities of the way agencies work together to provide care, the relationships between agency policies, legal requirements and professional boundaries in shaping the nature of services provided in integrated and interdisciplinary contexts

xi   the contribution of different approaches to management and leadership within different settings, and the impact on professional practice and on quality of care management and leadership in public and human services

xii   the development of person-centred services, personalised care, individual budgets and direct payments all focusing upon the human and legal rights of the service user for control, power and self-determination

xiii   the implications of modern information and communications technology for both the provision and receipt of services, use of technologically enabled support and the use of social media as a process and forum for vulnerable people, families and communities, and communities of professional practice.

Subject-specific skills and other skills

5.7   The range of skills required by a qualified social worker reflects the complex and demanding context in which they work. Many of these skills may be of value in many situations, for example, analytical thinking, building relationships, working as a member of an organisation, intervention, evaluation and reflection. What defines the specific nature of these skills as developed by social work students is:

i   the context in which they are applied and assessed (for example, communication skills in practice with people with sensory impairments or assessment skills in an interprofessional setting)

ii   the relative weighting given to such skills within social work practice (for example, the central importance of problem-solving skills within complex human situations)

iii   the specific purpose of skill development (for example, the acquisition of research skills in order to build a repertoire of research-based practice)

iv   a requirement to integrate a range of skills (that is, not simply to demonstrate these in an isolated and incremental manner).

5.8   All social work graduates demonstrate the ability to reflect on and learn from the exercise of their skills, in order to build their professional identity. They understand the significance of the concepts of continuing professional development and lifelong learning, and accept responsibility for their own continuing development.

5.9   Social work students acquire and integrate skills in the following five core areas.

Problem-solving skills

5.10 These are subdivided into four areas.

5.11 Managing problem-solving activities: graduates in social work are able to:

    i   think logically, systematically, creatively, critically and reflectively, in order to carry out a holistic assessment

    ii   apply ethical principles and practices critically in planning problem-solving activities

    iii   plan a sequence of actions to achieve specified objectives, making use of research, theory and other forms of evidence

    iv   manage processes of change, drawing on research, theory and other forms of evidence.

5.12 Gathering information: graduates in social work are able to:

    i   demonstrate persistence in gathering information from a wide range of sources and using a variety of methods, for a range of purposes. These methods include electronic searches, reviews of relevant literature, policy and procedures, face-to-face interviews, and written and telephone contact with individuals and groups

    ii   take into account differences of viewpoint in gathering information and critically assess the reliability and relevance of the information gathered

    iii   assimilate and disseminate relevant information in reports and case records.

5.13 Analysis and synthesis: graduates in social work are able to analyse and synthesise knowledge gathered for problem-solving purposes, in order to:

    i   assess human situations, taking into account a variety of factors (including the views of participants, theoretical concepts, research evidence, legislation and organisational policies and procedures)

    ii   analyse and synthesise information gathered, weighing competing evidence and modifying their viewpoint in the light of new information, then relate this information to a particular task, situation or problem

    iii   balance specific factors relevant to social work practice (such as risk, rights, cultural differences and language needs and preferences, responsibilities to protect vulnerable individuals and legal obligations)

    iv   assess the merits of contrasting theories, explanations, research, policies and procedures and use the information to develop and sustain reasoned arguments

    v   employ a critical understanding of factors that support or inhibit problem-solving, including societal, organisational and community issues as well as individual relationships

    vi   critically analyse and take account of the impact of inequality and discrimination in working with people who use social work services.

5.14 Intervention and evaluation: graduates in social work are able to use their knowledge of a range of interventions and evaluation processes creatively and selectively to:

    i   build and sustain purposeful relationships with people and organisations in communities and interprofessional contexts

    ii   make decisions based on evidence, set goals and construct specific plans to achieve outcomes, taking into account relevant information, including ethical guidelines

iii   negotiate goals and plans with others, analysing and addressing in a creative and flexible manner individual, cultural and structural impediments to change

iv   implement plans through a variety of systematic processes that include working in partnership

v   practice in a manner that promotes well-being, protects safety and resolves conflict

vi   act as a navigator, advocate and support to assist people who need care and support to take decisions and access services

vii   manage the complex dynamics of dependency and, in some settings, provide direct care and personal support to assist people in their everyday lives

viii   meet deadlines and comply with external requirements of a task

ix   plan, implement and critically monitor and review processes and outcomes

x   bring work to an effective conclusion, taking into account the implications for all involved

xi   use and evaluate methods of intervention critically and reflectively.

Communication skills

5.15   Graduates in social work are able to communicate clearly, sensitively and effectively (using appropriate methods which may include working with interpreters) with individuals and groups of different ages and abilities in a range of formal and informal situations, in order to:

i   engage individuals and organisations, who may be unwilling, by verbal, paper-based and electronic means to achieve a range of objectives, including changing behaviour

ii   use verbal and non-verbal cues to guide and inform conversations and interpretation of information

iii   negotiate and, where necessary, redefine the purpose of interactions with individuals and organisations and the boundaries of their involvement

iv   listen actively and empathetically to others, taking into account their specific needs and life experiences

v   engage appropriately with the life experiences of service users, to understand accurately their viewpoint, overcome personal prejudices and respond appropriately to a range of complex personal and interpersonal situations

vi   make evidence-informed arguments drawing from theory, research and practice wisdom, including the viewpoints of service users and/or others

vii   write accurately and clearly in styles adapted to the audience, purpose and context of the communication

viii   use advocacy skills to promote others' rights, interests and needs

ix   present conclusions verbally and on paper, in a structured form, appropriate to the audience for which these have been prepared

x   make effective preparation for, and lead, meetings in a productive way.

Skills in working with others

5.16   Graduates in social work are able to build relationships and work effectively with others, in order to:

i   involve users of social work services in ways that increase their resources, capacity and power to influence factors affecting their lives

ii   engage service users and carers and wider community networks in active consultation

iii   respect and manage differences such as organisational and professional boundaries and differences of identity and/or language

iv   develop effective helping relationships and partnerships that facilitate change for individuals, groups and organisations while maintaining appropriate personal and professional boundaries

v   demonstrate interpersonal skills and emotional intelligence that creates and develops relationships based on openness, transparency and empathy

vi   increase social justice by identifying and responding to prejudice, institutional discrimination and structural inequality

vii   operate within a framework of multiple accountability (for example, to agencies, the public, service users, carers and others)

viii   observe the limits of professional and organisational responsibility, using supervision appropriately and referring to others when required

ix   provide reasoned, informed arguments to challenge others as necessary, in ways that are most likely to produce positive outcomes.

Skills in personal and professional development

5.17 Graduates in social work are able to:

i   work at all times in accordance with codes of professional conduct and ethics

ii   advance their own learning and understanding with a degree of independence and use supervision as a tool to aid professional development

iii   develop their professional identity, recognise their own professional limitations and accountability, and know how and when to seek advice from a range of sources, including professional supervision

iv   use support networks and professional supervision to manage uncertainty, change and stress in work situations while maintaining resilience in self and others

v   handle conflict between others and internally when personal views may conflict with a course of action necessitated by the social work role

vi   provide reasoned, informed arguments to challenge unacceptable practices in a responsible manner and raise concerns about wrongdoing in the workplace

vii   be open and honest with people if things go wrong

viii   understand the difference between theory, research, evidence and expertise and the role of professional judgement.

Use of technology and numerical skills

5.18 Graduates in social work are able to use information and communication technology effectively and appropriately for:

i   professional communication, data storage and retrieval and information searching

ii   accessing and assimilating information to inform working with people who use services

iii   data analysis to enable effective use of research in practice

iv   enhancing skills in problem-solving

v   applying numerical skills to financial and budgetary responsibilities

vi   understanding the social impact of technology, including the constraints of confidentiality and an awareness of the impact of the 'digital divide'.

© The Quality Assurance Agency for Higher Education, 2019. http://www.qaa.ac.uk/

References

Abendstern, M, Hughes, J, Wilberforce, M, Davies, K, Pitts, R, Batool, S, Robinson, C and Challis, D (2021) Perceptions of the social worker role in adult community mental health teams in England. *Qualitative Social Work*, 20(3): 773–791.

Alexander, K, Henley, S and Newman, K (2014) Cognitive behavioural-based strategies. In L Grant and G Kinman (eds) *Developing resilience for social work practice*. Shanghai: Palgrave.

Alston, M and Bowles, W (2003) *Research for social workers: An introduction to methods*, 2nd edition. London: Routledge.

Argyris, C and Schön, D (1996) *Organisational learning II*. Boston: Addison-Wesley.

Atwal, A and Caldwell, K (2005) Do all health and social care professionals interact equally: A study of interactions in multidisciplinary teams in the United Kingdom. *Scandinavian Journal of Caring Science*, 19(3): 268–273.

Austin A, Dal Santo, T and Lee, C (2012) Building organisational supports for research minded practitioners. *Journal of Evidence-Based Social Work*, 9(1–20): 174–211.

Babiker, A, El Husseini, M, Al Nemri, A, Al Frayh, A, Al Juryyan, N, Faki, M, OAssiri, A, Al Saadi, M, Shaikh, F and Al Zamil, F (2014) Health care professional development: Working as a team to improve patient care. *Sudanese Journal of paediatric Medicine*, 14(2): 9–16.

Bailey, R and Brake, M (eds) (1975) *Radical social work*. London: Arnold.

Baldwin, M (2004) Critical reflection: Opportunities and threats to professional learning and service development in social work organisations. In N Gould and M Baldwin (eds) *Social work, critical reflection and the learning organisation*. Aldershot: Ashgate.

Bamford, T (1982) *Managing social work*. London: Tavistock Publications.

Barker, P and Buchanan-Barker, P (2012) *Tidal model of mental health nursing*. Available at: http://www.currentnursing.com/nursing_theory/Tidal_Model.html (accessed 23 March 2018).

Barki, H and Hartwick, J (2004) Conceptualizing the construct of interpersonal conflict. *International Journal of Conflict Management*, 15(3): 216–244.

Barking and Dagenham Safeguarding Children Board (2011) *Serious case review: Services provided for Child T and Child R*. Available at: http://newsite.bardag-lscb.co.uk/wp-content/uploads/2016/12/child-t-executive-summary.pdf (accessed September 2022).

Barlow, C and Hall, B (2007) What about feelings? A study of emotion and tension in social work field education. *Social Work Education*, 26(4): 399–413.

BASW (2018) *Professionals capability framework for social workers in England*. Available at: https://www.basw.co.uk/system/files/resources/BASW%20PCF.%20Detailed%20level%20descriptors%20for%20all%20domains.25.6.18%20final.pdf (accessed 10 July 2018).

BASW/CoSW (2011) *England research on supervision in social work, with particular reference to supervision practice in multidisciplinary teams*. Available at: https://www.basw.co.uk/system/files/resources/basw_13955-1_0.pdf (accessed 5 May 2022).

Batalden, M, Batalden, P, Margolis, P, Seid, M, Armstrong, G, Opipari-Arrigan, L and Hartung, H (2016) Coproduction of healthcare service. *BMJ Quality and Safety*, 25(7): 509–517.

Beadle-Brown, J, Richardson, L, Guest, C, Malovic, A, Bradshaw, J and Himmerich, J (2014) *Living in fear: Better outcomes for people with learning disabilities and autism*. Main research report. Canterbury: Tizard Centre, University of Kent.

Beck, J (2011) *Cognitive therapy basics and beyond*, 2nd edition. New York: Guilford Press.

Becker, H (1963) *Outsiders: Studies in the sociology of deviance*. New York: Free Press.

Bedford, A (2015) *Serious case review into child sexual exploitation in Oxfordshire: From the experiences of Children A, B, C, D, E, and F. Oxfordshire Safeguarding Children Board*. Available at: http://www.oscb.org.uk/wp-content/uploads/SCR-into-CSE-in-Oxfordshire-FINAL-FOR-WEBSITE.pdf (accessed 26 April 2016).

Bell, L and Allain, A (2010) Exploring professional stereotypes and learning for inter-professional practice: An example from UK qualifying level social work education. *Social Work Education*, 30(3): 266–280.

Berdahl, JL, Cooper, M, Glick, P, Livingston, RW and Williams, JC (2018) Work as a masculinity contest. *Journal of Social Issues*, 74(3): 422–428.

Biestek, F (1961) *The casework relationship*. London: Allen & Unwin.

Birmingham Safeguarding Children's Board (2013) *Serious case review in respect of the death of Keanu Williams*. Available at: https://www.basw.co.uk/system/files/resources/basw_94519-10_0.pdf (accessed September 2022).

Bock, G and James, S (1992) *Beyond equality and difference*. London: Palgrave.

Bolton, G (2014) *Reflective practice, writing and professional development*, 4th edition. London: SAGE.

Borton, T (1970) *Reach, touch, and teach: Student concerns and process education*. New York: McGraw-Hill.

Boud, D and Knight, S (1996) Course design and reflective practice. In N Gould and I Taylor (eds) *Reflective learning for social work*. Aldershot: Ashgate.

Boud, D and Walker, D (1998) Promoting reflection in professional courses: The challenge of context. *Studies in Higher Education*, 23(92): 191–206.

Boyle, D, Coote, A, Sherwood, C and Slay, J (2010) *Co-production: Right here, Right now* [Internet]. London: NESTA/New Economics Foundation. https://www.nesta.org.uk/sites/default/files/right_here_right_now.pdf (accessed 31 January 2023).

Branch, R and Willson, R (2010) *Cognitive behavioural therapy for dummies*, 2nd edition. Chichester: John Wiley and Sons.

Brookfield, S (1987) *Developing critical thinkers*. Buckingham: Open University Press.

Brown, J, Lewis, L, Ellis, K, Stewart, M, Freeman, TR and Kasperski, MJ (2011) Conflict on interprofessional primary health care teams–can it be resolved? *Journal of Interprofessional Care*, 25(1): 4–10.

Bull, S (2013) Applying legislation in social work. In A Mantell (ed) *Skills for social work*. London: SAGE.

Butler, J (2004) *Undoing gender*. London: Routledge.

CALM. Available at: http://www.thecalmzone.net/2015/11/why-we-need-to-discuss-men,%20research%20into%20male%20suicide (accessed 26 November 2015).

Cameron, C (2005) With heart, head and hands. *Community Care*, 16/8/2005, Available at: https://www.communitycare.co.uk/2005/08/16/with-hearthead-and-hands/ (accessed 28 January 2023).

Canadian Interprofessional Health Collaborative (2010) *A national interprofessional competency framework*. Available at: https://phabc.org/wp-content/uploads/2015/07/CIHC-National-Interprofessional-Competency-Framework.pdf

Carpenter, J, Webb, C, Bostock, L and Comber, C (2015) SCIE Research Briefing 43: Effective supervision in social work and social care. *SCIE*. Available at: www.scie.org.uk (accessed 5 May 2022).

Chandler, J (2017) *Identity at work*. Chapter 6: Gender. London: Routledge.

Christie, A (2006) Negotiating the uncomfortable intersections between gender and professional identities in social work. *Critical Social Policy*, 26(2): 390–411.

Christie, A (ed) (2001) *Men and social work: Theories and practices*, Basingstoke: Palgrave.

Clark, PG (2009) Reflecting on reflection in interprofessional education: Implications for theory and practice. *Journal of Interprofessional Care*, 23(3): 213–223.

Clements, L (2011) *Social care law developments: A sideways look at personalisation and tightening eligibility criteria.* Available at: www.lukeclements.co.uk/resources-index/files/PDF%2002.pdf (accessed 24 May 2013).

Cocker, C and Hafford-Letchfield, T (eds) (2022) *Rethinking feminist theories for social work practice.* London: Palgrave MacMillan.

Collins, PH and Bilge, S (2020) *Intersectionality*, 2nd edition. Key concepts. Cambridge: Polity.

Conner, MG (2001) *Transference: Are you a biological time machine? The Source.* Available at: www.crisiscounselling.com (accessed 11 February 2007).

Cook, A and Miller, E (2012) *Talking points: Personal outcome approach.* Available at: www.jits cotland.org.uk/action-areas/talking-points-user-and-carer-involvement/ (accessed 24 May 2013).

Cooper, A and Romeo, L (2022) Feminist perspectives on social work leadership. In C Cocker and T Hafford-Letchfield (eds) *Rethinking feminist theories for social work practice.* London: Palgrave MacMillan.

Cooper, A and Lousada, J (2005) *Borderline welfare: Feeling and fear of feeling in modern welfare.* London: Karnac.

Cooper, B (2016) Intersectionality. In M Hawkesworth and L Disch (eds) *The Oxford handbook of feminist theory.* Oxford: Oxford University Press.

Cooper, F (2012) *Professional boundaries in social work and social care: A practical guide to understanding, maintaining and managing your professional boundaries.* London: Jessica Kingsley Publishers.

Cooper, J (2011) *The need for more critically reflective social work.* Community Care. Available at: http://www.communitycare.co.uk/2011/04/08/the-need-for-more-critically-reflective-social-work/ (accessed 28 April 2016).

Copley, A (Summer, 2018) A critical evaluation of Miller and Rollnick's motivational interviewing as an approach to working with substance misuse. *Irish Association for Counselling and Psychotherapy*, 18(2): 11–15.

Corey, G (2020) *Theory and practice of counselling and psychotherapy*, 10th edition. Belmont: Brooks/Cole.

Cottrell, S (2010) *Skills for success: The personal development planning guide.* Basingstoke: Palgrave Macmillan.

Cottrell, S (2015) *Skills for success: Personal development and employability*, 3rd edition. Basingstoke: Palgrave Macmillan.

Cottrell, S (2017) *Critical thinking skills developing effective analysis and argument*, 3rd edition. Basingstoke: Palgrave.

Cournoyer, BR (2017) *The social work skills workbook.* Boston: Cengage Learning.

Coventry Local Safeguarding Children's Board (2013) *Serious case review re Daniel Pelka.* Available at: https://pdscp.co.uk/wp-content/uploads/2020/02/SCR-Daniel-Pelka-2013.pdf (accessed September 2022).

CQC (2011) *Review of compliance.* Available at: https://www.cqc.org.uk/news/releases/cqc-report-winterbourne-view-confirms-its-owners-failed-protect-people-abuse (accessed September 2022).

Crabtree, SA and Parker, J (2014) Being male in female spaces: Perceptions of masculinity amongst male social work students on a qualifying course. *Revista de Asistenta Sociala*, 4: 7–26.

Cree, V (2018) Feminism and social work: Where next for an engaged theory and practice? *Aotearoa New Zealand Social Work*, 30(3): 4–7.

Crisp, BR, Lister, PG and Dutton, K (2005) *Integrated assessment.* Glasgow: Scottish Institute for Excellence in Social Work Education.

Cunningham, G (2004) Supervision and governance. In D Statham (ed) *Managing front line practice in social care*. London: Jessica Kingsley.

Curtis Report (1946) *Care of children: Interdepartment committee report, Curtis Committee, Cmd 6922*. London: HMSO.

Darvill, G (1997) *The management of work-based learning: A guide for managers of social care and social work on raising standards of practice*. London: The Stationery Office.

Dean, E (2017) Schwartz rounds for nursing students. *Nursing Standard*, 31(33): 26–28.

Dent, A (2005) Supporting the bereaved: Theory and practice. *Healthcare Counselling and Psychotherapy Journal*, 22–23.

Department for Education (2013) *Statistics: Children social work workforce*. Available at: https://www.gov.uk/government/collections/statistics-childrens-social-care-workforce (accessed September 2022).

Department for Education (2018) *Children and family social work workforce 2017*. Available at: https://assets.publishing.service.gov.uk/government/uploads/system/uploads/attachment_data/file/681546/SFR09-2018_Main_Text.pdf.

Department of Education (2009) *Social work taskforce, building a safe confident future, the final report of the social work taskforce*. Available at: https://dera.ioe.ac.uk//10625/ (accessed September 2022).

Department of Education (2015) *Children's social work workforce ending 30 September 2014*. Available at: https://www.gov.uk/government/statistics/childrens-social-work-workforce-2013-to-2014 (accessed September 2022).

Department of Health (2022) *Care and support statutory guidance: Issued under the Care Act 2014*. Available at: www.gov.uk/government/publications/care-act-2014-statutory-guidance-for-implementation.

Department of Health and Social Care (2022) *Final report of the Ockenden review*. Available at: https://www.gov.uk/government/publications/final-report-of-the-ockenden-review (accessed September 2022).

Dewey, J (1933) *How we think*. Boston: D.C. Heath.

Dewey, J (1938) *Logic: The theory of inquiry*. Troy: Reinhart and Winston.

Dingwall, E, Eekelaar, J and Murray, T (1983) *The protection of children: State intervention and family life*. Oxford: Basil Blackwell.

Dore, I (2016) Shape-shifter and agenda setter: The influence of emotion in social work practice and practice education. *Social Work Education*, 34(4): 469–481.

Douglas, H (2008) Preparation for contact: An aid to effective social work intervention. *Social Work Education*, 27(4): 380–389.

Duffy, A (2009) Guiding students through reflective practice – The preceptors experiences. A qualitative descriptive study. *Nurse Education in Practise*, 9(3): 166–175.

Edelman, S (2006) *Change your thinking*. Chatham: Vermilion.

Ellis, A and Dryden, W (2007) *The practice of rational emotive behaviour therapy*, 2nd edition. New York: Springer Publishing Company.

Emilsson, UM (2013) The role of social work in cross-professional teamwork: Examples from an older people's team in England. *British Journal of Social Work*, 43(1): 116–134.

Eraut, M (2001) Learning challenges for knowledge-based organisations. In J Stevens (ed) *Workplace learning in Europe*. London: Chartered Institute of Personnel and Development.

European Institute for Gender Equality (2020) *Sexism at work: How can we stop it?* Available at: https://eige.europa.eu/publications/sexism-at-work-handbook.

Farmer, J and Grant, S (2020) The future of dementia care in rural areas of the world. In A Innes, D Morgan and J Farmer (eds) *Remote and rural dementia care: Policy, research and practice*. Bristol: Policy Press.

Faulkner, S and Faulkner, C (2018) *Research methods for social workers*, 3rd edition. Oxford: Oxford University Press.

Fawcett Society (2016) Available at: http://fawcettsociety.org.uk/news/gender-is-more-fluid-than-just-male-and-female-say-almost-half-of-britons.

Felton, K (1 March, 2005) Meaning based quality of life measurement: A way forward in conceptualizing and measuring client outcomes? *The British Journal of Social Work*, 35(2): 221–236.

Ferguson, H (2005) Working with violence, the emotions and the psycho-social dynamics of child protection: Reflections on the Victoria Climbié case. *Social Work Education*, 24(7): 781–795.

Ferguson, H (2011) *Child protection practice*. Basingstoke: Palgrave Macmillan.

Ferguson, H (2018) How social workers reflect in action and when and why they don't: The possibilities and limits to reflective practice in social work. *Social Work Education*. DOI: 10.1080/02615479.2017.1413083. Published online: 4 February 2018.

Ferguson, H (2021) The death of Arthur Labinjo-Hughes. *Guardian* (accessed 8 February 22).

Ferguson, I (2008) *Reclaiming social work: Challenging neoliberalism and promoting social justice.* London: SAGE.

Ferreira, S and Ferreira, R (2015) Teaching social work values by means of socratic questioning. *Social Work*, 50(4). Available at: http://www.scielo.org.za/scielo.php?script=sci_arttext&pid=S0037-8054 2015000400002 (accessed 13 April 2018).

Fine C (2010) *Delusions of gender: The real science behind sex differences*. London: Icon Books.

Fleming, N and Baume, D (November 2006) Learning styles again: VARKing up the right tree! Educational developments. *SEDA Ltd*, 7: 4–7.

Fook, J (2007) Reflective practice and critical reflection. In J Lishman (ed) *Handbook for practice learning in social work and social care*, 2nd edition. *Knowledge and theory* (pp. 363–375). London: Jessica Kingsley.

Fook, J (2012) Reflective practice and critical reflection. In J Lishman (ed) *Handbook for practice learning in social work and social care*, 2nd edition. London: Jessica Kingsley.

Fook, J (2016) *Social work: A critical approach to practice*, 3rd edition. London: SAGE.

Fook, J and Askeland, G (2007) Challenges of critical reflection: Nothing ventured, nothing gained. *Social Work Education*, 26(5): 520–533.

Forrester, D, Westlake, D, McCann, M, Thurnham, A, Shefer, G, Glynn, G and Killian, M (2013) *Reclaiming social work? An evaluation of systemic units as an approach to delivering children's services.* Tilda Goldberg Centre for Social Work and Social Care, University of Bedfordshire.

Foster, A (2005) Surface and depth in the Victoria Climbié report. *Child and Family Social Work*, 10: 1–9.

Francis, R (2013) *Report of the Mid Staffordshire NHS Foundation Trust Public Inquiry – Executive Summary*. London: The Stationary Office.

Freud, S (1988) *My three mothers and other passions*. New York: New York University Press.

Furness, S (2012) Gender at work: Characteristics of 'failing' social work students. *British Journal of Social Work*, 42: 480–499.

Garey, A, Hansen, K and Ehrenreich, B (2011) *At the heart of work and family: Engaging with the ideas of Arlie Hochschild*. New Brunswick: Rutgers University Press.

Gibbs, G (1988) *Learning by doing: A guide to teaching and learning methods*. London: Further Education Unit.

Gibbs, J (2001) Maintaining front-line workers in child protection: A case for refocusing supervision. *Child Abuse Review*, 10: 323–335.

Giddens, A (1992) *The Transformation of intimacy*. Cambridge: Polity Press.

Gilbert, P (2009) *Overcoming depression*. Croydon: Robinson.

Gilovich, T (1991) *How we know what isn't so: The fallibility of human reason in everyday life*. New York: The Free Press.

Goldstein, H (2001) *Experiential learning: A foundation for social work education and practice.* Alexandira: Council on Social Work Education.

Goleman, D (1996) *Emotional intelligence.* London: Bloomsbury.

Goleman, D (1998) *Working with emotional intelligence.* London: Random House.

Gomez, LE and Bernet (2019) Diversity improves performance and outcomes. *Journal of the National Medical Association,* 111(4): 383–392.

Goodman, A (2013) *Social work with drug, alcohol and substance misuse,* 3rd edition. London: SAGE.

Gorman, H and Postle, K (2003) *Transforming community care: A distorted vision.* Birmingham: Venture Press.

Gough, B (2001) Biting your tongue: Negotiating masculinities in contemporary Britain. *Journal of Gender Studies,* 10(2): 169–185.

Gould, N (1996) Introduction: Social work education and the 'crisis of the professions'. In N Gould and I Taylor (eds) *Reflective learning for social work.* Aldershot: Arena.

Gould, N (2004) Introduction: The learning organisation and reflective practice – The emergence of a concept. In N Gould and M Baldwin (eds) *Social work: Critical reflection and the learning organisation.* Aldershot: Ashgate.

Gov.uk (2022) *Reporting Year 2021: Children's social work workforce.* Available at: https://explore-education-statistics.service.gov.uk/find-statistics/children-s-social-work-workforce (accessed 30 September 2022).

Grant, L and Kinman, G (2012) Enhancing wellbeing in social work students: Building resilience in the next generation. *Social Work Education: The International Journal,* 31(5): 605–621.

Greenberger, D and Padesky, CA (2016) *Mind over mood,* 2nd edition. New York: Guildford Press.

Gregory, M and Holloway, M (2005) Language and the shaping of social work. *British Journal of Social Work,* 35(1): 37–53.

Griffin, M (2003) Using critical incidents to promote and assess reflective thinking in preservice teachers. *Reflective Practice,* 4(2): 207–220.

Grol, SM, Molleman, GRM, Kuijpers, A, van der Sande, R, Fransen, GAJ, Assendelft, WJJ and Schers, HJ (2018) The role of the general practitioner in multidisciplinary teams: A qualitative study in elderly care. *BMC Family Practise,* 19(1): 40.

Habermas, J (1972) *Knowledge and human interests* (trans J Shapiro). London: Heinemann.

Hafford-Letchfield, T and Cocker, C (2022) Feminisms and intersectionalities (pp. 117–121). In C Cocker and T Hafford-Letchfield (eds).

Handley, IM, Brown, ER, Moss-Racusin, CA and Smith, JL (2015) Quality of evidence revealing subtle gender biases in science is in the eye of the beholder. *Proceedings of the National Academy of Sciences,* 112(43): 13201–13206.

Harding, S (ed) (2004) *The feminist standpoint theory reader.* London: Psychology Press.

Hardy, SE, Delree, J and Loos, M (2017) A guide to best practice dementia care. Lessons from a serious care review. *Journal of the All-Ireland Gerontologcal Nurses Association.* Available at: https://openresearch.lsbu.ac.uk/item/87039 (accessed 6 August 2022).

Haynes, K (2022) *Social workers as leaders.* Available at: https://www.socialworktoday.com/archive/exc_040714.shtml (accessed 06 August 2022).

HCPC (2021) *Supervision agreement template.* Available at: www.hcpc.uk.org (accessed 11 May 2022).

HCPC (2021) *Diversity data report.* Available at: https://www.hcpc-uk.org/resources/reports/2021/diversity-data-report-2021/ (accessed 17 June 2022).

Hcpc (2021) *Supervision-recording-template.* Available at: www.hcpc.uk.org (accessed 11 May 2022).

Health and Safety Executive (2017) *Work related stress, depression or anxiety statistics in Great Britain*. Available at: www.hse.gov.uk/stress/research/htm (accessed 3 March 2018).

Healy, K (2022) *Social work theories in context: Creating frameworks for practice*, 3rd edition. Basingstoke: Palgrave Macmillan.

Heilman, ME and Okimoto, TG (2007) Why are women penalized for success at male tasks? The implied communality effect. *Journal of Applied Psychology*, 92(1): 81–92.

Henderson, J and Seden, J (2003) What do we want from social care managers? Aspirations and realities. In J Reynolds, I Henderson, J Seden, J Charlesworth and A Bullman (eds) *The managing care reader*. London: Routledge and the Open University.

Hicks, S (2001) Men social workers in children's services: 'Will the real man please stand up?' In A Christie (ed) *Men in social work*. Basingstoke: Palgrave Macmillan.

Hicks, S (2015) Social work and gender: An argument for practical accounts. *Qualitative Social Work*, 14(4): 471–487.

Higgins, M (2013) *The dilemmas of contemporary social work: A case study of the social work degree in England. A thesis submitted in partial fulfilment of the requirements of London South Bank University for the degree of Doctor of Philosophy*.

Higgins, M (2016) 'Cultivating our humanity' in child and family social work in England. *Social Work Education*. Available at: http://www.tandfonline.com/doi/full/10.1080/02615479.2016.1181161.

Higgins, M, Goodyer and Whittaker, A (2015) Can a Munro-inspired approach transform the lives of looked after children in England? *Social Work Education: The International Journal*, 34(5).

Himmelweit, S (2008) *Reducing gender inequalities to create a sustainable care system*. New York: Joseph Rowntree Foundation.

HM Government (2011) *Prevent strategy*. London: The Stationary Office.

HM Inspectorate of Constabulary and Fire and Rescue Services (2018) *Metropolitan policed service – National child protection inspection post-inspection quarter 4 update*. Available at: https://www.justiceinspectorates.gov.uk/hmicfrs/publications/metropolitan-police-service-national-child-protection-inspection-post-inspection-quarter-four-update/ (accessed September 2022).

Hochschild, A (1983) *The managed heart: Commercialization of human feeling*. Berkeley: University of California Press.

Hochschild, A (2015) The managed heart. In AS Wharton (ed) *Working in America: Continuity, conflict, and change in a new economic era*. New York: Routledge.

Hohman, L (2012) *Motivational interviewing in social work practice*. London: The Guildford Press.

Honey, P and Mumford, A (2006) *The learning styles questionnaire, 80-item version*. Maidenhead: Peter Honey Publications.

Hood, P, Everitt, A and Runnicles, D (1998) Femininity, sexuality and professionalism in the children's departments. *British Journal of Social Work*, 28(4): 471–490.

Horner, N (2012) *What is social work? Context and perspectives*, 4th edition. Exeter: Learning Matters.

Horner, N (2018) *What is social work? Context and perspectives*. Exeter: Learning Matters.

Horwath, J and Morrison, T (1999) *Effective staff training in social care: From theory to practice*. London and New York: Routledge.

Howe, D (2009) *A brief introduction to social work theory*. London: Palgrave Macmillan.

Howe, D (2013) *Empathy: What it is and why it matters*. Basingstoke: Palgrave Macmillan.

Hugman, R (2005) *New approaches to ethics in the caring professions*. Basingstoke: Palgrave.

Hunt, C (2001) Shifting shadows: Metaphors and maps for facilitating reflective practice. *Reflective Practice*, 2(3): 257–287.

Independent Jersey Care Inquiry (2017) *The Report of the Independent Jersey Care Inquiry*. Available at: http://www.jerseycareinquiry.org (accessed September 2022).

Ingram, I and Smith, M (2018) *Relationship based practice: Emergent themes in social work literature*. Glasgow: The Institute for Research and Innovation in Social Services.

Ingram, R (2013) Locating emotional intelligence at the heart of social work practice. *British Journal of Social Work*, 43: 987–1004.

Ingram, R (2015) *Understanding emotions in social work: Theory, practice and reflection*. Maidenhead: Open University Press.

International Federation of Social Workers (2014) *General Meeting and the IASSW General Assembly*. http://ifsw.org/policies/definition-of-social-work/.

Ixer, G (1999) There's no such thing as reflection. *British Journal of Social Work*, 29(6): 13–27.

Ixer, G (2003) Developing the relationship between reflective practice and social work values. *Journal of Practice Teaching*, 5(1): 7–22.

Jacklin, K and Chiovitte, J (2020) Consideration in dementia care for indigenous populations in Canada. In A Innes, D Morgan and J Farmer (eds) *Remote and rural dementia care: Policy, research and practice*. Bristol: Policy Press.

Janis, IL (1972) *Victims of Groupthink*. New York: Houghton Mifflin.

Jay, A (2013) *Rotherham Metropolitan Borough Council. Independent inquiry into child sexual exploitation 1997–2013*. Available at: https://www.rotherham.gov.uk/downloads/file/279/independent-inquiry-into-child-sexual-exploitation-in-rotherham (accessed September 2022).

Jenkins, R (2014) *Social identity*, 4th edition. Routledge.

Jennings, C and Kennedy, E (1996) *The reflective professional in education*. London: Jessica Kingsley.

Johns, C (2017) *Becoming a reflective practitioner*, 5th edition. Oxford: Blackwell.

Johnsson, E and Svensson, K (2004) Theory in social work: Some reflections on understanding and explaining interventions. *European Journal of Social Work*, 8(4): 419–433.

Johson, K and Scholes, P (2008) *Exploring corporate strategy*, 8th edition. Harlow: Pearson Education.

Jost, JT (2015) Resistance to change: A social psychological perspective. *Social Research: An International Quarterly*, 82(3): 607–636.

Kabat-Zinn, J (1992) *Wherever youou go, there you are: Mindfulness meditation in everyday life*. New York: Hyperion Book.

Kahneman, D (2011) *Thinking fast and slow*. New York: Penguin.

Kahneman, D (2011) *Thinking, fast and slow*. London: Allen Lane.

Karau, SJ and Williams, KD (1993) Social loafing: A meta-analytic review and theoretical integration. *Journal of Personality and Social Psychology*, 65(4): 681–706.

Kashdan, TB (2007) T Social anxiety spectrum and diminished positive experiences: Theoretical synthesis and meta-analysis. *Clinical Psychology Review*, 27: 348–365.

Katzenbach, JR and Smith, DK (1993) *The Wisdom of Teams: Creating the High-performance Organisation*. Boston: Harvard Business School.

Kearney, P (2004) First line managers, the mediator of standards and quality of practice. In D Statham (ed) *Managing front line practice in social care*. London: Jessica Kingsley.

Keinemans, S (2015) Be sensible: Emotions in social work ethics and education. *British Journal of Social Work*, 45: 2176–2191.

Kendi, I (2019) *How to be an anti-racist*. London: One World.

Kerfoot, D (2001) The organization of intimacy: Managerialism, masculinity and the masculine subject. In SM Whitehead and FJ Barrett (eds) *The masculinities reader*. London: Cambridge Press.

Kettle, M and Jackson, S (2017) Revisiting the rule of optimism. *The British Journal of Social Work*, 47(6): 1624–1640.

Kimura, D (2000) *Sex and cognition*. Cambridge: MIT Press.

Kirtley, P (2013) 'If you shine a light, you will probably find it': Report of a grass roots survey of health staff with regard to their experiences in dealing with child sexual exploitation Derby: National Working Group.

Knott, C (2016) Reflective practice in social work. In T Scragg and C Knott (eds) Reflective practice in social work, 4th edition. Exeter: Learning Matters.

Kolb, DA (1984) Experiential learning. London: Prentice-Hall.

Kolb, DA (2015) Experiential learning, experience as the source of learning and development, 2nd edition. London: Pearson Education.

Koprowska, J (2005) Communication and interpersonal skills in social work. Exeter: Learning Matters.

Kruger, J and Dunning, D (1999) Unskilled and unaware of it: How difficulties in recognizing one's own incompetence lead to inflated self-assessments. Journal of Personality and Social Psychology, 77(6): 1121–1134.

Kubler-Ross, E (1997) The wheel of life. New York: Station Hill Press.

Kubler-Ross, E and Kessler, D (2014) On grief and grieving: Finding the meaning of grief through the five stage of loss, London: Simon and Schuster.

Lambley, S and Marrable, T (2013) Practice enquiry into supervision in a variety of adult care settings where there are health and social care practitioners working together. Social Care Institute or Excellence. Available at: scie.org.uk (accessed 6 April 2018).

Laming, H (2003) The Victoria Climbié inquiry report. Cm5730. London: The Stationery Office. Crown copyright. Available at: www.victoria-climbié-inquiry.org.uk/fine/report.pdf.

Laming, H (2009) The protection of children in England; a progress report. London: The Stationary Office.

Laming, L (2003) The Victoria Climbié Inquiry. London: The Stationery Office.

Laming, L (2009) The protection of children in England: A progress report. London: The Stationary Office.

Larson, MS (1977) The Rise of Professionalism: A Sociological Analysis. Berkeley, CA: University of California Press.

Lavee, E and Strier, R. (2018) Social workers' emotional labour with families in poverty: Neoliberal fatigue? Child and Family Social Work, 23: 504–512.

Lawson, J, Lewis, S and Williams, C (2014) Making safeguarding personal guide 2014. Available at: www.local.gov.uk/...Safeguarding (accessed 28 August 2015).

Lazzari, MM, Colarossi, L, and Collins, KS (2009) Feminists in social work: Where have all the leaders gone? Affilia: Journal of Women and Social Work, 24: 348–359.

Lefevre, M (2018) Communicating with children and young people, 2nd edition. Bristol: Policy Press.

Lintern, S (2018) Health Care: A Risky Business. Presentation at London South Bank University 27/6/18.

Lipsky, M (1980) Street-level bureaucracy: Dilemmas of the individual in public service. New York: Russell Sage Foundation.

Littlechild, B (2013) Professional dangerousness: Lessons from research. London: Community Care Inform.

Local Safeguarding Children Board Haringey (2009) Serious case review: Baby Peter. Available at: https://assets.publishing.service.gov.uk/government/uploads/system/uploads/attachment_data/file/595135/second_serious_case_overview_report_relating_to_peter_connelly_dated_march_2009.pdf (accessed September 2022).

Lowe, C (2016) The Professional's influence within the client system: Exploring counter-transference and adult attachment within the therapeutic relationships with children experiencing abuse and their caregivers. Journal of Social Work Practice, 30(1): 59–68.

Luft, J and Ingham, H (1955) The Johari window, a graphic model of interpersonal awareness. In *Proceedings of the western training laboratory in group development*. Los Angeles: University of California.

Lynas, L (2014) *Introduction to team development. NHS Leadership Academy*. Available at: https://www.leadershipacademy.nhs.uk/wpcontent/uploads/2013/04/7428f23d7207f39da1eda97adbd7bf34.pdf (accessed 6 August 2022).

Macalister, J (2022) *The independent review of children social care: Final report*. Available at: https://childrenssocialcare.independent-review.uk/ (accessedAugust 2022).

MacInnes, J (1998) *The end of masculinity*. Buckingham: Open University Press.

Maclean, S, Finch, J and Tedam, P (2018) *SHARE: A new model for social work*. Hockley: 4edge Ltd.

Majchrzak, A, Rice, RE, Malhotra, A, King, N and Ba, S (2000) Technology adaption: The case of a computer-supported inter-organizational virtual team. *MIS Quarterly*, 24(2): 569–600.

Manners, K (2020) *National vulnerability action plan 2020-22*. National Police Chiefs' Council. Available at: https://www.npcc.police.uk/Crime%20Ops%20Committee/NVAP.pdf (accessed 6 April 22).

Mantell, A (2006) *Huntington's disease: The carers' story*. Unpublished DPhil thesis. University of Sussex.

Mantell, A (2010) Under a cloud: Carers' experiences of Huntington's disease. *Social Care and Neurodisability*, 1(2): 33–41.

Mantell, A (2011) Skills for engagement. In A Mantell (ed) *Skills for social work*, 2nd edition. Exeter: Learning Matters.

Mantell, A (2011) Introduction. In T Scragg and A Mantell (eds) *Safeguarding adults in social work*, 2nd edition. Exeter: Learning Matters.

Mantell, A (2013) Chapter 6: Skills for engagement. In A Mantell (ed) *Skills for social work practice*. London: Learning Matters.

Manthorpse, J and Martineau, S (2016) Serious case reviews into Dementia care: An analysis of context and content. *British Journal of Social Work*, 46(2): 514–531.

Marcus, G (1998) *Ethnography through thick and thin*. New Jersey: Princeton Publications.

Marsh, S (23 March, 2016) The gender-fluid generation: Young people on being male, female or non-binary. *The Guardian*. Available at: https://www.theguardian.com/commentisfree/2016/mar/23/gender-fluid-generation-young-people-male-female-trans (accessed 24 February 2023).

McPhail, BA (2004) Setting the record straight: Social work is not a female-dominated profession. *Social Work*, 49(2): 323–326.

McCarthy, MM, Arnold, AP, Ball, GF, Blaustein, JD and De Vries, GJ (2012) Sex differences in the brain: The not so inconvenient truth. *Journal of Neuroscience*, 32(7): 2241–2247.

McConnell, D (2006) *E-learning groups and communities*. Maidenhead: McGraw-Hill.

McDonald, C (2006) *Challenging social work: The context of practice*. Basingstoke: Palgrave Macmillan.

McLannahan, H (2004) *Emotions and mind 6*. Buckingham: Open University Press.

McLaughlin, H (2009) What's in a name: 'Client', 'patient', 'customer', 'consumer', 'expert by experience', 'service user' – What's next? *British Journal of Social Work*, 39(6): 1101–1117.

McLean, J (2003) Men as minority: Men employed in statutory social care workforce. *Journal of Social Work*, 3(1): 45–68.

Mezirow, J (1991) Transformation theory and cultural context: A reply to Clark and Wilson. *Adult Education Quarterly*, 41: 188–192.

Miller, E (2010) Can the shift from needs-led to outcomes-focused assessment in health and social care deliver on policy priorities? *Research, Policy and Planning*, 28(2): 115–127.

Miller, E (2011) *Insights 12 measuring personal outcomes: Challenges and strategies.* Glasgow: The Institute for Research and Innovation in Social Services.

Miller, T (2017) *Making sense of parenthood: Caring, gender and family lives.* Cambridge: Cambridge University Press.

Miller, WA and Ashcroft, R (2016) Challenges faced by social workers as members of interprofessional collaborative. *Health Care Teams*, 41(2): 101–109.

Miller, WR and Rollnick, S (2013) *Motivational interviewing: Helping people to change*, 3rd edition. New York: Guildford Press.

Milner, J, Myers, S and O'Byrne, P (2015) *Assessment in social work*, 4th edition. Basingstoke: Palgrave Macmillan.

Mind (2022) *What is the 'fight, flight or freeze' response?* Available at: www.mind.org.uk/information-support (accessed 24 February 2022).

Ministry of Justice (2008) *Deprivation of liberty safeguards code of practice to supplement the main Mental Capacity Act 2005 code of practice.* London: The Stationary Office.

Mizrahi, T and Abramson, JS (2000) Collaboration between social workers and physicians: Perspectives on a shared case. *Social Work in Health Care*, 31(3): 1–24.

Moon, J (2004) *A handbook of reflective and experiential learning: Theory and practice.* London: Routledge Falmer.

Moon, J (2005) *Critical thinking.* Bristol: Escalate.

Moon, JA (1999) *Reflection in learning and professional development: Theory and practice.* London: Kogan Page.

Moore, B (2010) *Team Work and the Role of Reflection.* Saybrook University. https://www.saybrook.edu/blog/2012/03/29/team-work-and-role-reflection/.

Morris, J (1993) *Independent lives: Community care and disabled people.* London: Macmillan.

Morrison, T (2007) Emotional intelligence, emotion and social work: Context, characteristics, complications and contribution. *British Journal of Social Work*, 37: 245–263.

Munro, E (2008) *Effective child protection*, 2nd edition. London: SAGE.

Munro, E (2011a) *The Munro review of child protection: Interim report. The Child's Journey.* Available at: www.education.gov.uk/publications/eOrderingDownload/Munro_Interim-report.pdf (accessed 24 May 2013).

Munro, E (2011b) *The Munro review of child protection: Final report – A child-centred system.* London: Department of Education. Available at: www.education.gov.uk/publications/eOrdering Download/Munro-Review.pdf (accessed 24 May 2013).

Munro, E (1996) *Avoidable and unavoidable mistakes in child protection work.* London: LSE Research Articles Online.

National Institute for Clinical Excellence (2021) *(Draft) Guidance: Adults with complex needs: Social work interventions including assessment, care management and support.* Available at: https://www.nice.org.uk/guidance/indevelopment/gid-ng10145 (accessed 13 February 2021).

National Society for the Prevention of Cruelty to Children (2018) *Case reviews Published in 2018.* Available at: https://www.nspcc.org.uk/preventing-abuse/child-protection-system/case-reviews/2018/.

NHS England (2020) *NHS Plan.* NHE England. Available at: https://www.england.nhs.uk/long-term-plan/ (accessed 6 August 2022).

Nicolson, P, Bayne, R and Owen, J (2006) *Applied psychology for social workers*, 3rd edition. Basingstoke: Palgrave Macmillan.

Nolan, M (2001) The positive aspects of caring. In S Payne and C Ellis-Hill (eds) *Chronic and terminal illness: New perspectives on caring and carers.* Oxford: Oxford University Press.

NSPCC (1901) *Annual report.* NSPCC.

NSPCC (2022) *Recently published case reviews.* Available at: https://learning.nspcc.org.uk/case-reviews/recently-published-case-reviews (accessed September 2022).

Oelofsen, N (2012) Using reflective practice in frontline nursing. *Nursing Times,* 108(24): 22–24.

Oliver, C (2013) Social workers as boundary spanners: Reframing our professional identity for interprofessional practice. *Social Work Education,* 32(6): 773–784.

Olson, M, Seikkula, J and Ziedonis, D (2014) *The key elements of dialogic practice in Open Dialogue.* Worcester, MA: The University of Massachusetts Medical School.

Oshikanlu, R (9 May 2014) Re-kindle your curiosity. *Nursing Times.* Available at: www.nursingtimes.net/rekindle-your-curiosity (accessed 18 May 2016).

Oxford Reference (2009) *Sociology of gender.* Available at: https://www.oxfordreference.com/view/10.1093/oi/authority.20110803095846541.

Oxfordshire Safeguarding Children Board (2015) *Serious case review into child sexual exploitation in Oxfordshire: From the experiences of children A, B, C, D, E, and F.* Available at: www.oscb.org.uk/.../SCR-into-CSE-in-Oxfordshire (accessed 28 August 2015).

Parker, J (2021) *Social work practice: Assessment, planning, intervention and review,* 6th edition. London: Learning Matters.

Parker, J and Bradley, G (2020) *Social work practice: Assessment, planning, intervention and review,* 6th edition. Exeter: Learning Matters.

Parker, R (1981) Tending and social policy. In E Goldman and S Hatch (eds) *A new look at the personal social services.* London: Policy Studies Institute.

Parkes, CM (1982) *Bereavement: Studies of grief in adult life.* London: Tavistock.

Parton, N (2001) The current state of social work in UK universities: Some personal reflections. *Social Work Education,* 20: 167–174.

Parton, N and O'Byrne, P (2000) *Constructive social work: Towards a new practice.* London: Macmillan.

Paul, R and Elder, L (2005) *A miniature guide to critical thinking: Concepts and tools.* The Foundation for Critical Thinking. Available at: www.criticalthinking.org.

Pennebaker, J (1997) *Opening up: The healing power of expressing emotions.* New York: Guilford Press.

Pennebaker, J (2007) *Writing to heal: A guided journal for recovering from trauma and upheaval.* Oakland: New Harbinger Publications.

Philip, G, Clifton, J and Brandon, M (2018) The trouble with fathers: The impact of time and gendered thinking on working relationships between fathers and social workers in child protection practice in England. *Journal of Family Issues,* 40(16): 2288–2309.

Phillips, M. (30 January, 2016) It's dangerous and wrong to tell all children they're 'gender fluid'. *The Spectator.* Available at: https://www.spectator.co.uk/2016/01/its-dangerous-and-wrong-to-tell-all-children-theyre-gender-fluid/.

Pileño, ME, Morillo, J, Morillo, A and Losa-Iglesias, M (2018) The mental health team: Evaluation from a professional viewpoint. A qualitative study. *Archives of Psychiatric Nursing,* 32(2): 206–214.

Porges, SW (2009) Reciprocal influences between body and brain in the perception and expression of affect: A polyvagal perspective. In D Fosha, D Siegel and M Solomon (eds) *The healing power of emotion: Affective neuroscience, development, and clinical practice.* New York: Norton.

Prpic, J (2005) Managing academic change through reflexive practice: A quest for new views. *Research and Development in Higher Education,* 28: 399–406.

Quadflieg, S and Neil Macrae, C (2011) Stereotypes and stereotyping: What's the brain got to do with it? *European Review of Social Psychology,* 22(1): 215–273.

Quote investigator (2014) Available at: http://quoteinvestigator.com/2014/04/06/they-feel/#note-8611-15.

Qureshi, H and Simons, K (1987) Resources within families: Caring for elderly people. In J Brannen and G Wilson (eds) *Give and take in families: Studies in resource distribution.* London: Allen and Unwin.

Rafferty, J and Steyaert, J (2007) Social work in a digital society. In M Lymbery and K Postle (eds) *Social work: A companion to learning.* London: SAGE.

Rai, L (2006) Owning (up to) reflective writing in social work education. *Social Work Education,* 25(8): 785–797.

Rajan-Rankin, S (2014) Self-identity, embodiment and the development of emotional resilience. *The British Journal of Social Work,* 44(8): 2426–2442.

Raleigh, VS and Foot, C (2010) *Getting the measure of quality: Opportunities and challenges.* London: The Kings Fund.

Rawles, J (2016) Developing professional judgment skills: Enhancing learning in practice by researching learning in practice. *Journal of Teaching in Social Work,* 36(1): 102–122.

Reid, W (1994) The empirical practice movement. *Social Service Review,* 69: 165–184.

Revell, L and Burton, V (2016) Supervision and the dynamics of collusion. *British Journal of Social Work,* 46: 1587–1601.

Reynolds, T (2013) 'Men's business?' Black men's caring within black-led community organisations. In C Rogers and S Weller (eds) *Critical approaches to care: Understanding caring relations, identities and cultures.* London: Routledge.

Rolfe, G, Freshwater, D and Jasper, M (2001) *Critical reflection for nursing and the helping professions.* Basingstoke: Palgrave Macmillan.

Rolfe, G, Jasper, M and Freshwater, D (2010) *Critical reflection in practice: Generating knowledge for care.* London: Palgrave Macmillan.

Romanou, E and Belton, E (2020) *Isolated and struggling: Social isolation and the risk of child maltreatment, in lockdown and beyond.* NSPCC Learning. Available at: https://learning.nspcc.org.uk/media/2246/isolated-and-struggling-social-isolation-risk-childmaltreatment-lockdown-and-beyond.pdf (accessed September 2022).

Rosen, G (ed) (2000) *Integrity, the organisation and the first-line manager: Discussion papers.* London: National Institute for Social Work.

Ruch, G (2002) From triangle to spiral: Reflective practice in social work education, practice and research. *Social Work Education,* 21(2): 199–216.

Ruch, G (2005) Relationship-based practice and reflective practice: Holistic approaches to contemporary child care social work. *Child and Family Social Work,* 10: 111–123.

Ruch, G, Turney, D and Ward, A (eds) (2018) *Relationship-based social work: Getting to the heart of practice,* 2nd edition. London: Jessica Kingsley.

Ruch, G, Ward, A and Turney, D (2010) *Relationship-based practice: Getting to the heart of practice.* London: Jessica Kingsley.

Rustin, M (2005) Conceptual analysis of critical moments in Victoria Climbié's life. *Child and Family Social Work,* 10: 11–19.

Rutter, L and Brown, K (2019) *Critical thinking and professional judgment for social work,* 5th edition. Exeter: Learning Matters.

Saleebey, D (2012) *Strengths perspective in social work practice,* 6th edition. London: Pearson.

Saleebey, D (2012) *The strengths perspective in social work practice.* Boston: Pearson.

Sawdon, C and Sawdon, D (1995) The supervision partnership: A whole greater than the sum of its parts. In J Pritchard (ed) *Good practice in supervision.* London: Jessica Kingsley.

Schwartz, J (1995) A patient's story. *The Boston Globe Magazine.* Available at: https://www.bostonglobe.com/magazine/1995/07/16/patient-story/q8ihHg8LfyinPA25Tg5JRN/story.html (accessed 2 March 2018).

Schaub, J (2022) Social work men as a feminist issue. In C Cocker and T Hafford-Letchfield (eds) *Rethinking feminist theories for social work practice.* London: Palgrave MacMillan.

Schofield, H, Bloch, S, Herman, H, Murphy, B, and Nankervis, J (eds) (1998) *Family caregivers: Disability, illness and ageing*. Melbourne: Allen and Unwin.

Schein, EH (1998) *Process consultation revisited: Building the helping relationship (ume 11:)*. Reading, MA: Addison-Wesley.

Schön, D (1983a) *How professionals think in action*. New York: Basic Books.

Schön, D (1983b) *The reflective practitioner: How professionals think in action*. London: Temple Smith.

Schön, D (1987) *Educating the reflective practitioner*. San Francisco: Jossey-Bass.

Schön, D (1991) *The reflective turn: Case studies in and on educational practice*. New York: Teachers Press Columbia University.

Schön, D (2002) From technical rationality to reflection-in-action. In R Harrison, F Reeve, A Hanson and J Clarke (eds) *Supporting lifelong learning: Volume I: Perspectives on learning*. London: Routledge/Open University.

Schön, DA (2017) *The reflective practitioner: How professionals think in action*. London: Routledge.

Schraer, R (2014) *Violence against social work staff*. Available at: https://www.communitycare. co.uk/2014/09/16/violence-social-workers-just-part-job-70-incidents-investigated/.

SCIE (2004) *Co-production: Involving service users and carers in social work education*. Available at: https://www.scie.org.uk/publications/guides/guide04/gs/10-3.asp#:~:text=In%20the%20last %2010%20years,individuals%20identified%20by%20these%20terms (accessed 1 April 2022).

SCIE (2012) *At a glance 01: Learning together to safeguard children: A 'systems' model for case reviews*. Available at: https://www.scie.org.uk/publications/ataglance/ataglance01.asp (accessed September 2022).

SCIE (2015) *Care Act guidance on strengths-based approaches*. Available at: https://www.scie.org. uk/strengths-based-approaches/guidance (accessed September 2022).

SCIE (2022) *Reflective practice*. Available at: www.scie.org.uk/workforce/induction/standards (accessed 16 January 2022).

SCIE (2022) *What is a strengths based approach?* Available at: www.scie.org.uk/strengths-based-approaches (accessed 20 January 2022).

Scourfield, JB (2006) Placing gender in social work: The local and national dimensions of gender relations. *Social Work Education*, 25(7): 665–679.

Scragg, T (2009) *Managing at the front line: A handbook for managers in social care*, 2nd edition. Brighton: OLM-Pavilion.

Scragg, T (2010) *Managing change in health and social care services*. Brighton: Pavilion Publishing.

Scragg, T (2011) Organisational cultures and the management of change. In T Scragg and A Mantell (eds) *Safeguarding adults in social work*, 2nd edition. London: SAGE.

Seikkula, J and Olson, ME (2003) The open dialogue approach to acute psychosis: In poetics and micropolitics. *Family Process*, 42(3): 403–418. Available at: http://www.powysmentalhealth. org.uk/fileadmin/PAMH/docs/Beyond_Medical/The_Open_Dialogue___2003__Poetics_and_ Micropolitics_2003.pdf (accessed 23 March 2018).

Seligman, M (2002) *Authentic happiness*. London: Nicholas Brealey.

Senge, PM (2006) *The fifth discipline: The art and practice of the learning organization*, 2nd edition. London: Random House Business Books.

Sennett, R (2004) *Respect in a world of inequality*. London: W.W. Norton.

Sharland, E and Taylor, I (2006) Social care research: A suitable case for systematic review. *Evidence & Policy*, 2(4): 503–523.

Shen-Miller, DS, Olson, D and Boling, T (2011) Masculinity in nontraditional occupations: Ecological constructions. *American Journal of Men's Health*, 5(1): 18–29.

Shermer, M (2008) Patternicity: Finding meaningful patterns in meaningless noise. *Scientific American*, 299(5).

Siegel, D (2015) *The developing mind*, 2nd edition. New York: Guilford Press.

Simola, S, Barling, J and Turner, N (2010) Transformational leadership and leader moral orientation: Contrasting an ethic of justice and an ethic of care. *The Leadership Quarterly*, 21(1), 179–188.

Simpson, R (2004) Masculinity at work; the experiences of men in female dominated professions. *Work, Employment and Society*, 18(2): 349–368.

Skills for Care (2012) *Workforce development 55: People not processes: The future of personalisation and independent living*. Available at: www.scie.org.uk/publications/reports/report55/ (accessed 28 August 2015).

Smale, G, Tuson, G, Biehal, N and Marsh, P (1993) *Empowerment, assessment, care management and the skilled worker*. National Institute for social work practice and development exchange. London: HMSO.

Smethurst, C (2004) *Gender care and emotion work: Men in a female profession*. Unpublished MA dissertation. University of Chichester.

Smith, M (2005) *Surviving fears in health and social care: The terrors of night and the arrows of day*. London: Jessica Kingsley Publishers.

Smith, R (2010) *Social work, risk, power. Sociology Research Online*, 15(1). Available at: https://www.socresonline.org.uk/15/1/4.html (accessed 24 February 2023).

Social Work England (2020) *Guidance on the professional standards*. Available at: https://www.socialworkengland.org.uk/standards/professional-standards/ (accessed 2 March 2022).

Soukup, T, Lamb, BW, Arora, S, Darzi, A, Sevdalis, N and Green, JS (2018) Successful strategies in implementing a multidisciplinary team working in the care of patients with cancer: An overview and synthesis of the available literature. *Journal of Multidisciplinary Healthcare*, 11: 49–61.

Spike, JR and Lunstroth, R (2016) *A casebook in interprofessional ethics: A succinct introduction to ethics for the health professions*. Springer.

Stevenson, L (2015) *High percentage of social workers leaving the frontline, official data Suggests*. Community Care Online.

Sullivan, E and Decker, P (2005) *Effective leadership and management in nursing*. New Jersey: 6TH Edition Prentice Hall.

Surrey Safeguarding Adults Board Serious Case Review (2013) *A serious case review of the death of Mrs Gloria Foster*. Available at: https://www.surreysab.org.uk/wp-content/uploads/2020/09/SCR-Report-The-Death-of-Mrs-Gloria-Foster.doc-Website-Accessibility-update-2020.pdf (accessed September 2022).

Sweifach, JS (2005) Social workers and interprofessional practice: Perceptions from within. *Journal of Interprofessional Nursing and Practice*, 1(1): 21–27.

Tate, S and Sills, M (eds) (2004) *The development of critical reflection in the health professions*. London: Higher Education Academy.

Taylor, B (2000) *Reflective practice: A guide for nurses and midwives*. Buckingham: Open University Press.

Taylor, B (2005) *Reflective practice: A guide for nurses and midwives*, 2nd edition. Buckingham: Open University Press.

Taylor, B (2010) *Reflective practice for health care professionals*, 3rd edition. Maidenhead: Open University Press.

Taylor, C (2006) Narrating significant experience: Reflective accounts and the production of (self) knowledge. *British Journal of Social Work*, 38: 189–206.

Taylor, C and White, S (2000) *Practicing reflexivity in health and welfare: Making knowledge*. Buckingham: Open University Press.

Taylor-Beswick, AML (2021) *Pre-pandemic, pandemic, post-pandemic social work education*. [PAPER] University of Graz, Austria Conference Programme Pre-pandemic, Pandemic, Post-pandemic Social Work Education Presentation conference abstracts.

The Care Act (2014) (c.23) London: The Stationary Office.

The Children and Social Work Act (2017) (C.16) London: The Stationary Office.

The Data Protection Act (2018) London: The Stationary Office.

The Freedom of Information Act (2000) (C.36) London: The Stationary Office.

The Mental Capacity Act (2003) (C.9) London: The Stationary Office.

The Quality Assurance Agency for Higher Education (2019) *Social work Subject Benchmark Statement*. 4th edition. Available at: https://www.qaa.ac.uk/docs/qaa/subject-benchmark-statements/subject-benchmark-statement-social-work.pdf?%20sfvrsn=5c35c881_6 (accessed September 2022).

Thomas, C (1993) De-constructing concepts of care. *Sociology*, 27(4): 649–669.

Thomas, W (2005) *Coaching solutions resource book*. Stafford: Network Educational Press Ltd.

Thompson, N (2015) *Understanding social work: Preparing for practice*, 4th edition. Basingstoke: Palgrave.

Thompson, S and Thompson, N (2008) *The critically reflective practitioner*. Basingstoke: Palgrave.

Thompson, S and Thompson, N (2018) *The critically reflective practitioner*, 2nd edition. Basingstoke: Palgrave Macmillan.

Trevithick, P (2016) 30th Anniversary Pieces. *Journal of Social Work Practice*, 30(4): 253.

Trevithick, P (2012) *Social work skills: A practice handbook*, 3rd edition. Maidenhead: Open University Press.

Trevithick, P (2014) Humanising managerialism: Reclaiming emotional reasoning, intuition, the relationship, and knowledge and skills in social work. *Journal of Social Work Practice*, 28: 3.

Trowell, J and Miles, G (1996) The contribution of observation training to professional development in social work. In G Bridge and G Miles (eds) *On the outside looking in*. London: Central Council for Education and Training in Social Work.

Tuckman, BW and Jensen, MAC (1977) Stages of small group development revisited. *Group and Organizational Studies*, 2: 419–427.

Turnell, A (1998) The signs of safety approach to child protection social work essay. *Paper prepared for the Twelfth International Congress on Child Abuse and Neglect in Auckland September* (pp. 6–9).

Turnell, A and Edwards, S (1999) *Signs of Safety: A safety and solution-oriented approach to child protection casework*. New York: WW Norton.

Turner, A (June 2022) *Over 40% of social work staff have faced abuse from public this year, finds survey in adults, children's*. Social Work Leaders workforce Community Care.

Turner, J and Stets, J (2005) *The sociology of emotions*. New York: Cambridge University Press.

Valios, N (29 June, 2011) *Five years on from Steven Hoskin has safeguarding improved?* Community Care. Available at: www.communitycare.co.uk/2011/06/29/five-years-on-from-steven-hoskin-has-safeguarding-improved/ (accessed 2 August 2015).

Vowell, C (2022) *What is motivational interviewing? A practical theory of change*. Available at: www.positivepsychology.com (accessed 12 April 2022).

Waldfogel, JM, Battle, DJ, Rosen, MI, Knight, L, Saiki, CB, Nesbit, SA, Cooper, RS, Browner, IS, Hoofring, LH, Billing, LS and Dy,SM (2016) Team leadership and cancer end-of-life decision making. *Journal of Oncology Practise*, 12(11): 1135–1140.

Warwick Safeguarding Adults (2010) *Serious case review: The murder of Gemma Hayter*. Available at: http://www.hampshiresab.org.uk/wp-content/uploads/2011-October-Serious-Case-Review-regarding-Jemma-Hayter-Warwickshire.pdf (accessed September 2022).

Webb, P and Childs, C (2012) Gender politics and conservatism: The view from the British conservative party grassroots. *Government and Opposition*, 47(1): 21–48.

Whittaker, A and Havard, T (2016) Defensive practice as 'fear-based' practice: Social work's open secret? *The British Journal of Social Work*, 46(5): 1158–1174. https://doi.org/10.1093/bjsw/bcv048 (accessed August 2022).

Williams, C (1995) *Still a man's world: Men who do women's work*. Berkeley: University of California Press.

Williams, J (2021) Rewiring my racist brain: A Life's work. In T Moore and G Simango (eds) *The anit-racist social worker*. St Albans: Critical Publishing.

Williams, S and Bendelow, G (1998) *Emotions in social life: Critical themes and contemporary issues*. London: Routledge.

Wilson, K, Ruch, G, Lymbery, M and Cooper, A (2008) *Social work: An introduction to contemporary practice*. Harlow: Longman.

Woolmore, S (2014) *Safeguarding children E-academy*. Available at: www.safeguarding childrenea.co.uk/resources/sue-woolmore-talks-about-disguised-compliance-2/ (accessed 17 December 15).

Worden, JW (2018) *Grief counselling and grief therapy: A handbook for mental health professionals*. New York: Springer.

Yip, K (2006) Self-reflection in reflective practice: A note of caution. *British Journal of Social Work*, 36: 777–788.

Index